THEOLOGY IN TRANSITION

CONTEMPORARY THEOLOGY

EDITOR: Elmer O'Brien, S.J.

VOLUME I

THEOLOGY
IN TRANSITION

A Bibliographical Evaluation of the
"Decisive Decade," 1954-1964

Edited by
Elmer O'Brien, S.J.

HERDER AND HERDER

1965

HERDER AND HERDER NEW YORK
232 Madison Avenue, New York 10016

Nihil obstat: William J. Collins, S.T.L.
                 Censor Librorum
Imprimatur: ✠ Ernest J. Primeau
                 Bishop of Manchester
                 August 5, 1965

230.01

Library of Congress Catalog Card Number: 65–13486
© 1965 by Elmer O'Brien, S.J.
Manufactured in the United States of America

Contents

Foreword

There seems no gainsaying that the decade 1954-1964 revealed itself to have been decisive for theology, particularly for Catholic theology. Yet to say in what way decisive—whether the transition it underwent was good or was bad—would be to move onto ground that is rather less sure because theological fanaticisms appeared during those years in numbers not appreciably less (and, in vigor, clearly not less) than instances of theological probity.

Yet the instances of theological probity were more numerous and more vigorous by far than entire previous generations had ever seen or expected (or, perhaps, wished) to see. So there may be reasons for a moderate optimism after all. For one thing, bystander theology was no longer much in evidence; there were now, you might say, two for the seesaw.

The pages which follow, reproducing the main papers given at the inaugural session of the Contemporary Theology Institute, Loyola College, Montreal, provide a generously comprehensive record of the production in theology and its immediately related fields throughout those ten years.

On which end of the seesaw the contributors sat, the reader will not be long in detecting.

He will notice something more: the contributors' common hope (seconded by all in attendance at the Institute) that theology will now at long last decide to abandon playground for market place. May this first issue of *Contemporary Theology* serve, however minimally, to give substance to so good a hope.

July 3, 1964

THE EDITOR

THEOLOGY IN TRANSITION

Theological Trends

JOSEPH HUGH CREHAN, S.J.

THE SOURCES OF THEOLOGY

As we all know, there has been a serious debate at the council about Scripture and tradition, a debate that was suspended in the first session and has yet to be concluded. The debate began in Germany, where certain Catholic theologians questioned whether the Church in virtue of the decrees of Trent is committed to saying that there are some doctrines which we establish without appeal to Scripture on the basis of tradition alone. Chief of these was Joseph Geiselmann, whose study of the circumstances of the first decree passed at Trent began the discussion.[1] It will be immediately obvious that the question of the canon of Scripture is at once involved, for if the Scripture warrant for a doctrine (for example, praying for the dead) comes from a book (in this case, Maccabees) that is rejected from the Hebrew canon, then one has to settle if the book is or is not Scripture before going further. Now while some Anglican writers (e.g., J. W. C. Archbishop Wand[2]) were willing to admit as a matter of history that the Reformers took up the shorter canon of the Bible in order to have controversial advantage in their arguments with Catholics, there were not wanting Catholic theolo-

[1] Joseph R. Geiselmann, *Die mündliche Ueberlieferung,* in conjunction with H. Bacht and Heinrich Fries; edited by Michael Schmaus, Munich, Hüber, 1957. He was opposed by H. Lennerz in a series of articles in *Gregorianum* entitled "*Scriptura sola?*" (40, 1959, 38-53, 624-635; also 42, 1961, 517-522). J. Beumer (*Die mündliche Ueberlieferung als Glaubensquelle,* Freiburg, Herder, 1962) is also in opposition to him.

[2] J. W. C. Wand, *The Authority of the Scriptures,* London, Mowbray, 1949, 46.

gians who said we should change our idea of the canon and make it more fluid. In this way, the distinction of Scripture from tradition would become less sharp.[3]

On the circumstances of Trent there is an account in the *Cambridge History of the Bible*.[4] A change was certainly made in the draft of the decree; the words declaring that the truth of Christ's good news was contained partly in Scripture and partly in tradition being dropped in favor of the more neutral: both in Scripture and in tradition. Geiselmann has continued to claim that this change was one of substance and policy;[5] but the evidence is against him. We shall probably never know exactly what went on at the meeting of the drafting committee which made the change, but there are three broad facts against him. The first is that there was left in the decree the statement that the council receives with equal reverence Scripture and tradition. This phrase had been bitterly attacked by the Bishop of Chioggia (who argued with the vehemence of the bargees and lightermen among whom he lived that no one would want to equate the prologue of St. John with the practice of facing east to pray), a vote was taken, the phrase was approved by a handsome majority and stayed in the decree. Finally, it is known that Ambrose Catharinus was called in by the legates for the redrafting, and he was entirely opposed to the idea that the whole of revealed truth can be found in the Scriptures.

A further attempt to uphold the same essential view as Geiselmann was made by some[6] who went back to the theologians who were the accepted authorities in the time of Trent to see if they would help. But this has not succeeded either. To Gabriel Biel they have appealed, to Biel let them go; that, in effect, is the message of

[3] Karl Rahner, *Ueber die Schriftinspiration*, Freiburg, Herder, 1957; ET *Inspiration in the Bible*, New York, Herder and Herder, 1961. See also the article, "Canon of the Scriptures," in A *Catholic Dictionary of Theology* 1 (New York, Nelson, 1962), 321-324.

[4] The present writer has a chapter in *The Cambridge History of the Bible* (edited by S. L. Greenslade, New York, Cambridge University Press, 1963) which deals with the Bible in the Catholic Church from Trent to the present day.

[5] *Die heilige Schrift und die Tradition*, Freiburg, Herder, 1962.

[6] Louis Bouyer, *Du protestantisme à l'Eglise*, Paris, Cerf, 1955 [2]; ET *The Spirit and Forms of Protestantism*, Westminster, Newman, 1956; G. H. Tavard, *Holy Writ or Holy Church*, New York, Harper, 1960.

a Harvard scholar[7] who has studied the whole of Biel's thought very deeply and who comes back with the verdict that for Biel "Tradition is not only the instrumental vehicle of Scripture, but also . . . the authoritative vehicle of divine truth, embedded in Scripture but overflowing in extrascriptural tradition." P. de Vooght, who championed Wyclif's view of the sources of revelation,[8] met a like fate at the hands of Michael Hurley.[9] The work of John Driedo on tradition has been examined by J. L. Murphy,[10] who reports that this pre-Tridentine theologian had a very developed concept of tradition; he did not separate or oppose Scripture to tradition, but rather treated them as correlative, so that what Scripture contained was to be gradually unfolded by tradition. Perhaps the Fathers at Trent were not so much in the dark as some moderns have depicted them.[11]

INSPIRATION

The inspiration of the Scriptures, though dealt with in the encyclical *Divino afflante Spiritu*, (1943), was not much discussed in the post-war period, and, when I wrote the article on that subject for A *Catholic Commentary on Holy Scripture* (1953), I had to make my own way in the interpretation of the effects of the encyclical. I pointed out that, by saying that the spiritual sense of a Scripture passage (where such a sense may be known to be present) is from God alone, the Pope had wrecked the Thomist theory of "total inspiration," according to which God produces the whole effect, that is, the words of Scripture, and the human author, God's instrument, also produces the whole effect, but in his own order. Here was a reality, a real sense of the Bible (not something foisted onto it by devout meditation of later times), and it was not in any

[7] Heiko A. Oberman, *The Harvest of Medieval Theology*, Cambridge (Mass.), Harvard University Press, 1963, especially 406-407.

[8] P. de Vooght, *Les sources de la doctrine chrétienne*, Bruges, Desclée de Brouwer, 1954.

[9] Michael Hurley, *Wyclif and his Critics. Scriptura sola*, New York, Fordham University Press, 1960 (in answer to P. de Vooght).

[10] *The Notion of Tradition in Driedo*, Milwaukee, Serafic, 1959.

[11] Henri Holstein, *La Tradition dans l'Eglise*, Paris, Grasset, 1960; Yves M. J. Congar, *La Tradition et les Traditions*, 2 volumes, Paris, Fayard, 1960, 1963.

way from the human author. The hint has not gone unnoticed in the sequel.

Joseph Coppens in his anxiety to defend the Thomist position strove to show that the human author was normally conscious of this fuller sense of what he was writing, even if somewhat vaguely.[12] He pointed to the peculiarity of the Hebrew mentality, which did not deal in systematic concepts but reached out for vague horizons, and this must be conceded. But the distance between what Isaiah or David wrote and what Christ and the Church found in their words is so great that it would require a miracle of foresight to suppose that these early authors had even a glimpse of what they were really talking about. P. Benoit answered Coppens much in this vein,[13] and Raymond E. Brown, summing up ten years' work on the problem, says:

We now tend to see the *demand* for consciousness on the part of the human author as a pseudo-problem. How could one ever measure this vague consciousness? To what extent is a man aware of the implication of his words? In an imprecise Semitic language which employs many symbols, what constitutes a different formal concept? . . . It is worth noting that in the field of literature modern criticism seems to be moving away from an emphasis on what the author intended to an emphasis on what his words actually convey.[14]

Another line of investigation started by the encyclical was the analogy between the Word of God Incarnate and the word of God written. In my article, I took a sentence out of the encyclical [15] and used it to point to a solution of the Modernist crisis about Scripture. I did this without being consciously dependent on any other writer, and I am glad to see that the analogy is accepted now not

[12] "Le problème du sens plenier," *Ephemerides Theologicae Lovanienses* 34, 1958, 1-20.
[13] Pierre Benoit, "La plénitude de sens des livres saints," *Revue biblique* 67, 1960, 161-196.
[14] "The *Sensus Plenior* in the Last Ten Years," *Catholic Biblical Quarterly* 25, 1963, 264. See also his book, *The* Sensus Plenior *of Sacred Scripture* (Baltimore, St. Mary's, 1955).
[15] "Just as the substantial Word of God became like to men in all things, sin excepted, Heb 4:15, so the words of God, expressed in human language, became in all things like to human speech, error excepted." *Divino afflante Spiritu*, par. 41.

only by Catholics, but also by a theologian in the Church of Scotland [16] as fully satisfying the requirements of divine and human elements in the Bible and as explaining their juxtaposition as far as that can ever be explained. A whole book was devoted to elaborating this idea by Jean Levie, S.J.,[17] at least by emphasizing the need to avoid a kind of biblical Docetism or Monophysitism which would deny any scope at all to the human element; for some reason he did not touch on the opposite error of dividing too sharply the human and divine elements by what might be called biblical Nestorianism. The patristic foundation for the analogy is extensive and interesting. In recent attacks on the Biblical Institute[18] and on Levie's book, this foundation, as far as I know, has not been touched.

The Rahner view of inspiration is best summed up in the words of the late Canon Hawkins:

> God's will to inspire the Scriptures is part of His will to found the Church. We cannot think adequately of the word of God without considering to whom it is addressed, and the Scriptures are most properly thought of as addressed to the Church, whose function it is to recognize them as the word of God by placing them in the Canon.

Canon Hawkins goes on to say:

> Rahner is also anxious to soften the difference between the Protestant rule of faith in Scripture alone and the Catholic conjunction of Scripture with Tradition. Of course he agrees that oral tradition came first, but he seems to want to say that since the New Testament is in some sense an expression of the whole life of the Church, it must in some way contain the whole of her faith. It is difficult to follow him here. No doubt one would expect the main teachings of the Christian faith to find a mention somewhere or other in the New Testament, but in so unsystematic a collection of writings it can hardly be expected

---

[16] J. K. S. Reid, reviewing A *Catholic Commentary on Holy Scripture* in *Scottish Journal of Theology* 7, 1954, 83-97.

[17] *La Bible. Parole humaine et message de Dieu*, Bruges, Desclée de Brouwer, 1958; ET *The Bible. Word of God in Words of Men*, New York, Kenedy, 1962.

[18] The best summary about this is by Joseph A. Fitzmyer, "A Recent Roman Scriptural Controversy," *Theological Studies* 22, 1961, 426-444.

that absolutely everything, even of some importance, should be expressed.[19]

Rahner's way of bringing in the Old Testament is not very successful. He claims that the Jewish canon of books was inchoate and incomplete and could not be regarded as finally settled until there was an infallible Church to settle it. This is a travesty of what actually happened. The Jewish canon was fixed before the advent of Christ and was cut down at the so-called Synod of Jamnia after the fall of Jerusalem in order to exclude some books which were being used against orthodox Jewry by Christians and other sectaries. Ignatius of Antioch is on record (Eusebius, *Hist. eccl.*, 3:36) that for the safety of Apostolic tradition it must be put into writing; it is at least curious that Ignatius did not seem to realize that (as Rahner would have us believe) the task was already completed by the formation of the New Testament.

INFALLIBILITY

The word "collegiality" has become one of the battle-cries of the council. One may apply to it what Augustine said about time: "When you do not ask me, I know what it is, but when you do ask, it escapes me." The desire to have some counterbalance at this council to the emphasis on the papal primacy in 1870 has been expressed by Paul VI himself in a pastoral letter written to his Diocese of Milan just before the first session.[20] For many, the correct approach has been to take up the discussion where the first Vatican Council broke it off. Some of the proceedings of that council were printed in 1878, but the whole verbatim report has not been available for more than thirty-eight years.[21] The draft of

---

[19] D. J. B. Hawkins, "A Suggestion about Inspiration," *Downside Review* 80, 1962, 197-213. The Canon here makes his suggestion, and then compares it with what Rahner wanted. A comment by the Abbot of Downside is also given.

[20] Pastoral letter of Giovanni Battista Montini, Cardinal Archbishop of Milan, *Pensiamo al Concilio*, Milan, Ufficio Studi Arcivescovile, 1962, especially 44.

[21] The full proceedings of Vatican I were published as three supplementary volumes of Mansi's *Concilia* in 1926. The *Collectio Lacensis*, volume 7

a decree that could not be proceeded with owing to the break-up of the Council said that "the bishops are not without their share in the supreme work of teaching and governing the whole Church. It is clear that the power of binding and loosing that was given to Peter alone was also given to the college of the Apostles, in conjunction with their head." From this the draft went on to deduce that the decrees of general councils are to be accepted as the work of the Holy Ghost.[22]

It is here that some of the modern writers want to call a halt and to say that it is only in council that the bishops have this power. It has been urged that only at the so-called Council of Jerusalem were the Apostles actually functioning as a college.[23] There has been a rush to produce theories about what really happened there.[24]

Are there two infallibilities or one? The famous formula which was devised by Cardinal Cullen and taken up in 1870 said that the pope enjoys that infallibility with which Christ wished his Church to be endowed. Are these two subjects (pope and bishops) or just one subject (pope-with-bishops, or occasionally without them) operating in different ways? Rahner, who is a canonist at heart, has revelled in this subtlety of debate.[25] One thing should be clear. This is not a debate about jurisdiction, whether that comes to bishops direct from God or from God through the pope, but about infallibility. The supreme work of a bishop is to witness to, and to teach, a revealed doctrine. Liturgy and administration may fill his day, but the teaching office is primary. It may be that by comparing this doctrine of pope and bishops with that of the Trinity some light may be won. Two subjects of one power: the terms of the

---

(edited by T. Granderath [1892]), had many of the important documents, but not a verbatim report of the debates.

[22] This schema is cited in G. Dejaifve, *Pape et Evêques au premier concile du Vatican* (Bruges, Desclée de Brouwer, 1961), 135.

[23] Alfredo Cardinal Ottaviani was quoted in the press as being of this opinion.

[24] Paul Gächter has produced (in "Geschichtliches zum Apostelkonzil," *Zeitschrift für katholische Theologie* 85, 1963, 339-354) the curious theory that there was a meeting going on at Jerusalem under the presidency of James when Peter, whose whereabouts had been unknown to those assembled, suddenly burst in on them.

[25] Karl Rahner and Josef Ratzinger, *Episkopat und Primat*, Freiburg, Herder, 1961; ET *The Episcopate and the Primacy*, New York, Herder and Herder, 1962.

problem are familiar to the theologians of the Trinity, though obviously there are also differences between the two spheres.[26]

THEOLOGY OF THE LAITY

The dictionary of Larousse defines *"laïc"* as "one who does not belong to the Church," and with this handicap to live down one can understand that French theologians have been foremost in magnifying the position of the laity in the Church.[27] In English, where the same ambiguity does not arise, the need has been less pressing. Some of the work has been done for the benefit of the liturgists, and one may say of the two great treatises of Paul Dabin on royal priesthood [28] that they were aimed at giving the laity their rightful place in the liturgy.

Sometimes this has led to excess. For example, Pius XII intervened twice to correct some ideas of Karl Rahner about the theology of concelebration, insisting that the offering of the priest (in the Person of Christ) and that of those who offer with him is different in kind and not merely in degree; and, again, that there are as many acts of Christ as there are priests saying Mass, but that this is not true of the assistance of priests at the Mass of another because their acts are not acts of Christ.[29] Development of the theology of Confirmation, to which we are coming presently, has

[26] Gustave Thils (*Primauté pontificale et prérogatives épiscopales,* Louvain, Warny, 1961) and A. Chavasse, with others (*L'Ecclésiologie au XIX siècle,* Strasbourg, Presse Universitaire, 1960), have brought out the importance of a third force at Vatican I and have scrutinized what was left over from that meeting.

[27] Yves M. J. Congar, *Jalons pour une théologie du laïcat,* Paris, Cerf, 1953; ET *Lay People in the Church,* Westminster, Newman, 1957; Palémon Glorieux, *Le laïc dans l'Eglise,* Paris, Ouvrières, 1960.

[28] *Le Sacerdoce royal des fidèles dans l'Ecriture,* Louvain, Museum Lessianum, 1942, and *Le Sacerdoce royal des fidèles dans la Tradition,* Bruges, Desclée de Brouwer, 1950.

[29] Rahner had two articles, one in *Zeitschrift für katholische Theologie* 71, 1949, 257-317, "Die viele Messen und das eine Opfer," and another in *Münchener Theologische Zeitschrift* 6, 1955, 81-106, "Die Frage der Konzelebration." The two papal pronouncements are in *Acta Apostolicae Sedis* 46, 1954, 669, and 48, 1956, 716. It is worth noting that in the recent concelebration at the blessing of the new Abbot of San Paolo fuori in Rome, each of the three concelebrants had his own host, while the chalice was in common.

made plainer the dignity of the layman in the Church, and this has gained, too, from the tendency of Scripture scholars to concentrate on the aspect of the Church as People of God, in Old Testament categories, rather than as simply the Body of Christ.[30]

The centenary of Newman's famous essay, *On Consulting the Laity in Matters of Doctrine*, saw its republication with an introduction by a Catholic layman in vastly different circumstances from its first appearance.[31] A text from St. Hilary that Newman had used in his argument was taken up eagerly by Scheeben, while Franzelin regarded it as the statement of an objection against the doctrine of the Church. There was some consultation of the laity before the definition of the Assumption, just as there had been over the Immaculate Conception in 1854, and this made the reprint all the more timely. The laity are sometimes out in front of the clergy in matters of devotion based on doctrine, and sometimes they lag behind; no fixed rule can be set down, but their function in development cannot be neglected.

The existence of *seniores laici* as a church-council in North Africa had been traced by layman W. H. Frend to probable Jewish origins,[32] and it would seem that the Church began by doing her business in the presence of the laity or at least of their senior representatives, just like the synagogue; the setting of Origen's *Dialektos* confirms this idea.[33] It might be used to support the proposal for lay presence at Vatican II in its later sessions.

The old division of active and passive elements in the Church has gone forever with the theology of the Mystical Body coming into its own, and though in 1954 Pius XII issued a warning against independent lay theology that was not in continuity with the teaching authority of the Church,[34] the spread of means to satisfy

---

[30] For instance, Lucien Cerfaux, *La théologie de l'Eglise suivant S. Paul*, Paris, Cerf, 1947; ET *The Church in the Theology of St. Paul*, New York, Herder and Herder, 1959.

[31] Reprinted with an Introduction by J. Coulson, New York, Sheed & Ward, 1962.

[32] W. H. Frend, "The *Seniores laici* and the Origins of the Church in North Africa," *Journal of Theological Studies* 12, 1961, 280-284.

[33] *Entretien d'Origène avec Héraclide*, text and French version by Jean Schérer, Paris, Cerf, 1960.

[34] This warning occurs in *Acta Apostolicae Sedis* 46, 1954, 317. It was spoken to the bishops who attended the canonization of Pius X.

the demand everywhere felt for a correct lay theology has grown apace in the last ten years.

Church Membership

Membership of the Church is a topic that is at the base of all problems of ecumenism. Faith and Baptism go together; the notion of Baptism as a contract where the candidate or his sponsors put down faith and have it baptized runs through the whole of tradition.[35] While, therefore, the Catholic Church may recognize other baptisms as valid, or probably valid, there is at once apparent a discrepancy in faith which may not be harmful straightway, but which makes hazardous the future of the baptized non-Catholic. If he reject one of the articles of faith defined by the true Church when such article has been properly presented to him, he sins against faith and the whole of his supernatural faith is gone. He may win it back, or he may continue with a human acceptance of such Christian doctrines as commend themselves to his mind. If he reject Catholic doctrine in some point or other through not understanding that it is indeed revealed doctrine, then his faith can be said to be still in being. Augustin Cardinal Bea in many of his conferences has insisted that such people are *of* the Church even if they may not be *in* the Church. He can point to the fact that the Church in her laws expressly exempts them from the operation of enactments which are held to be in principle for all the baptized.[36]

It is true that heresy is not inherited, but those who are baptized outside the Church have sponsors who undertake to bring them up in what is objectively an heretical form of Christianity. In these times, this undertaking may be a dead letter, but hitherto the Church has presumed it to be operative. What is perhaps needed is

[35] In Chapter 5 of my *Early Christian Baptism and the Creed* (London, Burns & Oates, 1950), I put together the evidence for this idea, and so far I have not found anyone to gainsay it.

[36] Augustin Cardinal Bea, *L'unione dei cristiani*, Rome, Civiltà Cattolica, 1962; GT *Die Einheit der Christen: Probleme und Prinzipien, Hindernisse und Mittel, Verwirklichungen und Aussichten*, Freiburg, Herder, 1963; ET *The Unity of Christians*, edited by Bernard Leeming, New York, Herder and Herder, 1963. The baptismal question is discussed by Kevin McNamara in the Maynooth symposium, *Christian Unity* (Maynooth, Furrow Trust, 1962).

the revival of the ancient idea of two levels of communion with the Church, one allowing attendance at Mass, a share in sacramentals, and the being prayed for, while the other gave the right to the sacraments and a voice in Catholic affairs. The old imagery of the ark makes it appear that one must either be inside or out, but the Church as Mystical Body must be able to have new cells engrafted which somehow live with the life of the Body but are not yet incorporated into it.[37]

Part of the trouble is the need to determine the kind of reality which we describe as the Mystical Body of Christ. There was in pre-war Germany a series of books calling this reality physical,[38] and this interpretation was rejected by the encyclical of Pius XII on the subject. On the other hand, the Church is more than the moral unity which a company would have. What lies in between these two types of union can be called "mystical," but that does not get us much further. One may recall at this point that there has been a long-standing controversy among theologians whether the sacraments operate by physical or moral causality, and this dispute is obviously connected with the one about the character of the Mystical Body.

Having come to an impasse, theological opinion in the last ten years has been trying a new approach by way of the notion of the presence of Christ in his mysteries. For some, this means that Christ when on earth foresaw, with the prevision that is his, every sacramental event wherein his Passion was to be applied.[39] Objection has been taken to this solution on the ground that Christ merited for us as *viator* and not as *comprehensor*, and although he was both at once, it would be improper to attach the sacraments to what looks like the wrong side of his activity. A phrase in the encyclical *Mediator Dei* of 1947 has been seized upon, in the words

[37] The articles, "Body, Mystical," and "Biology. Impact upon Theology," in volume 1 of A *Catholic Dictionary of Theology* (283-293, 270-273) are relevant here.

[38] Karl Pelz, *Der Christ als Christus* (1939), may be cited as an example. German theology at that time was entering on a period of apocalyptic writing which lasted until 1950. This book was put on the Index in 1940.

[39] See T. Filthaut, *La théologie des mystères* (Tournai, Desclée et Cie., 1954), a survey which, incidentally, provoked an extensive discussion.

that tell us that "the faithful should come into vital contact with the sacrifice of Christ," and some analysis of this vital contact has been offered.[40]

SACRAMENTS

The theology of the sacraments has been very active recently.[41] There is less eagerness now to make Christian Baptism a copy of the Jewish treatment of proselytes, for Qumran has, if anything, pointed to the differences rather than the similarities between Jewish lustrations and Baptism. The distinction of Confirmation from Baptism is becoming clearer, and one Swedish scholar has proposed to regard the so-called *Gospel of Truth* as in reality a second-century homily to Confirmation candidates.[42] The High Anglicans are committed to elaborating the distinction of the two sacraments,[43] for in any united church they might form with the Methodists it is likely to go hard with their cherished practices.

The sign, the grace, and the middle term between these two (which was called by medieval theologians the *res-et-sacramentum*) offer some kind of analogy with human birth. The sign is posited by the human minister of the sacraments, and God supplies the grace, just as he breathes a soul into the conjoined human elements that parents provide; but, in this sacramental process, what place is taken by the middle term? It is a necessary theological concept, for it alone can explain how a sacrament may be valid but unfruitful, and in three of the sacraments this middle term is the

---

40 P. Wegenaer, *Heilsgegenwart*, Münster, Aschendorff, 1958.

41 Otto Semmelroth, *Die Kirche als Ursakrament* (Frankfurt, Knecht, 1954; ET *The Church as Primordial Sacrament*, New York, Herder and Herder, 1965); and E. H. Schillebeeckx, *Christus, Sacrament van de Godsontmoeting* (Bilthoven, Nelissen, 1960; ET *Christ the Sacrament of the Encounter with God*, New York, Sheed & Ward, 1963), are the leading works; there is a summary of opinions in the most recent and most comprehensive manual, by William Van Roo, *De sacramentis in genere* (Rome, Università Gregoriana, 1960²). I may perhaps be permitted to refer to the survey I made for the years 1945-1955, "Ten Years' Work on Baptism and Confirmation," *Theological Studies* 17, 1956, 494-515. Shortly, another such must be undertaken.

42 E. Segelberg, "*Evangelium Veritatis*—A Confirmation Homily and its Relation to the Odes of Salomon," *Orientalia Suecana* 4, 1959, 3-42.

43 Lionel Thornton's *Confirmation. Its Place in the Baptismal Mystery* (Westminster, Dacre, 1954) is a good example of High Church theology.

character, the definition of which according to St. Thomas is "a participation in the priesthood of Christ." Priesthood of the baptized has already been mentioned, but this intermediate sharing in the priesthood of Christ which is proper to the confirmed has come in for much discussion.[44] It has been taken as an active sharing, as opposed to the passive sharing enjoyed by the baptized, but it seems better to take it as the plenitude of the seven gifts which were imparted at Baptism in an elementary way.

The activists seem sometimes to land themselves in strange predicaments. Thus Rahner says of Confirmation that it is "imposition of hands to receive the charismatic spirit of a world-transforming mission in the accomplishment of the task proper to the Church." Its grace is "not so much the grace of individual care for the salvation of one's own soul as the charismatic gift, that is, one rich in blessing for others, of collaborating in the mission of the Church." [45] But *charismata* are by definition freely given for the benefit of others and not for our own sanctification. The Church has emphasized this by declaring, for example, in the canonization of Gemma Galgani that her stigmata had nothing to do with her sanctity and that the canonization did not involve the judgment that these phenomena were supernatural. It does seem that the Church is committed to a distinction of individual from group which rests ultimately on the doctrine of the Judgment.

The theology of the Mass I must leave to the liturgists to explain, though here I may touch on one aspect of it by anticipation. There has been since the Council of Florence[46] a question between East and West about the *epiklesis*, that invocation of the Holy Spirit which the East says is the cause of the change in the elements, making them the Body and Blood of Christ. At Florence, one of the Easterns who was eager for reunion read out a statement

[44] One may cite the article, "Confirmation (effets)," in *Dictionnaire de Spiritualité* 2-2 (Paris, Beauchesne, 1953), 1412-1422, where the language of "fighting for one's faith" is still used of the sacrament. The suggestion I made about regarding Confirmation as the completion of Baptism (*Theological Studies* 17, 1956, 513-515) has been adopted by Charles Davis in *The Making of a Christian* (London, Sheed & Ward, 1964).

[45] Karl Rahner, *Kirche und Sakramente*, Freiburg, Herder, 1961; ET *The Church and the Sacraments*, New York, Herder and Herder, 1963, 92.

[46] Of which there is now available a sound history by Joseph Gill: *Council of Florence*, New York, Cambridge University Press, 1959.

about this, after the Eastern bishops had signed the decree of union and before the Western bishops did so. Bessarion said that it was the words of Our Lord, used in the Mass, that effected the change, but there is no evidence that the majority of the Eastern bishops supported his declaration. In the sequel, the matter has been fought out by liturgists of varying degrees of historical scholarship and partisanship, but it is now time for theologians to take a hand. If one has to find in the Mass a remembering of Christ's Resurrection, as well as one of his Passion, it may be that one can find it in the *epiklesis* rightly understood. In the Roman Missal, there is the remains of an *epiklesis* in the prayer *Supplices*. The first known form of this prayer (in the *Stowe Missal* [47]) runs: *"Supplices Te rogamus et petimus, omnipotens Deus, iube perferri per manus sancti angeli Tui in sublimi altari Tuo in conspectu divinae maiestatis Tuae ut quotquot ex hoc altari sanctificationis sacrosanctum filii Tui corpus et sanguinem sumpserimus omni benedictione et gratia repleamur."* This envisages two altars, one here and one in heaven, and the petition is for the ratification on the heavenly altar of what has been done here below. That in liturgical terms is the equivalent of the Resurrection of Christ which was God's acceptance of the sacrifice of his Son.[48] If we ask for the Holy Spirit to be sent by the Father for this purpose, we do not deny that the consecration on our altar has already taken place, and yet we do find room for a proper *epiklesis*—proper, that is, to the sacrifice itself and not merely to the Communion.

OUR LADY

When the Fathers of Vatican II decided by a small majority to take the subject of the Blessed Virgin as an integral part of the schema on the Church, they yielded to the prevailing trend of

[47] In *Vigiliae Christianae* (12, 1958, 45-48) I have put the case for regarding the Mass-Canon of the *Stowe Missal* as genuinely Gelasian. No one has refuted this position, and a number of writers have relied on it.

[48] The suggestion that the *epiklesis* should be connected with the Resurrection comes from J. P. de Jong ("Le rite de la commixtion dans la messe romaine dans ses rapports avec les liturgies syriennes," *Archiv für Liturgiewissenschaft* 4, 1956, 245-278; 5, 1957, 39-79), but he is too eager to bring the rite of commixtion into the story.

northern theologians who have come, since the definition of the Assumption and in dependence on the Scripture scholars' report about Chapter 12 of the Apocalypse and its meaning for the patristic age, to take the Church as primary analogate and Our Lady as secondary in the nuptial understanding of the Church.[49] In patristic times there was no false modesty about Christian language. Clement of Alexandria says that the Church ever gives birth to new children and yet remains a virgin, while one Spanish Father can speak of the *gloriosa copula* between Christ and the Church.[50]

The great difficulty felt about the Apocalypse passage is its apparent conflict with the painless birth of Christ.[51] This conflict seems to have been overcome about the sixth century and thenceforth the bride of Christ may be the Church, or, in a secondary way, Our Lady. The principle that many follow today, that whatever is written of the Church may be predicated of Our Lady without impropriety, is due to Honorius Augustodunensis, a man of the eleventh century.[52] Honorius says that Scripture and tradition—whatever is written—speak of the Church, and that this may be applied to Our Lady.[53] Loose talk about the bridal *fiat* of Mary at the Annunciation does not keep to this rule. For the original language of the Fathers was that in the marriage of the Son of God with human nature Mary was the proxy for mankind, or the bridal chamber of these sacred nuptials.[54] One text has been noticed

[49] J. Lécuyer collected the texts in a contribution to *Etudes mariales* 10, 1952, 25-41.

[50] Aponius, *In Canticum I, Patrologia Latina*, Supplement (edited by Hamman) 1:805.

[51] See J. Crehan, "The Painless Birth of Christ," *Clergy Review* 41, 1956, 719-726; "Mary's Virginity and the Painless Birth of Christ," *Clergy Review* 45, 1960, 718-725. Oecumenius, who is the first to relate the text to Our Lady, made out that the pain she is there said to have suffered was due to her having to put up with the doubts of St. Joseph. See his *Commentary on Apocalypse* (edited by H. C. Hoskier, Ann Arbor, 1928), 135-136.

[52] Who was probably an Irishman from Cashel and not a Frenchman from Autun. This placing of Honorius comes from R. W. Southern's *St. Anselm and his Biographer* (New York, Cambridge University Press, 1963), a work which has also much to say about Eadmer, who was a pioneer in promoting the theology of the Immaculate Conception.

[53] *Sigillum B.V.M., Patrologia Latina* 172:499.

[54] The evidence for patristic ideas about Our Lady as *thalamus* or *pronuba* of the espousals between Christ and human nature is set out in an article of *Theological Studies*, "Maria paredros" (16, 1955, 421-422). Here it may be

from the Latin Fathers where she is called outright the bride of Christ, and this from a sermon of Peter Chrysologus.[55] One may remark that when Christ praises those who do his Father's will, he says that they are his brothers, sisters, mother, but not his spouse. Books with titles such as *Mary. Archetype of the Church*[56] will have to be reinscribed: *The Church. Archetype of Mary*.

MARRIAGE

It has become common form in the last decade to present Christian marriage as an acted parable of the relation between Christ and the Church. The points of similarity have to be worked out more fully, and some attempt at this has been made by Rahner, if only in outline. He would say that "conjugal consent is itself one of those acts in which the Church's own nature is brought into activity, for in this consent of her members she manifests herself as the mystery of the union between Christ and mankind." [57]

But not merely in the contracting of marriage is this likeness to be found. A thoughtful theology of marriage by Henri Rondet emphasizes that it is to be found also in the consummation of mar-

---

summarized. The main line of thought is the interpretation of Psalm 18:6; a fragment of Origen (*Patrologia Graeca* 12:1244), the *Breviarium in psalmos* (*Patrologia Latina* 26:873) and many times in Augustine (for example, *Patrologia Latina* 32:701; 35:1452; 38:1319). Ephraem (in *Hymni et Sermones*, edited by T. J. Lamy, volume 2, p. 574) has the same idea, but without using the psalm, while the pseudo-Modestus (*Patrologia Graeca* 86:3288) has it too, though the Latin version supplied by Migne has changed the word for bride-chamber into that for bride. Another error in Migne's versions from the Greek is in the rendering of a poem by John the Geometer (*Patrologia Graeca* 106:856) where the title "*gamostolos*," or "*pronuba*," is applied to Mary.

55 *Sermo de Annunt.*, *Patrologia Latina* 52:576. See Donal Flanagan, "Image of the Bride in Early Marian Tradition," *Irish Theological Quarterly* 27, 1960, 111-124. At that date, there was no critical edition of the sermons of Peter Chrysologus; this has now been in part supplied by the Benedictines of Monserrat, and the passage is still there. At Ravenna, then the gateway to the East, Peter may have been influenced by some Oriental writer to forsake the sobriety of the West.

56 A work with this title by Otto Semmelroth has lately been translated into English (New York, Sheed & Ward, 1963). The German original, *Urbild der Kirche* (Würzburg, Echter), was produced in 1950, and since then theology has moved on.

57 Karl Rahner, *The Church and the Sacraments*, 110.

riage.[58] The partners are there in one flesh, but still they are two; the self-giving that is involved in this is the warrant for the words of St. Thomas that marriage is essentially grace-giving because Christ prefigured it in his Passion.[59]

Actually, however, the theology of marriage has suffered neglect during these ten years. There has been, of course, a spate of books and booklets about sex and the Catholic, and about the giving of pre-nuptial instructions, but there is no outstanding work to set beside such a volume as the *Christian Marriage* of G. H. Joyce, S.J., from an earlier decade.[60] The very fact that this work goes on being reprinted is a sign that it has not been supplanted. Nonetheless, there are many problems of matrimonial theology which await the attention of dogmatic theologians when they have time to deal with them. The idea of the sacrament of marriage as a permanent sacrament, which was taken up by Pius XI from Bellarmine, has led most popular writers to stress the holiness of the married state. That the *res-et-sacramentum* here is the marriage-bond itself, which gives a right to actual graces when they are needed, makes marriage appear to be very much like those sacraments which confer a character; yet, in fact, it does not confer one. It remains for the theologian to work out the implications of this paradox for the theology of the sacraments generally. Bellarmine[61] arrived at his view by comparing marriage and the Eucharist; both had an event as their "coming-to-be" and both were in essence a permanent state. If now a theologian were to try to work out the theology of the sacraments with marriage as his foundation, striking results might be expected. The liturgists have neglected marriage, too. One may look through such a periodical as *La Maison-Dieu* in vain for a discussion of the magnificent *velatio nuptialis* of the Leonine Sacramentary. Is this due to the fact that liturgical studies are so much in the hands of monks?

To understand the development of the Christian attitude towards sex, much patient research is needed. A beginning has been

[58] *Introduction à l'étude de la théologie du mariage*, Paris, Lethielleux, 1960.
[59] S.T., Supplement, Q. 32, a. 3, ad 1.
[60] New York-London, Sheed & Ward, 1933, 1948².
[61] See "Bellarmine, Influence of," in *A Catholic Dictionary of Theology* 1, 253-255.

made by Joseph Kerns, S.J.,[62] but more is needed. If, for instance, the troubadours devoted their energies to spreading the idea that love between man and woman could only spring to life when their relationship was forbidden, can the medieval Church be blamed, as it sometimes is, for accepting their ideas? Again, one might ask: How often are patristic *dicta* on the subject influenced by Roman civil law? Or again, why did the Ambrosiaster change his mind on 1 Corinthians 7:5 between the two editions of his work? In what sense was marriage of Our Lady and St. Joseph regarded as an ideal marriage? These are some of the questions that still await a satisfactory answer.

Theology of the State

Conflicts between Church and state can arise over marriage and education more easily than in any other way, but the conflict between liberty and truth would come next in importance. There was a symposium in Rome in 1960 on this question, and it may be hoped that some light for the Council in its schema on toleration was there provided.[63] Studies on the rights of an erroneous conscience (as distinct from the rights of error) have been undertaken, and for the American scene there are two notable works, by John Courtney Murray on the present situation, and by T. Hanley on the historical perspective.[64] What needs to be stressed is that countries of the Roman civil law have a different outlook on such questions from countries of the English common law. It took the Church some eighteen centuries to shake off the shackles of the pagan Roman law (on torture, for example), while the common law was not subject to such pagan trammels. Ultimately, this difference goes back to the concept of person and personal dignity

[62] *The Theology of Marriage*, New York-London, Sheed & Ward, 1964.

[63] The symposium, *Thomistica morum principia* (Rome, Officium libri catholici, 1960), was concerned with two other themes, general ethics and the theology of work, as well as the specific question of liberty and truth.

[64] John Courtney Murray, *We Hold These Truths*, New York, Sheed & Ward, 1960, and T. Hanley, *Their Rights and Liberties*, Westminster, Newman, 1959. T. Clancy has studied Catholics and the deposing power in *Recusant History* 6, 1960.

which is a Christian product foreign to the ethics and law of paganism and which was able to make its impact in the early stages of the formation of the common law. The late Richard O'Sullivan was an untiring propagator of these ideas, which he derived from his great hero, St. Thomas More.[65] In the Latin world, they are less well understood. Joseph Lecler has studied toleration as a post-Reformation phenomenon, but without its wider setting in earlier Christian thought.[66] Theological commentaries on the legacy of Pope John (*Pacem in terris*) are beginning to be made,[67] but it will be some time before its ideas are fully assimilated.

CHRIST AND TIME

Irenaeus, reflecting on the words of Our Lord, "Many prophets desired to see what you see," refers the whole of salvation history to Christ the Word: "He sometimes deals with his creation, then he gives the law; now he exhorts, now he rebukes; finally he frees the slave and adopts him as a son, giving him at the appointed time the inheritance of incorruption, unto the perfection of man." [68] This cosmic vision of Christ is appealed to by the followers of Teilhard de Chardin to show that what he is saying was not unfamiliar to the Fathers of the Church and that Teilhard's insights about the redemption would not have been unwelcome to them.

One may agree at once that our new physical horizons make old theological controversies look rather shabby. Thus it has been suggested that the Thomist view of the motive for the Incarnation is true when one regards this planet only, but if one allows that there could be other intelligent beings on other planets who are devoid of the sin of Adam, then the Scotist view comes into its own and it appears more reasonable to say that the Son of God became man as

[65] Richard O'Sullivan, *Under God and the Law*, London, Thomas More Society, 1949; *The Inheritance of the Common Law*, London, Stevens, 1950.

[66] Joseph Lecler, *Histoire de la tolérance au siècle de la Réforme*, 2 volumes, Paris, Aubier, 1955; ET *Toleration and the Reformation*, 2 volumes, New York, Association, 1960.

[67] For example, Peter Riga, *Peace on Earth*, New York, Herder and Herder, 1964.

[68] *Against the Heresies* 4, 21, 1.

the crown of all creation.[69] Teilhard, with his optimism and his desire to see evolution not as a random scattering but as convergent, cherished the Pauline doctrine of the *pleroma* (Col 1:15; Eph 1:23; Rom 8:21), which has now to be scrutinized much more carefully by the theologians than was fashionable in their treatises on Incarnation and redemption a decade ago. The Scotists have for centuries defended the theory of their master without being involved in the heretical concept of a necessary Incarnation; it is to this fact that the defenders of Teilhard will have to appeal, while at the same time they take care not to fall into the Origenist idea of salvation-for-all at the end of the world.[70] If in the past evolution has had so many rejects and failures (such as Neanderthal man), it does not seem impossible that in the future human growing-together towards an Omega point should be the work not of the whole of humanity, but of an élite. That might involve the disappearance of the distinction between Church and state, but who can answer for that?

It may be suitable to say a word here about the theology of history, though that is a topic the Scripture scholars are wont to make their own when they begin to discuss eschatology. Already in the days of the Gospel, the Church had to make up her mind about history. Was there a cycle of degeneration from golden age through silver and bronze to iron and so on, as the Greeks said? And at the end of the cycle would there be a renewal of all things, an *apokatastasis*, when the world would start all over again in the manner hoped for by Vergil's fourth *Eclogue*? Our Lord in speaking to the Apostles used the Jewish term of regeneration or renewal, implying not the pagan, cyclic view of history, but the coming—and that soon—of a time of decision, after which the world would never be the same again. Jean Daniélou has analyzed this notion of *kairos*, and the objections to it which have been made

---

[69] The suggestion was made by a correspondent in *The Catholic Herald* (London) during 1959, and I worked it out in a paper given at the Dortmund Hochschulewoche in November, 1961.

[70] The bibliography of writings about Teilhard is enormous. The list given annually in *Archivum historicum Societatis Iesu* continues to grow. In 1962, it had one hundred items and in 1963 one hundred and fifty. Henri de Lubac's *La pensée religieuse du P. Teilhard* (Paris, Aubier, 1962) is a good beginning.

since the time of Origen, in his *The Lord of History*, the best beginner's guide to a theology of history.[71]

Typology—about which patristic and liturgical scholars have much to say—enters in here, and from the days of the Apostolic preaching it was customary to regard the Old Testament as the ground plan or even the scaffolding for the Christian Church.[72] There was, therefore, a direction in history, and things did not go round and round forever. Yet the sense of finality that is so marked in the utterances of Our Lord precluded any facile expectation of indefinite progress towards good. I may instance the article on Antichrist in the new *A Catholic Dictionary of Theology*[73] for a modern treatment of the idea of a bad time coming that was in many Christian minds in patristic times. The dark words of St. Paul about the factor which held him in check led to the idea (in Tertullian and Jerome) that the Roman Empire served that purpose. Just one thousand years ago, a Benedictine abbot was telling a Frankish queen: "One of the kings of the Franks will rule the whole Roman Empire. After he has faithfully governed his kingdom, he will come to Jerusalem and lay down his crown at the Mount of Olives. Then the man of sin will appear. . . ." [74] This is just a glimpse of how theological ideas about history can influence ordinary conduct. Crusaders and supporters of the Holy Roman Empire were under the spell of this idea.

One of the most fruitful but little noticed ideas of Newman is that of the historical spiral. History is not cyclic but climbs upwards and outwards in a widening spiral which does not exactly reproduce the original track. In *Discussions and Arguments*, he says: "Every event of this world is a type of those that follow,

[71] Chicago, Regnery, 1958, ET of *Essai sur le mystère de l'histoire*, Paris, Seuil, 1953. See also Martin D'Arcy, *The Meaning and Matter of History* (New York, Farrar, Straus, 1959); Christopher Dawson, *The Dynamics of World History* (New York, Sheed & Ward, 1956; New American Library, 1962); Hans Urs von Balthasar, *Theologie der Geschichte* (Einsiedeln, Johannes, 1959²; ET *A Theology of History*, New York, Sheed & Ward, 1963).

[72] Melito of Sardis in his *Homily on the Pasch* (Greek text published by B. Lohse, Leiden, Brill, 1958) uses the word "scaffolding" for the Old Testament.

[73] Volume 1, 104-106.

[74] Adso, Abbot of Montier, to Queen Gerberga, in his *Libellus de Anti-Christo* (*Patrologia Latina* 101:1289).

history proceeding forward as a circle ever enlarging. The days of the Apostles typified the last days; there were false Christs, and risings, and troubles, and persecutions, and the judicial destruction of the Jewish Church. In like manner, every age presents its own picture of those still future events, which, and which alone, are the real fulfillment of the prophecy which stands at the head of all of them. Hence St. John says: 'It is the last time, and as ye have heard that the Antichrist shall come, even now are there many Antichrists.' Antichrist was come, and was not come; it was, and it was not the last time."

Doctrinal Development

Development of doctrine is the last and most difficult problem for the theologian. Only when he has seen how each single dogma has come into its own can he proceed to generalize and say that thus and thus do doctrines develop out of the primitive teaching of the Apostles. Newman in his Anglican days came to see that Catholics had a truly Catholic church and Anglicans had not, but he comforted himself by the thought that Anglicans had Apostolicity which Catholics lacked. (He could have appealed to the Preface to the *Ordinal* of Edward VI: "It is evident unto all men, diligently reading holy Scripture and ancient authors, that from the Apostles time there hath been these Orders of Ministers in Christ's Church. . . .") This drawn battle between the claims of the rival churches was gradually changed for him by two factors: the realization that Catholics had holiness on their side (in the person of Father Dominic), and that a theory of development would account for what he had thought to be un-Apostolic in the teaching of the Catholic Church.[75] What was for him the removal of a hindrance to his conversion has become a source of enlightenment for the Church at large. Work still proceeds on the theory, and an

[75] The movement of Newman's thought is becoming clearer as the publication of his letters proceeds (*Letters and Diaries*, edited by Charles Stephen Dessain, New York, Nelson, 1961-). A start was made with his conversion, the first volume of letters published being styled "volume 11." In volume 12 one may find much about the impact of Rome on his mind and his discussion of theological problems with Father Perrone.

essential part of it has only recently been disclosed in the paper he wrote (after 1860) to explain what he understood by "the mind of the Church." [76]

The plea of Karl Rahner for more prophecy in the Church is largely due to the lack on his part of a theory of development of doctrine.[77] One cannot simply leave it to the charismatics to scourge the Church into the acceptance of new emphasis or new disconcern on matters of doctrine. The Montanists tried that in Tertullian's day and were condemned. Other factors leading to development have to be assessed and it is a work of extreme delicacy.

Bossuet, the champion of fixity in doctrine, has come under fire in recent times as a Gallican,[78] and his views would not leave room for the development of doctrine which has taken place over such matters as the papal infallibility, the Immaculate Conception and the Assumption.

The advocates of logical elaboration of doctrine have also suffered from the destructive criticism that has been addressed to the examples they had given of such syllogistic expansion. By contrast, the great surge of appreciation for the typological understanding of the Old Testament in recent times indicates how easy it was for the nucleus of a later-expanded doctrine to lurk for a time under the guise of an Old Testament type. I may here point to the earliest patristic idea of the meaning of Psalm 131:8: "Arise, Lord, into Thy rest; Thou and the ark Thou hast sanctified."

What has come to light recently is the fact that it was Manning who put Newman on the line of his great work. When the affair of *Tract* 90 happened, "Manning said: 'Shut up your controversy and go to the Fathers, which is your line.' Well, they had been the beginning of my doubts, but I did so. I began to translate Athanasius. The truth kept pouring in on me. I saw in the Semi-arians the Via-medians, I saw in the Catholic Church of the day the identical

[76] The paper was published in *Journal of Theological Studies* 9, 1958, 324-335, by C. Stephen Dessain ("An Unpublished Paper by Cardinal Newman on the Development of Doctrine").

[77] Karl Rahner's *Visionen und Prophezeiungen* (Freiburg, Herder, 1958; ET *Visions and Prophecies*, New York, Herder and Herder, 1963) is a plea for more charismatics in the Church.

[78] A. Martimort, *Le Gallicanisme de Bossuet*, Paris, Una Sancta, 1954.

self of the Catholic Church now—as you know a friend by his words and deeds or see an author in his works." [79] Newman's development is, therefore, not just biological growth;[80] it is a personal identity amid a manifold of experience. Acton was anxious to claim that Newman gave up his theory under criticism from Rome, but this hostile conjecture has no substance in it, any more than the unfounded assertion that "development was expressly discarded at Rome in 1854. It was making the historian master of the divine." As appears from *The Acton-Newman Relations* by H. MacDougall.[81] Acton wanted to believe that in the sixties Newman had given up his development theory, but, when Newman accepted the results of Vatican I, Acton could no longer maintain this line, for that was a palpable case of development.

Bibliography

The Sources of Theology

BEUMER, J. *Die mündliche Ueberlieferung als Glaubensquelle*, Freiburg, Herder, 1962.

BOUYER, LOUIS. *Du protestantisme à l'Eglise*. Paris, Cerf, 1955²; ET *The Spirit and Forms of Protestantism*, Westminster, Newman, 1956.

CONGAR, YVES M. J. *La Tradition et les Traditions*, 2 volumes, Paris, Fayard, 1960, 1963.

[79] *Letters*, volume 12, 357. This debt of Newman to Manning has never been noticed. In his work on Athanasius and the Arians, Newman had plenty of opportunity to see how development had taken place already in the doctrine of the Trinity before Nicaea.

[80] The seven marks of development answer to what was known in Newman's day about the growth of a living organism. He wrote before Darwin, and did not contemplate change out of all recognition. Recent books on his theory, for example J. Walgrave's *Newman. Le développement du dogme* (Tournai, Casterman, 1957; ET *Newman the Theologian. The Nature of Belief and Doctrine as Exemplified in his Life and Works*, New York, Sheed & Ward, 1960), do not quite allow for this.

[81] New York, Fordham University Press, 1962.

CREHAN, JOSEPH. "Canon of the Scriptures," A *Catholic Dictionary of Theology* 1, New York, Nelson, 1962.

——. "The Bible in the Roman Catholic Church from Trent to the Present Day," in S. L. Greenslade, *The Cambridge History of the Bible*, New York, Cambridge University Press, 1963.

GEISELMANN, J. R. *Die heilige Schrift und die Tradition*, Freiburg, Herder, 1962.

——, et al. *Die mündliche Ueberlieferung*, edited by Michael Schmaus, Munich, Hüber, 1957.

HOLSTEIN, HENRI. *La Tradition dans l'Eglise*, Paris, Grasset, 1960.

HURLEY, M. *Wyclif and his Critics. Scriptura sola*, New York, Fordham University Press, 1960.

LENNERZ, H. "Scriptura sola?" *Gregorianum* 40, 1959, 38-53, 624-635; 42, 1961, 517-522.

MURPHY, J. L. *The Notion of Tradition in Driedo*, Milwaukee, Serafic, 1959.

OBERMAN, HEIKO A. *The Harvest of Medieval Theology*, Cambridge (Mass.), Harvard University Press, 1963.

RAHNER, KARL. *Ueber die Schriftinspiration*, Freiburg, Herder, 1957. ET *Inspiration in the Bible*, New York, Herder and Herder, 1961.

TAVARD, G. H. *Holy Writ or Holy Church*, New York, Harper, 1960.

VOOGHT, P. DE. *Les sources de la doctrine chrétienne*, Bruges, Desclée de Brouwer, 1954.

WAND, J. W. C. *The Authority of the Scriptures*, London, Mowbray, 1949.

INSPIRATION

BENOIT, PIERRE. "La plénitude de sens des livres saints," *Revue biblique* 67, 1960, 161-196.

BROWN, RAYMOND E. *The* Sensus Plenior *of Sacred Scripture*, Baltimore, St. Mary's, 1955.

——. "The *Sensus Plenior* in the Last Ten Years," *Catholic Biblical Quarterly* 25, 1963, 262-285.

COPPENS, JOSEPH. "Le problème du sens plenier," *Ephemerides Theologicae Lovanienses* 34, 1958, 1-20.

FITZMYER, JOSEPH A. "A Recent Roman Scriptural Controversy," *Theological Studies* 22, 1961, 426-444.

HAWKINS, D. J. B. "A Suggestion about Inspiration," *Downside Review* 80, 1962, 197-213.

LEVIE, JEAN. *La Bible. Parole humaine et message de Dieu*, Bruges,

Desclée de Brouwer, 1958; ET *The Bible. Word of God in Words of Men*, New York, Kenedy, 1962.

REID, J. K. S. [A review of *A Catholic Commentary on Holy Scripture*.] *Scottish Journal of Theology*, 7, 1954, 83-97.

INFALLIBILITY

CHAVASSE, A., *et al. L'Ecclésiologie au XIX siècle*, Strasbourg, Presse Universitaire, 1960. [This was a special number of *Revue des sciences religieuses* (34, 1960).]

DEJAIFVE, G. *Pape et Evêques au premier concile du Vatican*, Bruges, Desclée de Brouwer, 1961.

GÄCHTER, PAUL. "Geschichtliches zum Apostelkonzil," *Zeitschrift für katholische Theologie* 85, 1963, 339-354.

MONTINI, GIOVANNI BATTISTA CARDINALE. *Pensiamo al Concilio*, Milan, Ufficio Studi Arcivescovile, 1962.

RAHNER, KARL, and RATZINGER, JOSEF. *Episkopat und Primat*, Freiburg, Herder, 1961; ET *The Episcopate and the Primacy*, New York, Herder and Herder, 1962.

THILS, GUSTAVE. *Primauté pontificale et prérogatives épiscopales*, Louvain, Warny, 1961.

THEOLOGY OF THE LAITY

Acta Apostolicae Sedis 46, 1954, 317, 669; 48, 1956, 716.

CERFAUX, LUCIEN. *La théologie de l'Eglise suivant S. Paul*, Paris, Cerf, 1947; ET *The Church in the Theology of St. Paul*, New York, Herder and Herder, 1959.

CONGAR, YVES M. J. *Jalons pour une théologie du laïcat*, Paris, Cerf, 1953; ET *Lay People in the Church*, Westminster, Newman, 1957.

DABIN, PAUL. *Le Sacerdoce royal des fidèles dans l'Ecriture*, Louvain, Museum Lessianum, 1942.

————. *Le Sacerdoce royal des fidèles dans la Tradition*, Bruges, Desclée de Brouwer, 1950.

FREND, W. H. "The *Seniores laici* and the Origins of the Church in North Africa," *Journal of Theological Studies* 12, 1961, 280-284.

GLORIEUX, PALÉMON. *Le laïc dans l'Eglise*, Paris, Ouvrières, 1960.

NEWMAN, JOHN HENRY. *On Consulting the Laity in Matters of Doctrine*, reprinted with an introduction by J. Coulson, New York, Sheed & Ward, 1962.

RAHNER, KARL. "Die viele Messen und das eine Opfer," *Zeitschrift für katholische Theologie* 71, 1949, 257-317.

————. "Die Frage der Konzelebration," *Münchener Theologische Zeitschrift* 6, 1955, 81-106.

SCHÉRER, JEAN (editor and translator). *Entretien d'Origène avec Héraclide*, Paris, Cerf, 1960.

CHURCH MEMBERSHIP

BEA, AUGUSTIN CARDINAL. *L'unione dei cristiani*, Rome, Civiltà Cattolica, 1962; GT *Die Einheit der Christen. Probleme und Prinzipien, Hindernisse und Mittel, Verwirklichungen und Aussichten*, Freiburg, Herder, 1963; ET *The Unity of Christians*, edited by Bernard Leeming, New York, Herder and Herder, 1963.

CREHAN, JOSEPH. *Early Christian Baptism and the Creed*, London, Burns & Oates, 1950.

DAVIS, H. FRANCIS. "Body, Mystical," *A Catholic Dictionary of Theology* 1, New York, Nelson, 1962.

FILTHAUT, T. *La théologie des mystères*, Tournai, Desclée et Cie., 1954.

O'CALLAGHAN, K. "Biology. Impact on Theology," *A Catholic Dictionary of Theology* 1, New York, Nelson, 1962.

WEGENAER, P. *Heilsgegenwart*, Münster, Aschendorff, 1958.

SACRAMENTS

CREHAN, JOSEPH. "Ten Years' Work on Baptism and Confirmation. 1945-1955," *Theological Studies* 17, 1956, 494-515.

CUTTAZ, FRANÇOIS. "Confirmation (effets)," *Dictionnaire de Spiritualité* 2-2, Paris, Beauchesne, 1953.

DAVIS, CHARLES. *The Making of a Christian*, London, Sheed & Ward, 1964.

GILL, JOSEPH. *Council of Florence*, New York, Cambridge University Press, 1959.

JONG, J. P. DE. "Le rite de la commixtion dans ses rapports avec les liturgies syriennes," *Archiv für Liturgiewissenschaft* 4, 1956, 245-278; 5, 1957, 33-79.

RAHNER, KARL. *Kirche und Sakramente*, Freiburg, Herder, 1961; ET *The Church and the Sacraments*, New York, Herder and Herder, 1963.

SCHILLEBEECKX, E. H. *Christus, Sacrament van de Godsontmoeting*, Bilthoven, Nelissen, 1960; ET *Christ the Sacrament of the Encounter with God*, New York, Sheed & Ward, 1963.

SEGELBERG, E. *"Evangelium Veritatis*—A Confirmation Homily and its Relation to the Odes of Salomon," *Orientalia Suecana* 4, 1959, 3-42.

SEMMELROTH, OTTO. *Die Kirche als Ursakrament,* Frankfurt, Knecht, 1954; ET *The Church as Primordial Sacrament,* New York, Herder and Herder, 1965.

THORNTON, LIONEL. *Confirmation. Its Place in the Baptismal Mystery,* Westminster, Dacre, 1954.

VAN ROO, WILLIAM. *De sacramentis in genere,* Rome, Università Gregoriana, 1960².

OUR LADY

CREHAN, JOSEPH. "The Painless Birth of Christ," *Clergy Review* 41, 1956, 719-726.

———. "Mary's Virginity and the Painless Birth of Christ," *Clergy Review* 45, 1960, 718-725.

FLANAGAN, DONAL. "Image of the Bride in Early Marian Tradition," *Irish Theological Quarterly* 27, 1960, 111-124.

SEMMELROTH, OTTO. *Urbild der Kirche.* Würzburg, Echter, 1950, 1954²; ET *Mary. Archetype of the Church,* New York, Sheed & Ward, 1963.

SOUTHERN, R. W. *St. Anselm and his Biographer,* New York, Cambridge University Press, 1963.

MARRIAGE

JOYCE, G. H. *Christian Marriage,* New York-London, Sheed & Ward, 1933, 1948².

KERNS, JOSEPH. *The Theology of Marriage,* New York-London, Sheed & Ward, 1964.

RAHNER, KARL. *Kirche und Sakramente,* Freiburg. Herder, 1961; ET *The Church and the Sacraments,* New York, Herder and Herder, 1963.

RONDET, HENRI. *Introduction à l'étude de la théologie du mariage,* Paris, Lethielleux, 1960.

THEOLOGY OF THE STATE

HANLEY, T. *Their Rights and Liberties,* Westminster, Newman, 1959.

LECLER, JOSEPH. *Histoire de la tolérance au siècle de la Réforme,* 2 volumes, Paris, Aubier, 1955; ET *Toleration and the Reformation,* 2 volumes, New York, Association, 1960.

MURRAY, JOHN COURTNEY. *We Hold These Truths*, New York, Sheed & Ward, 1960.

O'SULLIVAN, R. *Under God and the Law*, London, Thomas More Society, 1949.

———. *The Inheritance of the Common Law*, London, Stevens, 1950.

RIGA, PETER. *Peace on Earth*, New York, Herder and Herder, 1964. *Thomistica morum principia*, Rome, Officium libri catholici, 1960.

CHRIST AND TIME

BALTHASAR, HANS URS VON. *Theologie der Geschichte*, Einsiedeln, Johannes, 1959[2]; ET *A Theology of History*, New York, Sheed & Ward, 1963.

CREHAN, JOSEPH. "Anti-Christ," *A Catholic Dictionary of Theology* 1, New York, Nelson, 1962.

DANIÉLOU, JEAN. *Essai sur le mystère de l'histoire*, Paris, Seuil, 1953. ET *The Lord of History. Reflections on the Inner Meaning of History*, Chicago, Regnery, 1958.

D'ARCY, MARTIN. *The Meaning and Matter of History*, New York, Farrar, Straus, 1959.

DAWSON, CHRISTOPHER. *The Dynamics of World History*, New York, Sheed & Ward, 1956; New American Library, 1962.

LUBAC, HENRI DE. *La pensée religieuse du P. Teilhard*, Paris, Aubier, 1962.

DOCTRINAL DEVELOPMENT

DESSAIN, C. STEPHEN. "An Unpublished Paper by Cardinal Newman on the Development of Doctrine," *Journal of Theological Studies* 9, 1958, 324-335.

MACDOUGALL, H. *The Acton-Newman Relations*, New York, Fordham University Press, 1962.

MARTIMORT, A. *Le Gallicanisme de Bossuet*, Paris, Una Sancta, 1954.

NEWMAN, JOHN HENRY. *Letters and Diaries*, edited by Charles Stephen Dessain, New York, Nelson, 1961-.

RAHNER, KARL. *Visionen und Prophezeiungen*, Freiburg, Herder, 1958. ET *Visions and Prophecies*, New York, Herder and Herder, 1963.

WALGRAVE, J. *Newman, Le développement du dogme*, Tournai, Casterman, 1957. (This is a translation, revised and expanded, of the author's thesis, Louvain, published in 1944 under the title *Kardinal Newmans theorie over de ontwikkeling van het dogma.*) ET *Newman the Theologian. The Nature of Belief and Doctrine as Exemplified in his Life and Works,* New York, Sheed & Ward, 1960.

Old Testament Studies

ROLAND E. MURPHY, O. CARM.

Any summary of significant publications and trends in the Old Testament field during the last ten years is bound to be deficient. Even if it is relatively complete from the point of view of religious denomination, geography, and language, it must reflect many personal and fallible judgments on what is important, what represents "assured results." But this is the risk involved in an Institute such as this which is preoccupied with the decisive decade of 1954-1964. If this decade knew its moments of crisis, especially on the Catholic biblical front, on the whole it was decisive: the historico-critical approach to the Bible laid down in the 1943 encyclical of Pius XII, *Divino afflante Spiritu*, was implemented (in America the time lag was almost ten years), and Catholic exegesis made remarkable progress. This progress has been recognized by our non-Catholic colleagues, most notably perhaps in the public statements of two of the official observers to Vatican Council II, Oscar Cullmann of Basel and Edmund Schlink of Heidelberg.[1] Our present survey intends to spell out the progress made in Catholic studies in the Old Testament area, while not neglecting the foremost non-Catholic studies which, be it frankly said, are more numerous and often more significant.[2]

---

[1] For a more detailed judgment, see S. Schulz, "Die römisch-katholische Exegese zwischen historisch-kritischer Methode und lehramtlichem Machtspruch," *Evangelische Theologie* 22, 1962, 141-156.

[2] The best summary of modern developments up to 1950 is *The Old Testament and Modern Study*, edited by H. H. Rowley (Oxford, Clarendon, 1951). In his *Geschichte der historisch-kritischen Erforschung des Alten Testaments von der Reformation bis zur Gegenwart* (Neukirchen, Erziehungsvereins, 1956), H. J. Kraus has given a very useful and clear summary of the trends that have

OLD TESTAMENT INTRODUCTIONS

Although Introductions are a rather pedestrian topic for investigation, they are significant for their global presentation of trends and of what may be considered the assured results of current research. Catholic scholarship has produced two widely different works: *Introduction à la Bible* 1 (Tournai, Desclée et Cie., 1957, 1959[2]) under the editorship of the late Père Robert and A. Feuillet, and *Introductio in libros sacros Veteris Testamenti* (Rome, Herder, 1958) by Bonaventura Mariani, O.F.M. The French work is open to scholarly trends and investigation of problems on a literary and historical level, as instanced in its frank recognition of sources or traditions in the composition of the Pentateuch.[3] Because it upset some cherished notions it was the target of several sharp criticisms and eventually the first edition was submitted to the Holy Office. A decree emanating from the Holy Office through the Sacred Congregation of Seminaries and Universities pronounced this edition as not suitable as a manual for seminarians for reasons of pedagogy and methodology. Presumably, this stricture does not apply to the second and revised edition of 1959, which acknowledges the help of Augustin Cardinal Bea and others in presenting the revised edition.

In contrast, the volume by Mariani can best be described as closed on questions that should remain free, and—a grave matter—insinuating that the orthodoxy of opposing views is questionable.[4]

---

marked modern biblical study, with special emphasis on German scholarship (for the present time, see M. Noth, *Developing Lines of Theological Thought in Germany* [Richmond, Union Theological Seminary, 1963]).

The most valuable and the most complete bibliographical index for the Bible is the "Elenchus Bibliographicus Biblicus" edited by P. Nober, S.J., in each issue of *Biblica* (Rome, Pontificio Instituto Bibilco). Also deserving of mention are *Internationale Zeitschriftenschau für Bibelwissenschaft und Grenzgebiete*, edited by F. Stier (Düsseldorf, Patmos); the annual *Book List* of the Society for Old Testament Study, now edited by G. W. Anderson (Edinburgh); *Theologische Rundschau* (Tübingen, Mohr); the various periodical surveys that appear in biblical journals, such as *Zeitschrift für die alttestamentliche Wissenschaft* (Berlin, Töpelmann) edited by G. Fohrer.

[3] See D. N. Freedman, "Pentateuch," *The Interpreter's Dictionary of the Bible* 3, Nashville, Abingdon, 1962, 711-727.

[4] See, for example, the review of Mariani by Luis Alonso-Schökel, S.J., in *Biblica* 39, 1958, 499-502, and by P. Duncker, O.P., in *Angelicum* 36,

The fact of the matter is that almost all biblical studies by Catholics reflect the approach of Robert-Feuillet, and not that of Mariani.

Long regarded as the best of Old Testament introductions, the *Einleitung in das Alte Testament* of Otto Eissfeldt appeared in a second and revised edition (1956), and in an enlarged third edition (Tübingen, Mohr, 1964). In comparison to the first edition of 1934, Eissfeldt made a successful and praiseworthy effort to include the growing number of Catholic studies. The style of the introduction follows that indicated by earlier studies of J. Hempel (1934) and A. Bentzen (1948, 1957[2]): The introductions to the individual books are preceded by a lengthy and valuable analysis of literary forms in the Old Testament. This new development was the result of the epoch-making studies of the literary aspects of the Bible by Hermann Gunkel. The *Einleitung in das Alte Testament* (Gottingen, Vandenhoeck & Ruprecht, 1957[4]; ET *The Old Testament: Its Formation and Development*, New York, Association, 1961) by Artur Weiser is similar to the Eissfeldt plan, but slighter; it is stamped by Weiser's interpretation of Old Testament religion, especially the central place occupied by the covenant renewal feast. A *Critical Introduction to the Old Testament* (London, Duckworth, 1959) by G. W. Anderson is an excellent presentation in very brief compass.

COMMENTARIES

During the decade several of the standard commentaries continued to publish individual works, either for the first time or in revised

---

1959, 51-63. A detailed analysis of the second edition of Robert-Feuillet is to be found in *L'ami du clergé* 70, 1960, 530ff. The decree concerning the book can be found in the *L'Osservatore Romano*, July 2nd, 1958.

One wonders if the decade 1954-1964 will, in the judgment of future historians, have marked a turning point in the history of modern biblical studies in the Catholic Church. The high point seems to have come just before the Vatican Council II (first session), and the background is very well described by Joseph A. Fitzmyer, S.J., "A Recent Roman Scriptural Controversy," *Theological Studies* 22, 1961, 426-444. See now the Instruction from the Biblical Commission (May 14th, 1964), published in *Catholic Biblical Quarterly* 26, 1964, 299-312.

editions. Among them should be singled out: *Handbuch zum Alten Testament,* in which the best commentary on Jeremiah is to be found: W. Rudolph, *Jeremia* (Tübingen, Mohr, 1958²). *Das Alte Testament Deutsch* (Göttingen, Vandenhoeck & Ruprecht) is another series, and it stresses the theological message of the books, with a minimum of textual notes; the fine commentaries of W. Zimmerli on Coheleth (1962) and G. von Rad on Genesis (1953; ET *Genesis,* Philadelphia, Westminster, 1961) are typical. The *Sacra Bibbia,* edited by S. Garofalo, is almost complete, and the best work in it is *Libro dei Salmi* by G. Castellino (Turin, Marietti, 1955). The series of *La Sainte Bible,* edited now by A. Clamer, is approaching its end with the appearance of *Les Petits Prophètes* by A. Deissler and M. Deissler (Paris, Letouzey, 1961). Clamer's commentary on Exodus (1956) in this series is the best one done by a Catholic on this particular book.

A remarkable fact is that two new commentary series began in Germany during the last ten years, and both of them are of high quality. *Biblischer Kommentar* is edited by M. Noth and it operates according to a definite structure: *Text* (textual criticism), *Form* (poetical style and literary form), *Ort* (life-setting), *Wort* (verse by verse commentary), and *Ziel* (a spiritual application, growing out of the literal sense, and correlation with the New Testament). Already an outstanding commentary on the Psalms has appeared: H. J. Kraus, *Psalmen* 1-2 (Neukirchen, Neukirchener Verlag, 1960). The other series is edited by W. Rudolph, K. Elliger and F. Hesse: *Kommentar zum Alten Testament,* and it is an up-to-date continuation of a series originally started by E. Sellin and stopped by the war. Some of the foremost German scholars are among the prospective contributors, and a monumental study on Job has just been published by G. Fohrer (*Das Buch Hiob,* Gütersloh, Mohn, 1963). There is no comparable series by German Catholic scholars. The so-called *Bonner Bibel* (*Die Heilige Schrift des Alten Testaments* [Bonn, Hanstein, 1923ff.]) was for all practical purposes finished before World War II. The *Echter Bibel* series (Würzburg, Echter), edited by the dean of Catholic biblical scholars in Germany, Friedrich Nötscher, was completed before our decade began, and it is of a more popular nature. However, in

Holland a first-class commentary edited by A. van den Born (*De Boeken van het Oude Testament*, Roermond, Romen & Zonen) is almost complete.

OLD TESTAMENT THEOLOGY

Biblical theology has been rediscovered in the past quarter century. It had been crowded out by *Religionsgeschichte*, and reduced to a history of Israelite religion, in the wake of the astonishing wealth of comparative material yielded up by the archeological spade. There was always the standard work of Walther Eichrodt, *Theologie des Alten Testaments* (Göttingen, Vandenhoeck & Ruprecht, 1, 1957[5]; 2-3, 1961[4]; ET of volume 1: *Theology of the Old Testament* 1, Philadelphia, Westminster, 1961), first published in 1933-1935. This book practically ruled the field until the last ten years, when a wave of new works appeared.[5] Preëminent among them is Gerhard von Rad, *Theologie des Alten Testaments* 1-2 (Munich, Kaiser, 1958-60; ET *Old Testament Theology* 1, New York, Harper, 1962). There is a marked antithesis between himself and Eichrodt, and this difference has been sharpened by the introduction Eichrodt wrote for the later editions (to be found as an excursus in the English translation of volume 1). Whereas Eichrodt subsumed Old Testament doctrine under the all-pervasive concept of covenant, von Rad denies that a theology of the Old Testament is to be a systematization or synthesis of biblical data. The more traditional books approached the material from a dogmatic framework (God, his attributes, man, etc.). The challenge of von Rad's study is that he attempts to be guided by Israel's witness to the salvific revelation of the Lord. One must follow Israel's "confession" in the "histories," her answer to Yahweh's revelation of himself in the wisdom literature, and the dialogue with past traditions that is to be found in the prophets.[6] [Old Testament theology is an exposition of a confession to Yahweh's acts, not of the concepts

---

[5] See the summary by M. L. Ramlot, O.P., "Une décade de théologie biblique," *Revue thomiste* 64, 1964, 65-96, à suivre.

[6] See Roland E. Murphy, O. Carm., "A New Theology of the Old Testament," *Catholic Biblical Quarterly* 23, 1961, 217-233.

and thought-forms of the Israelite or "Israelite religion." Working with methods of form criticism and the history of traditions he analyzes the Hexateuch (Gn-Jos) which he finds to be an expansion of the ancient liturgical credos (Dt 26:1-9; Jos 24:2-13). There is a certain Bultmannian existentialism in von Rad; the confession of Israel may or may not agree with true history—and he has had to respond to the attacks of F. Hesse in his second volume. But even if the development of the Hexateuch, and also the importance of the cultic credos, comes to be seen differently, there is no denying the marvelous insights which von Rad has provided into Old Testament theology.

Most other theologies are in a traditional pattern. Although Th. C. Vriezen's work was published first in 1950, it was not until the 1954 edition was published in German (1956) and in English (*An Outline of Old Testament Theology*, Oxford, Blackwell, 1958) that it became influential. His two major preoccupations are the relationship between the Testaments and the method and development of this theology ("the nature of the knowledge of God in the Old Testament as an intimate relationship between the Holy God and Man" [p. 124]). He treats everything in terms of the themes: God, man, and their mutual relationship.

G. A. F. Knight's *A Christian Theology of the Old Testament* (Richmond, John Knox, 1959) betrays a Christian's preoccupation with the Old Testament—these books are "Christian Scripture" to be read and understood within the Church and not merely in terms of critical and historical analysis. To this end he periodizes the Old Testament: birth, marriage (Sinai), death (Exile), resurrection (Restoration), consummation (Coming of Christ)—and this corresponds to five moments in Christ's life. It is hard to escape the impression of artificiality in this approach.

Among the other studies should be noted the efficient work of E. Jacob, *Theology of the Old Testament* (New York, Harper, 1958; French original, 1955), which follows along "traditional" lines, but is marked by alertness to historical development and literary problems, and is organized around God's presence and action in Israel. *Théologie de l'Ancien Testament* 1-2 of P. van Imschoot (Tournai, Desclée et Cie., 1954-1956) lacks the third volume for completion. Although objections have been made against van Imschoot (and Jacob) for following the framework of dogmatic theology, there is no distortion of the mentality and viewpoint of the Old Testament in the particular areas which are treated. In the United States, *The Two-Edged Sword* of J. L. McKenzie, S.J. (Milwaukee, Bruce, 1956) was and remains a publication of some moment. It is well-written and it presents a penetrating insight into the theological message of the Old Testament, although it does not try to be complete or formal in treatment.[7]

Progress in biblical theology is made possible by detailed studies in small areas, such as biblical themes and concepts.[8] Many of these (often developed out of doctoral theses) have been published in various monograph series.[9]

Some of the most profound analyses of Old Testament thoughtforms have been made by A. R. Johnson: *The One and the Many in the Israelite Conception of God* (Cardiff, University of Wales, 1961[2]); *The Vitality of the Individual in the Thought of Ancient Israel* (Cardiff, University of Wales, 1949). This type of study recreates the mental background of fundamental Old Testament concepts. A twentieth-century reader is apt to supply his own coloring to "grace," "justice," "spirit," etc. Instead, he must come to terms with Israel's understanding of God, of sin, and of salvation— as expressed in one book, these ideas may be more or less developed than in another. It is with such ideas that J. Guillet, S.J., concerned himself in *Themes of the Bible* (Notre Dame, Fides,

---

[7] *Myths and Realities* (Milwaukee, Bruce, 1963) by the same author is a collection of valuable essays on Old Testament subjects, especially messianism and myth.

[8] Here we may point to the salutary reminder of J. Barr (*The Semantics of Biblical Language*, New York, Oxford, 1961) that word studies cannot prescind from the context, and also that the alleged connection between thought-forms and language is false. His strictures on Kittel's famous *Theologisches Wörterbuch* do not make that work any the less a necessary and valuable tool in biblical theology. But it is good to be alerted against sweeping generalizations about the relation between Hebrew mentality and vocabulary (against T. Boman, *Hebrew Thought Compared with Greek*, Philadelphia, Westminster, 1960).

[9] Only a few can be indicated here; for the series themselves, one can consult the list in G. S. Glanzman and J. A. Fitzmyer, *An Introductory Bibliography for the Study of Scripture* (Westminster, Newman, 1961), 11-12, to which may be added *Wissenschaftliche Monographien zum Alten und Neuen Testament* (Neukirchen, Neukirchener Verlag) and *Cahiers de la Revue Biblique* (Paris, Gabalda).

1960), a work that was significantly subtitled in the French original (1954), "Studies on the expression and the development of revelation."

Dogmatic theologians have made complaints, not without some justice, that biblical scholars have not provided them with necessary theological syntheses. This lack will doubtless be remedied, and already one may point to the fine study of A. M. Dubarle, O.P., *Le péché originel dans l'Ecriture* ("Lectio Divina" 20, Paris, Cerf, 1958; ET *The Biblical Doctrine of Original Sin*, New York, Herder and Herder, 1964). This is a sober and careful analysis of the biblical data (Old Testament and New Testament) relevant to the dogma of original sin. Dubarle's treatment of the first chapters of Genesis is in the tradition of such studies as Bruce Vawter, C.M., *A Path Through Genesis* (New York, Sheed and Ward, 1956) and H. Renckens, S.J., *Israel's Concept of the Beginning. The Theology of Genesis I-III* (New York, Herder and Herder, 1964). However, the dogmatic theologians of today can no longer afford to tolerate the dichotomy that has come to exist between Scripture and dogma; otherwise a "nonhistorical" theology will result. The best theological study does exemplify biblical orientation, such as Karl Rahner's sketch of a treatise on the "One God" in *Theological Investigations* 1 (Baltimore, Helicon, 1961), 79-148, or the treatment of theological concepts in *Handbuch theologischer Grundbegriffe*, edited by H. Fries (Munich, Kösel, 1962-1963) in two volumes. Likewise, among Evangelical theologians, there is the monograph, *Offenbarung als Geschichte*, edited by W. Pannenberg (Göttingen, Vandenhoeck & Ruprecht, 1961, 1963[2]), which deals with history as the milieu of revelation. The Old Testament is treated by R. Rendtorff ("Die Offenbarungsvorstellungen im alten Israel"). He seems to separate the Word unduly from the Act(s) of God; action needs interpretation, such as supplied by the prophets. Nonetheless, a correct understanding of the revelational aspect of history is central to dogmatic theology and will doubtless receive extended treatment in the future.

There is a strange paradox about biblical theology that deserves some consideration. Many studies, and good ones, purport to give biblical theology of the Old Testament. But when the concept itself is subjected to scrutiny, there is a wide diversity of opinion.

Can one speak of an Old Testament theology, prescinding from the New Testament? Roland de Vaux, O.P., denies this ("A propos de théologie biblique," *Zeitschrift für die alttestamentliche Wissenschaft* 68, 1956, 225-227). J. van der Ploeg, O.P., asks if Old Testament theology is possible ("Une théologie de l'Ancien Testament, est-elle possible?" *Ephemerides Theologicae Lovanienses* 38, 1962, 417-434), and his answer is in the negative. At least, he points to the very real difficulties: the extreme fluidity of Old Testament concepts and language, for example, justice, blessing, etc. There are few ideas in the Old Testament which have the firmness of what we call a dogma. Yahweh may be the creator, but there is a disconcerting freedom in representing this fact. Israel never felt the need of an explicit and circumscribed faith, as the bareness of the cultic credos (Dt 26:1-9) indicates. Of course, there was no central, authoritative body which could fix "truths of faith," as is illustrated by the oscillation in the belief in a blessed immortality. Finally, the Old Testament is concerned more with orthopraxy than orthodoxy—in contrast to our emphasis on the world of ideas. All this leaves one with the impression that "theology" is perhaps too ambitious a title for an analysis of Old Testament belief, which refuses to bend itself to our categories.

Krister Stendahl has written an acute article on biblical theology in *Interpreter's Dictionary of the Bible* 1 (Nashville, Abingdon, 1962), 418-432, in which he distinguishes two levels: What did he (the biblical writer) mean? what does he mean (to one who reads the Bible today)? Descriptive theology is in contrast, but not necessarily in opposition, to existential theology. This distinction is in itself important and must always be kept in mind. One might say that current biblical theology is largely descriptive and historical: Israel's understanding of Yahweh and of itself. As for the present meaning, this seems to involve development in doctrine—a development which must take place within the Church, and with regard to authentic tradition. One cannot simply "hear" the Word today in an intellectual vacuum, without recognition of one's spiritual inheritance.

Another important study of the nature of biblical theology is by G. Ebeling in his collected essays, *Word and Faith* (Philadelphia, Fortress, 1963, 79-97. He studies the development of the phrase

and concept of biblical theology which, he finds, originated in the
seventeenth century as a demand for a reform of systematic theology in Protestant circles—a biblical instead of Scholastic dogmat-
ics. Under J. P. Gabler it set itself up as an historical discipline
which has lived in delicate coexistence (detached, critical, even
normative) with dogmatic theology. This, however, does not mean
that it approached the Bible without certain "dogmatic" presup-
positions of its own ("the timelessly valid," "religious impulse,"
etc.)—and the problematic nature of biblical theology began to
emerge. As Ebeling sees it, the Bible does not contain theology,
but its contents are capable of theological explication: "theology
arises from the meeting of the biblical testimony to revelation with
Greek thinking" (p. 93); for him, these two elements are constitutive of the nature of theology, and the biblical testimony involves
both Testaments.[10] If Ebeling is right, biblical theology is in its
infancy. He seems to be striking a blow for a relevant translation of
the biblical message (what does it mean? —not, what did it
mean?) in terms of our current understanding—even, in the sense
of Bonhoeffer's "non-religious interpretation of biblical concepts."

The Relation of the Old Testament to the New Testament

The renewal in Old Testament biblical theology leads into the specific question of the relationship between the Testaments. We
have already noted that de Vaux thinks they cannot be separated
in treating Old Testament theology. Both Vriezen and von Rad
devote a large part of their works to this relationship. In 1962-1963
no less than four significant volumes on this topic were published.
Two are by French Catholics: C. Larcher, O.P., *L'actualité
chrétienne de l'Ancien Testament* (Paris, Cerf, 1962); P. Grelot,
Sens chrétien de l'Ancien Testament (Tournai, Desclée et Cie.,
1962). The other volumes are collections of studies: *The Old Testament and Christian Faith*, edited by B. W. Anderson (New
York, Harper, 1963); *Essays on Old Testament Hermeneutics*,

[10] These remarks tie in with the renewed discussion concerning one's hermeneutical stance; see G. Ebeling, "Word of God and Hermeneutics," *op.
cit.*, 305-332.

edited by C. Westermann (Richmond, John Knox, 1963; German original, 1960).[11] This question was discussed from a narrower point of view in previous generations: messianic prediction and prophecy, and fulfillment in Christ. The present approach is much broader, in that newer insights into Israelite history and into the history of the biblical text itself (especially the rereading and reinterpretation of earlier biblical passages) are being utilized.

In Westermann's *Essays*, both R. Bultmann and F. Baumgärtel take a definite stand in rejecting the Old Testament as part of the Christian Bible. The Old Testament merely serves to aid man in his self-understanding before listening to the gospel of the New Testament (Bultmann). For Baumgärtel, the Old Testament presents a strange religion, entirely different from Christianity; hence it must be "lost" in order to be "regained." It is regained in so far as faith in Christ recognizes him as the fulfillment of the Old Testament promise, "I am the Lord thy God." This promise seems to exhaust the validity of the Old Testament for Christianity.

G. von Rad, C. Westermann, and especially W. Zimmerli stress the unity of the Testaments in *Essays*. Zimmerli's study is significantly entitled "Promise and Fulfillment," a category taken from the New Testament. The Pentateuch, however, develops the Abrahamic promise (Gn 12:1-3) of the land and the people, with some emphasis on the tension between the promise and its realization, and on the openness of the promise itself; the Exodus and the Conquest become the (partial) fulfillment of the patriarchal promises. In the Deuteronomistic history of Joshua to Kings it is the promise of Nathan to David that is uppermost, even if the Davidic dynasty is under judgment. The royal messianism that forms around the currently reigning king provides an orientation to a future ideal. But the tension between ideal and reality, the reality of irreligious monarchs on the throne, still perdures. The feeling that Yahweh is sovereign and free in his manner of fulfillment grows—as the author of Psalm 88(89) testifies in his agonizing questions about the anointed of the Lord and the Davidic dynasty.

[11] For a more detailed survey, see Roland E. Murphy, O. Carm., "The Relationship between the Testaments," *Catholic Biblical Quarterly* 26, 1964, 349-359. An important earlier publication is Joseph Coppens, *Les Harmonies des deux Testaments* (Tournai, Casterman, 1949²).

The ultimate will of Yahweh escapes detection; Christ is not to be "deduced" from the Old Testament, although he is the goal.

An interesting development, which owes much to this discussion, is the acceptance by many of typological exegesis (for example, von Rad, Eichrodt, in Westermann's *Essays*). This means that there exists a correspondence—whether by way of similarity or of contrast—between the persons, institutions, and events of the Old Testament and those of the New Testament. Such is the basic supposition of the New Testament writers themselves, and also of the Church Fathers. The difficulty here is one of control: not every correspondence is valid; the correspondence *as willed by God* is the key to the validity of this relationship and not enough attention is paid to it. The problem remains subtle because a progressive understanding (on our part) of the typological relationship is possible. In many instances, however, it is easier to be deceived by coincidence than to arrive at a firm typological correspondence.

All things considered, I think that Grelot's work is the best study of the Christian meaning of the Old Testament. He synthesizes many of the ideas of the Fathers and medieval theologians, while avoiding excesses. He finds the Incarnation anticipated—especially in figures or types—by Yahweh's presence among his People, through covenant and word. The Law provides many institutions, for example, priesthood, sacrifice, temple, which have the providential purpose of prefiguring the mystery of Christ. Israel's own tortured experience of sin and destruction left the way open to the mystery of the Suffering Servant; the Old Testament remains a promise that finds its transcendent fulfillment in the New Testament.

The usual understanding of the *sensus plenior* or "fuller sense" is to be found in Grelot. This sense is the literal sense understood on a deeper level (*"saisi à un second degré de profondeur"*). The Old Testament author gives a real assent—without the discursive, rational aspect of the notional assent—to the total reality which he experiences: the "mystery of God among men." He would distinguish correctly, I think, between the *sensus plenior* as it is found in an historical or prophetical context. In an historical context, a definite meaning which corresponds to a given moment in the process of revelation is expressed: salvation, light, life—these meanings are deepened in the perspective of the New Testament goal towards which they are swept up. In a prophetical context, the meanings are deepened in the perspective of the New Testament consummation, however inadequately described, such as the final salvation proclaimed in Isaiah 40:1-11. His discussion of the *sensus plenior* is a rich one, and he gives many examples.

But one cannot very well discuss the fuller sense without taking into consideration the dissertation of Raymond E. Brown, S.S., *The* Sensus Plenior *of Sacred Scripture* (Baltimore, St. Mary's, 1955), which capped a discussion of the term (since 1927) and of the concept (as old as the Church Fathers). He defined the fuller sense thus:

> The *sensus plenior* is that additional, deeper meaning, intended by God but not clearly intended by the human author, which is seen to exist in the words of a biblical text (or group of texts, or even a whole book) when they are studied in the light of further revelation or development in the understanding of revelation (p. 92).

The discussion is still going on, as evidenced in the pages of the *Catholic Biblical Quarterly*: Raymond E. Brown, S.S., "The *Sensus Plenior* in the Last Ten Years," (25, 1963, 262-285); Bruce Vawter, C.M., "The Fuller Sense: Some Considerations," (26, 1964, 86-96).[12]

The nub of the dispute is the presence of the fuller meaning in the text: Is the fuller meaning something that grows out of the literal sense of the text as an *approfondissement,* and so is homogeneous with it? Or is it merely a question of a fuller *understanding* of the biblical text in the light of the development of revelation? It will not be easy to move off center in this debate, and perhaps another approach will eventually present itself.

The debate proceeds along the line of the human author as God's instrument; his meaning and "intention" in writing is therefore God's meaning and intention. The analogy of "instrument" has proved serviceable, but perhaps it does not provide the correct

---

[12] J. M. Robinson has indicated the importance of the fuller sense in Catholic theology as a hermeneutical stance; see his address at the Harvard Colloquium, published in *Ecumenical Dialogue at Harvard. The Roman Catholic-Protestant Colloquium* edited by S. H. Miller and G. E. Wright, (Cambridge, Harvard University Press, 1964), 91-109, especially 104-108.

way to arrive at meaning; it is a bit mechanistic, and one gets involved in the problem of the deficient instrument that is man. One might begin with the undeniable fact of rereading and reinterpretation which one finds in the Bible.[13] Instead of being bound by the intention and consciousness of God's "instrument," we are then confronted by the new dimensions which the word of God acquires in the ongoing life of his People. Intention and meaning are far too complex to be exhausted at birth. This aspect of things leaves the biblical text open to the future and to a fuller meaning. The community in which it is received hears the Word on different levels—with the aid of the Spirit.

THE HISTORY OF ISRAEL

During the last ten years, positions on the early history of Israel have hardened into two camps that may be roughly identified as German and American. The German scholars are preëminently Martin Noth (*The History of Israel*, London, Black, 1960²) and Albrecht Alt (*Kleine Schriften zur Geschichte des Volkes Israel* 1-3, Munich, Beck, 1953-1959). Representative of the Americans are William F. Albright (*The Biblical Period from Abraham to Ezra*, revised edition, New York, Harper, 1963) and John Bright (*A History of Israel*, Philadelphia, Westminster, 1959). There are, of course, many other scholars (and of other nations) whose names could be mentioned.

The point of division is the evaluation of both archeological and literary sources in the reconstruction of Israel's history. Thus, Bright's *Early History in Recent History Writing* (Naperville, Allenson, 1956) represents a critique of the excessively literary approach of the German scholars, which is allegedly skeptical of the historical value of Israelite traditions, and insensitive to archeological evidence. Noth has repudiated what he considers to be an overconfident reliance on (if not misuse of) archeology in "Der Beitrag

[13] The late A. Gelin was particularly emphatic about *relecture*, and almost dogmatic about the various late additions to works, which supposedly represented a later rereading. But his general point is well taken. D. J. McCarthy, S.J., in "Personality, Society and Inspiration," *Theological Studies* 24, 1963, 553-576, has well described the formation of parts of the Bible in the light of the reinterpretation given to the word of God.

der Archäologie zur Geschichte Israels," *Vetus Testamentum Supplements* 7 (Leiden, Brill, 1960), 262-282.

At the present time, there is a stalemate, and this situation will prevail until new insights are brought to bear on Israel's records. The scholarly world has been grappling with the problem for only about one hundred years, and it has moved far beyond the ideas of Wellhausen; we may expect that future scholarly research will resolve the impasse.

We may state the problem as succinctly as possible: In what sense does the Pentateuch (and Joshua) contain valid historical memory? There has been some telescoping and reinterpretation of early traditions. Has this oversimplification, however understandable in the light of Israel's liturgical and religious needs, been so drastic that we do not have an historically valid representation of the patriarchal and Mosaic periods? Even the fundamental studies of de Vaux, Rowley, and others do not establish any more than the general historical flavor of the early accounts: These narratives reflect the customs, names, and general life-pattern of the patriarchal era (eighteenth-seventeenth centuries) as known from the Nuzu and Mari sources. But they cannot *prove* the historicity of key details. Yet, enough progress has been made, I think, to create a certain presumption in favor of the genuine historical authenticity of these narratives. One of the most significant break-throughs (comparable to the light thrown on the patriarchal narratives by Nuzu and Mari in the 1940s) came in G. Mendenhall's study of the covenant in the light of the suzerainty treaties between Hittite kings and vassal states in the fourteenth-thirteenth centuries. This evidence shows that Israel conceived of its relationship to the Lord in terms of a covenant concept that goes back to the Mosaic period.[14] On the other hand, archeological excavations have pointed up some problems in the biblical narratives; the excavations at Jericho and Ai have revealed no occupation levels that can be dated to Joshua's time. It may not be out of order to emphasize here that

[14] G. Mendenhall, *Law and Covenant in Israel and the Ancient Near East*, Pittsburg, Biblical Colloquium, 1955 (reprinted from *The Biblical Archaeologist* 17, 1954, 26-46, 49-76). The same line of thought is found also in K. Baltzer, *Das Bundesformular* (Neukirchen, Neukirchener Verlag, 1960); he sketches the development of the covenant form through the Old Testament, and on into the Qumran material.

belief in the inspiration and inerrancy of the Bible does not touch the question; from the point of view of methodology, these dogmatic truths are not able to determine the type of literature we are dealing with in the so-called "historical" narratives.

Another problem that has not received a satisfactory answer is the relationship between the Sinai and Exodus traditions. This is an interesting example of *Traditionsgeschichte*. Both von Rad and Noth have argued that these traditions—Sinai and Exodus, or Covenant and Election—are completely separate blocks of material within the Old Testament, as shown by literary analysis. They were joined at a later period, and hence one would conclude that the combined role of Covenant and Election in early Israelite tradition is highly problematical. In reply, one may well ask if form-critical analysis can be made the vehicle of conclusions that regard history. And one might also point out that the absence of the Covenant in the cultic credos (e.g., Dt 26:1-9) could be explained by the aspect of obligation which characterizes the Covenant; when one is witnessing to the saving acts of God, there is no necessary reason to emphasize the Law. Yet one would desire a more convincing reply, and the eventual solution may be found along the lines of the study of W. Beyerlin, *Herkunft und Geschichte der ältesten Sinaitraditionen* (Tübingen, Mohr, 1961). He argues from extra-biblical evidence that the Sinai traditions (Decalogue and Covenant law) go back to the time of Moses. Hence one cannot justifiably deny the historical link between God's saving and covenanting action.

If many points in the early history of Israel remain problematical, the general trend of Israel's history has been increasingly illustrated by the yield from archeological work. Perhaps the best example is the Babylonian Chronicle which was published in 1956, and which has established the date of Nabuchadnezzar's capture of Jerusalem as March 16, 697 B.C. (the first deportation), and thrown light on the historical background of the last ten years of Judah's existence.[15] Time after time, the meaning of the biblical text has been explained with the help of archeology, and one may

---

[15] See the discussion by D. N. Freedman, "The Babylonian Chronicle," *The Biblical Archaeologist Reader* (New York, Doubleday, 1961), 113-127.

form an idea of such progress from studies like G. E. Wright, *Biblical Archaeology* (Philadelphia, Westminster, 1957, 1962[2]).

The total history of Israel has been enriched by the realization that the Old Testament presents not *one* history, but several. In the Pentateuch itself there are several global interpretations—the vivid sketch according to the Yahwist, the Priestly gradation of covenants (Noah, Abraham, Sinai). Thanks to the fundamental studies of M. Noth (*Ueberlieferungsgeschichte des Pentateuch*, Stuttgart, Kohlhammer, 1948[2], and *Ueberlieferungsgeschichtliche Studien*, Tübingen, Niemeyer, 1957[2]), we have a better appreciation of the rich variety of sources and the dominant traditions governing these sources. There is general agreement in speaking of the Deuteronomist "history" (Jos, Jgs, 1-2 S, 3-4 K—studied by E. Jenni ["Zwei Jahrzehnte Forschung an den Büchern Josua bis Könige," *Theologische Rundschau* 27, 1961, 1-32, 97-146]), which reflects a judgment on Israel's past that depends on the theology of the book of Deuteronomy: Faithfulness brings life, but infidelity will bring death (Dt 30:15-20). The Chronicler's history (Ez-Neh, 1-2 Chr) is another version of Israel's past which reinterprets it in the light of the interests of the post-Exilic theocratic community for whom the work was composed. D. N. Freedman ("The Chronicler's Purpose," *Catholic Biblical Quarterly* 23, 1961, 436-442) has continued in the trend of earlier studies (A. Brunet, "Le Chroniste et ses sources," *Revue biblique* 60, 1953, 481-508; 61, 1954, 349-386), and he has argued that the intent of the Chronicler was to authenticate the claims of the Davidic dynasty and its relationship to the post-Exilic community with its temple and liturgy. The value of the Chronicler as an historical source has been more widely recognized, even if his point of view is highly individual and tendentious.

Before leaving the subject of Israel's history, we must point out the immensely valuable *Ancient Israel* (New York, McGraw-Hill, 1961; French original, 1958-1960) of the renowned French archeologist and exegete, Roland de Vaux, O.P., director of the Ecole Biblique in Jerusalem. Although his summary history of Israel in Vigouroux, *Dictionnaire de la Bible Supplément* 4, 1949, 729-777, is somewhat antiquated now, one may judge from *Ancient Israel* the revision which that dictionary article will doubtless undergo.

Ancient Israel examines the institutions of Israel: nomadism, family, state, royalty, law, military and religious institutions—in the light of the biblical text and archeological data. There is nothing like this study available in any language; it represents the cautious and sober judgment of one who is in control of the material. Even if he may not be always right, his judgment is always well-balanced.

MISCELLANEOUS AREAS

Demands of space limit us to a scatter-shot approach to several areas that are nevertheless not to be neglected in a survey such as this.

1. *Exegesis and Dogma.* The famous essay of Karl Rahner, S.J., on this topic seems to have given the name to the valuable collection of studies edited by H. Vorgrimler, *Exegese und Dogmatik* (Mainz, Matthias-Grünewald, 1962), in which it is reproduced (pp. 25-52) along with E. H. Schillebeeckx, O.P., "Exegese, Dogmatik und Dogmenentwicklung" (pp. 91-114). Rahner addresses himself first to the exegete and then to the dogmatic theologian, urging candor (even if "dangerous") and a coöperation based on mutual respect and knowledge. He raises some concrete and delicate questions, for example, in the realm of fundamental theology and biblical history, that should be met with courage and openness. Schillebeeckx describes Catholic dogma as the hearing (correct, but not exhaustive) of the word of revelation. The dogma is not found as such in the Bible, but it represents what the Church hears at a given period in its history. This historical level is investigated by the dogmatic theologian, while the exegete examines the biblical level. It is to be hoped that these considerations, along with those suggested by Luis Alonso Schökel, S.J., in "Argument d'Ecriture et théologie biblique dans l'enseignement théologique," *Nouvelle revue theologique* 81, 1959, 337-354, will contribute to the bridge-building between Scripture and dogma,[16] and to the revitalization of theological teaching.

2. *Messianism.* The general advance in our knowledge of the historical background and textual exegesis has contributed greatly

---

[16] See also H. Haag, "Zum Verhältnis Exegese-Dogmatik," *Tübinger Theologische Quartalschrift* 142, 1962, 1-22.

to a clearer picture of the development of Old Testament messianism. The entire 1957 volume of the *Catholic Biblical Quarterly* gives a fairly accurate picture of the current understanding of this subject. One of the most important gains has been the recognition of the nature of royal messianism. As developed in the Old Testament, this is essentially dynastic, and rooted in Nathan's oracle to David (2 S 7). The relevant texts are to be referred in the first instance to the reigning king. For example, the purely predictive interpretation of Psalms 2, 72, etc., in relation to an eschatological king-figure is generally recognized to be an oversimplification. This does not deny that such passages have messianic implications; rather, one is able to understand more precisely the nuanced manner in which the messianic hope was expressed through the Davidic dynasty. In this respect, the study of royal messianism by John L. McKenzie is a model synthesis.[17] In 1956, two important studies appeared: S. Mowinckel, *He That Cometh* (Oxford, Blackwell; a revision of the Norwegian original of 1951) and H. Ringgren, *The Messiah in the Old Testament* (Naperville, Allenson). Mowinckel's great study is weakened by a definition of messianism as eschatological—there is no messianism until Deutero-Isaiah, when the hope of restoration was eschatologized. The majority of scholars would agree, I think, that the messianic hope is older, and that eschatology is only one form of it. The many studies of Joseph Coppens of the University of Louvain have clarified the roots and the various strands of messianism within the Old Testament.[18] In summary, we have a clearer picture of the development of the messianic hope in Israel, but there is not yet an adequate synthesis of all the data; perhaps no real synthesis is possible.[19]

[17] *Catholic Biblical Quarterly* 19, 1957, 25-52; reprinted in his *Myths and Realities*, 203-231.

[18] See his *L'Attente du Messie* (Bruges, Desclée de Brouwer, 1954); for further references, see Roland E. Murphy, O. Carm., "Notes on Old Testament Messianism and Apologetics," *Catholic Biblical Quarterly* 19, 1957, 5-15, and also the valuable study of P. Grelot, "L'accomplissement des Écritures en Jésus-Christ," *Le Christ, envoyé de Dieu* (Bulletin du Comité des Etudes, Compagnie de Saint-Sulpice, 35; Paris, 1961), 365-386.

[19] The "synthesis" supplied by A. Gelin in Vigouroux, *Dictionnaire de la Bible Supplément* 5, 1165-1212, remains inadequate, despite much valuable information.

3. *Literary Genres.* There should be no need to recall the emphasis of the encyclical *Divino afflante Spiritu* on the duty of exegetes to determine the literary form(s) in which the biblical message is expressed. There are two general ways (often combined in a given case) in which the literary genre may be established: A comparison with extrabiblical literature may provide the key, or else a book can be understood when interpreted out of the Bible itself. 1) The most fertile area of research in modern biblical studies has been precisely the relating of the Bible to the surrounding world. This has been made possible by the discovery of whole literatures, down to 1929 with Ugarit, and 1947 with the Dead Sea Scrolls. The comparative studies have not only increased our understanding of the background of the biblical text, but in many instances they have shed new light on the meaning of the text. Such, for example, has been Mendenhall's fundamental study of the covenant form, which was mentioned above. It is impossible to do justice to all of this research, but some should be mentioned as typical of the study of the relationship of the Old Testament to its world, for example, W. Moran, S.J., "The Ancient Near Eastern Background of the Love of God in Deuteronomy," *Catholic Biblical Quarterly* 25, 1963, 77-87; J. Vergote, *Joseph en Egypte* (Louvain, Publications Universitaires, 1959); J. T. Milik, " 'Prière de Nabonide' et autres écrits d'un cycle de Daniel," *Revue biblique* 63, 1956, 407-415; M. J. Dahood, S.J., "Ugaritic Studies and the Bible," *Gregorianum* 43, 1962, 55-79. William F. Albright has been a past master in bringing to bear the religion and culture of the ancient Near East on the Bible, as his *From the Stone Age to Christianity* (New York, Doubleday, 1957[2]) proves. 2) Two very successful examples of arriving at the literary form by interpreting the Bible out of the Bible are the books of Judith and Jonah. P. W. Skehan has firmly fixed the character of the book of Judith in "The Hand of Judith," *Catholic Biblical Quarterly* 25, 1963, 94-110, by discovering the deliberate parallels which the author draws between the hand of God, the hand of Moses, and the hand of Judith. The detailed literary reference to Exodus, Psalms, and other books establish beyond any doubt the nonhistorical, theological type of writing in this book. A. Feuillet has done the same for the book of

Jonah in Vigouroux, *Dictionnaire de la Bible Supplément*, 4, 1104-1131, by indicating its use of "anthological composition" (the allusive use of words and phrases of earlier biblical literature)—with clear dependence on Jeremiah particularly. The book is a satire concerning a disobedient prophet which forms a parable concerning the all-embracing mercy of God.

Now that myth is no longer defined as a story about gods, there is reason to ask if there is myth in the Old Testament. H. Cazelles (Vigouroux, *Dictionnaire de la Bible Supplément* 6, 246-261) recognizes the presence of myth, at least in the earlier Old Testament writings. J. L. McKenzie's review of the current studies of the nature of myth ("Myth in the Old Testament," *Catholic Biblical Quarterly* 21, 1959, 265-282 = *Myths and Realities*, Milwaukee, Bruce, 1963, 182-200) illustrates the changed point of view. Myth is no longer equated with polytheism and untruth. It represents an approach to reality in the form of imagery and story, which must be respected, and several points of comparison can be made between the Old Testament and such works as the "epics" of Gilgamesh and Enuma Elish.[20]

In the refined area of stylistic and literary analysis of Old Testament poetry, a beginning has been made by Luis Alonso Schökel, S.J., *Estudios de Poética Hebrea* (Barcelona, Flors, 1963). The Spanish professor of the Pontifical Biblical Institute brings to bear the methods of current literary criticism (the "stylistic analysis" school of Spitzer and Alonso) on the poetry of the Old Testament; this is an entirely new approach. The reality of "anthological composition" (*style anthologique*, as its originator, André Robert, called it) is being recognized more and more as a standard feature of later Hebrew poetry, such as the Psalms and the wisdom literature.

4. *Psalms and the Canticle of Canticles.* While we cannot permit ourselves the luxury of examining various books in any detail, the Book of Psalms can be considered an exception—if only for the reason that the Psalms exemplify so many different aspects of bibli-

[20] Other important works on this subject are S. H. Hooke, *Myth, Ritual and Kingship* (Oxford, Clarendon, 1958[2]); B. S. Childs, *Myth and Reality in the Old Testament* (Naperville, Allenson, 1960).

cal research: literary types and poetic style, cultic background, Near-Eastern parallels, and biblical theology. Moreover, the last decade has seen the appearance of several important works.[21] Foremost among these is S. Mowinckel, *The Psalms in Israel's Worship* 1-2 (Nashville, Abingdon, 1962)—a book that represents the culmination of forty years of study (since his famous *Psalmenstudien* of 1921-1924). Every phase of Psalm study is represented here, but particularly the cultic aspects of these prayers. If one may doubt the existence of the feast of the Enthronement of Yahweh, with its attendant Psalms (about forty), there is no denying the alert and vital way in which Mowinckel has analyzed these prayers. The most up-to-date commentary is by H. J. Kraus, *Psalmen* 1-2, which, despite the author's predilection for a royal festival of Sion (in opposition to Mowinckel), reflects the current scholarly understanding of this book.

The Canticle of Canticles is important because it illustrates a rather significant change in the trend of Catholic interpretation, and in the last ten years it has figured in biblical research with a remarkable frequency for its size.[22] The allegorical interpretation of the Canticle has been the customary and time-honored interpretation among Catholic exegetes. Three articles by foremost Catholic scholars offered sound reason for regarding the literal sense of the Canticle as referring to human love between man and woman: A. M. Dubarle, O.P., "L'amour humain dans le Cantique des Cantiques," *Revue biblique* 61, 1954, 67-86; M. A. van den Oudenrijn, O.P., "Vom Sinne des Hohen Liedes," *Divus Thomas* 31, 1953, 257-280; J. P. Audet, O.P., "Le sens du Cantique des Cantiques," *Revue biblique* 62, 1955, 197-221.

These articles have not settled the question, by any means, but they have provided sound reasons, and sufficient in my estimation, why the Canticle should be referred to human love in the literal sense. The very latest commentary by a Catholic is a massive argumentation for the allegorical theory: A. Robert, A. Feuillet,

[21] See R. de Langhe, ed., *Le Psautier* (Louvain, 1962), in which the origins and literary problems of the Psalms are discussed in the perspective of recent studies.

[22] Recent trends up to 1953 were summarized in my article, "Recent Literature on the Canticle of Canticles," *Catholic Biblical Quarterly* 16, 1954, 1-11.

R. Tournay, *Le Cantique des Cantiques* (Paris, Gabalda, 1963).[23] These scholars attempt to solve the meaning by the method of anthological composition; although this method has served well in the wisdom literature, it is highly artificial here. The distinct and wide difference of opinion—particularly in the face of the general, standard interpretation among the majority of Church Fathers and the medieval writers—is instructive; it indicates that Catholic exegetes are striving to solve the problem on the only level that it can be solved: historical and literary arguments. It is quite clear that there is no dogmatic tradition that has determined the literal sense of this challenging little book. It is certainly time to put an end to the myth that the so-called "naturalistic" interpretation of the Canticle is excluded by the strictures of the Second Council of Constantinople (553) against Theodore of Mopsuestia.

5. *The Prophets.* There is no need to go into detail here after the summary of G. Fohrer, "Zehn Jahre Literatur zur alttestamentlichen Prophetie (1951-1960)," *Theologische Rundschau* 28, 1962, 1-75, 235-297, 301-374. Since then, several general studies of prophetical literature have appeared, such as J. Lindblom, *Prophecy in Ancient Israel* (Philadelphia, Muhlenberg, 1962), with its emphasis on the psychological background of prophetism; A. J. Heschel, *The Prophets* (New York, Harper, 1962), which is dominated by the Jewish scholar's view of sympathy; Bruce Vawter, C.M., *The Conscience of Israel* (New York, Sheed & Ward, 1961), is a well-balanced, knowledgeable introduction to Israelite prophecy.

Recent research reflects a wide agreement on the role of oral tradition in the formation of the Old Testament, and especially of the prophetical writings. Only in a very few instances do we have firsthand information of the prophet himself being involved in the writing down of his oracles (for example, Jer 36). It is commonly assumed that it would have been his disciples who would have compiled his sayings; the disparate collections in a given prophetical book (and also the description of the prophet in the third person, as, for example, in Amos 7:10ff.) suggest this. A. Gunneweg

[23] Two recent and important commentaries by non-Catholic scholars are: G. Gerlemann, *Das Hohelied* (Neukirchen, Neukirchener Verlag, 1963) and W. Rudolph, *Das Hohelied* (Gütersloh, Mohn, 1962).

(*Mündliche and schriftliche Tradition der vorexilischen Prophet-enbücher*, Göttingen, Vandenhoeck & Ruprecht, 1959) has argued against the extremes of the Uppsala position on oral tradition by stressing the priestly office of the prophets. Because they were cultic prophets, it is far more probable that writing was the vehicle of transmission, rather than oral tradition. A distinction is necessary here; the sons of the prophets (*b*e*nê n*e*bî'îm*) do seem to be associated with sanctuaries and probably were cult prophets. But it is not clear that any of the writing prophets whose works have been preserved for us must be so designated. On the other hand, the attitude of the writing prophets to the cult is ambivalent. They condemn it many times, and this has provided the basis in the past for a distinction between a "more spiritual" and "less spiritual" attitude. On all sides today, there is a recognition that this distinction is due to modern attitude and not pertinent to the prophets, who did not discard the cult, but who did condemn insincere worship. They spoke in typical Semitic form of "dialectical negation."

Another noticeable change in emphasis has been the recognition of the dependence of the prophets on previous Israelite traditions. They were not men simply "drunk with the Spirit," but rather they were seriously engaged in a dialogue with the present situation, in the light of past traditions. G. von Rad, particularly, has stressed this aspect of the prophets in the second volume of his *Theologie*, referred to above.

6. *Wisdom Literature.* The most important single volume on the sapiential literature during the past decade was the *Festschrift* in honor of H. H. Rowley: *Wisdom in Israel and in the Ancient Near East*, edited by M. Noth, D. W. Thomas (*Vetus Testamentum Supplements* 3, Leiden, Brill, 1955). Scholars of international repute contributed detailed studies on various aspects: Canaanite sources (Albright), Solomonic wisdom (Noth), wisdom in the prophets (Lindblom), etc. The volume illustrates two basic observations that should be made about Old Testament wisdom literature: 1) Scholarship is continually expanding the comparative literature of Egypt and Mesopotamia which is related to the Old Testament wisdom books. 2) Not enough actual study of the wisdom movement in Israel is being carried on.

1) There has been an increasing number of studies which con-

tribute to the courtly *Sitz in Leben* of Egyptian wisdom literature. The latest example is to be found in *Les Sagesses du proche-orient ancien* (Paris, Presses Universitaires, 1964). The research on Egyptian wisdom has given biblical scholars the perspective which now dominates the understanding of the milieu of Israelite wisdom: its royal associations.[24] However, the whole story is not yet told. There is strikingly little from courtly sources in Mesopotamia, as is clear from the monumental study of W. G. Lambert, *Babylonian Wisdom Literature* (Oxford, Clarendon, 1960). Hence one may perhaps look forward to even more fertile studies of ancient wisdom which will underline the paternal or home origins of wisdom, as suggested by J. P. Audet, O.P., in G. Couturier, C.S.C., "Sagesse babylonienne et Sagesse israélite," *Sciences ecclésiastiques* 14, 1962, 265-309.

2) There has not been enough attention paid to the striking fact that if the origins of wisdom are in the court, nevertheless most, if not all, of Israelite wisdom literature is post-Exilic, when there was no longer any court.[25] What is the precise nature of the wisdom movement, its motives, its teachers, as this developed in the obscure centuries after the Exile? A more straightforward evaluation of the wisdom literature on its own merits (allowing, however, for foreign counterparts) is needed, and perhaps there will be a solution of the problem as to its place in Old Testament theology—a point raised in modern discussion by G. E. Wright, *God Who Acts* (Naperville, Allenson, 1952).

7. *The Dead Sea Scrolls.* The past decade was also decisive for the famous Scrolls, in that the sensationalism which marked their introduction to the North American public by Edmund Wilson (which was paralleled abroad by the writings of A. Dupont-Sommer and J. Allegro) was readily quashed, and scholars over the world got down to the serious task of evaluation, which still continues.[26] While the texts are far from all being published, especially

[24] See, for example, E. Würthwein, *Die Weisheit Aegyptens und das Alte Testament* (Marburg, Elwert, 1960).

[25] See Roland E. Murphy, O. Carm., "The Concept of Wisdom Literature," in J. L. McKenzie, *The Bible in Current Catholic Thought* (New York, Herder and Herder, 1962), 46-54.

[26] It is quite impossible to give an adequate bibliographical survey of publications on the Scrolls. No other archaeological discovery sired a magazine

those of Caves 4 and 11, the official publications are being efficiently handled in the series of *Discoveries in the Judean Desert*.[27] Significant translations into English have appeared by T. H. Gaster, *The Dead Sea Scriptures* (New York, Doubleday, 1964²); A. Dupont-Sommer, *The Essene Writings from Qumran* (New York, Meridian, 1962); G. Vermès, *The Dead Sea Scrolls in English* (Baltimore, Penguin, 1962). The strictly archeological data is best summarized in R. de Vaux, O.P., *L'archéologie et les manuscrits de la Mer Morte* (New York, Oxford, 1961).

There can be no doubt that the Dead Sea Scrolls (not to be confused with the later documents from the caves of Wadi Murrabba'at or those of the caves near Engaddi excavated by the Israeli) date from before the Jewish revolt of 68-70 A.D. The most likely date for the settlement of the Jewish sect, now commonly identified with the Essenes, at Khirbet Qumran in the Judean wilderness is about the middle of the second century B.C. The Essenes revolted against the normative Judaism of Maccabean times, and, probably under the leadership of the man who was called "the Teacher of Righteousness," they settled at Qumran to prepare for the imminent messianic era. Their mode of life was spare and rigorous—meditating day and night on the law of the Lord—and highly organized. They were the Children of Light, opposed to the Children of Darkness, who included the rest of the Jews and the Gentiles. Their occupation of the Qumran area came to a violent end with the Jewish revolt. Presumably, they had stored their precious manuscripts in the caves for safekeeping, if indeed Cave 4 is not the community library.

The most significant general studies are due to two of the men who worked on the international and interconfessional team which

---

such as *Revue de Qumran,* which was inaugurated in 1958 by Jean Carmignac solely for Qumraniana. The regular surveys of literature in this journal keep one up to date on all publications relative to Qumran; they continue the first bibliographical study published by C. Burchard, *Bibliographie zu den Handschriften vom Toten Meer* (Berlin, Töpelmann, 1957).

[27] Published by Oxford University Press (1955-)—three volumes thus far. The publication of most of the Cave 1 materials was divided between the American Schools of Oriental Research (first Isaiah scroll, Habacuc commentary, and the so-called "Manual of Discipline") and the Hebrew University (second Isaiah scroll, Hodayot, the War scroll, and the Genesis Apocryphon).

deciphered the materials which the eleven Caves have yielded: F. M. Cross, *The Ancient Library of Qumran and Modern Biblical Studies* (New York, Doubleday, 1961²), and J. T. Milik, *Ten Years of Discovery in the Wilderness of Judaea* (Naperville, Allenson, 1959). Here one will find a sound evaluation of most of the more important questions raised by the discovery of the Scrolls.

The areas of theological interest that have been opened up, and which will continue to be affected by scholarly research, are threefold: the transmission of the Hebrew Bible, the intertestamental literature (and the Jewish world in which it flourished), and the relationship of the Essene doctrines to the literature and teachings of the New Testament.

Until more of the biblical texts are published, the current impressions of the early history of the Hebrew Bible remain tantalizing. There is every reason to believe that Cross's reconstruction of Hebrew paleography will be successful ("The Development of the Jewish Scripts," in G. E. Wright, *The Bible and the Ancient Near East*, New York, Doubleday, 1961, 133-202). And scholars are quite convinced that the Qumran biblical manuscripts prove that there was a great variety of recensions (at least three) of the pre-Masoretic Bible. In particular, the validity of the Septuagint type has been established by the discovery of fragmentary Hebrew manuscripts that reflect the Septuagint.

The intertestamental literature has been immeasurably enriched, and with it our understanding of the religious ferment in Judaism before and during the time of Christ. One need only compare the 1963 reissue of R. H. Charles, *The Apocrypha and Pseudepigraph of the Old Testament* (New York, Oxford) with the works in Vermès' translation in order to appreciate the number and variety of the apocryphal (or pseudepigraphical) works whose existence was never known before or known only in secondary translation. All of this will be important in reconstructing the religious currents of the Judaism in which Christianity was born.

There is no doubt that the most important contributions of the Qumran discoveries have to do with Christianity as described in the New Testament. A quick impression can be garnered from the parallels published by this writer in the *Catholic Biblical Quarterly* 18, 1956, 263-272, and a detailed analysis has been given by

67

H. Braun, "Qumran und das Neue Testament," *Theologische Rundschau* 28, 1962, 97-234; 29, 1963, 142-176, 189-260; the article is to be continued. One may perhaps summarize the parallels between Qumran and the New Testament under the following headings: *vocabulary* (for example, *b^ene r^esono*, the sons of his good pleasure, *"hominibus bonae voluntatis"*); *thought-world* (for example, the ethical dualism that divides this world into light and darkness; eschatological tension, etc.); *concrete practices* (especially ascetical —ritual ablutions, hierarchical structure of organization); *understanding of the Old Testament* (see J. A. Fitzmyer, S.J., "The Use of Explicit Old Testament Quotations in Qumran Literature and in the New Testament," *New Testament Studies* 7, 1960-1961, 297-333).

The connection between some ideas of the Qumranites and those of the New Testament writers, and of Jesus himself, are not to be denied. All belonged to the same religious background of Judaism; all looked to the Old Testament as heritage. The real problem is the determination of dependence in specific instances. Nothing is to be gained by such generalizations as inferring that John the Baptist or even Jesus was an Essene at some time or other. On the other hand, there can be no reasonable doubt that both of them must have been aware of the Essene teachings, and so have taken a position concerning them. My own opinion is that, by and large, the influence of Essenism on New Testament thought is largely indirect—the ideas which they shared were current in the milieu in which both were formed. However, there are several points at which a dependence on Qumran appears probable, as, for example, in 2 Corinthians 6:14ff., as shown by J. A. Fitzmyer, S.J., "Qumran and the Interpolated Paragraph in 2 Cor 6,14-7,1," *Catholic Biblical Quarterly* 23, 1961, 271-280; he has also pointed out that the precise dualism or division of all humanity into two groups of good and evil is unknown outside of Qumran and the New Testament—this cannot therefore be explained by indirect influence.

We may expect more similarities between Qumran and the New Testament to appear, as the scrolls and fragments are published, but it appears that the distinctive message of Christianity—the mystery of the redemptive Incarnation, death and resurrection—was not "anticipated," as some have alleged, by the Essenes.[28]

Bibliography

BIBLIOGRAPHICAL AIDS

Biblica, "Elenchus Bibliographicus Biblicus," edited by P. NOBER, Rome, Pontificio Istituto Biblico.

Book List, edited by G. W. ANDERSON, Edinburgh, Society for Old Testament Study.

GLANZMAN, G., AND FITZMYER, J. A. *An Introductory Bibliography for the Study of Scripture,* Westminster, Newman, 1961.

Internationale Zeitschriftenschau für Bibelwissenschaft und Grenzgebiete, edited by F. STIER, Düsseldorf, Patmos.

Theologische Rundschau, edited by W. G. KÜMMEL AND E. DINCKLER, Tübingen, Mohr.

SURVEYS

BRIGHT, J. "Modern Study of Old Testament Literature," in G. E. Wright, *The Bible and the Ancient Near East,* New York, Doubleday, 1961.

KRAUS, H. J. *Geschichte der historisch-kritischen Erforschung des Alten Testaments von der Reformation bis zur Gegenwart,* Neukirchen, Erziehungsvereins, 1956.

NOTH, M. *Developing Lines of Theological Thought in Germany,* Richmond, Union Theological Seminary, 1963.

ROWLEY, H. H. (editor). *The Old Testament and Modern Study,* Oxford, Clarendon, 1951.

SCHULZ, S. "Die römisch-katholische Exegese zwischen historisch-kritischer Methode und lehramtlichem Machtspruch," *Evangelische Theologie* 22, 1962, 141-156.

[28] See also F. Nötscher, *Zur theologischen Terminologie der Qumran-Texte* (Bonn, Hanstein, 1956); P. Benoit, "Qumran et le Nouveau Testament," *New Testament Studies* 7, 1960-1961, 276-296.

GENERAL

ANDERSON, G. W. A *Critical Introduction to the Old Testament,* London, Duckworth, 1959.

EISSFELDT, O. *Einleitung in das Alte Testament,* Tübingen, Mohr, 1964³.

FITZMYER, J. A. "A Recent Roman Scriptural Controversy," *Theological Studies* 22, 1961, 426-444.

FREEDMAN, D. N. "Pentateuch," *The Interpreter's Dictionary of the Bible* 3, Nashville, Abingdon, 1962.

MARIANI, B. *Introductio in libros sacros Veteris Testamenti,* Rome, Herder, 1958.

ROBERT, A., AND FEUILLET, A. (editors). *Introduction à la Bible* 1, Tournai, Desclée et Cie., 1957, 1959².

WEISER, A. *Einleitung in das Alte Testament,* Göttingen, Vandenhoeck & Ruprecht, 1957⁴; ET *The Old Testament. Its Formation and Development,* New York, Association, 1961.

COMMENTARIES

Das Alte Testament Deutsch, Göttingen, Vandenhoeck & Ruprecht, 1949ff.

Bonner Bibel (Die Heilige Schrift des Alten Testaments), Bonn, Hanstein, 1923ff.

BORN, A. VAN DEN (editor). *De Boeken van het Oude Testament,* Roermond, Romen & Zonen.

CASTELLINO, G. *Il Libro dei Salmi,* "Sacra Bibbia," Turin, Marietti, 1955.

CLAMER, A. *Exode,* "La Sainte Bible" 12, Paris, Letouzey, 1956.

FOHRER, G. *Das Buch Hiob,* "Kommentar yum Alten Testament" 16, Gütersloh, Mohn, 1963.

KRAUS, H. J., *Psalmen* 1-2, "Biblischer Kommentar" 15, 1-2, Neukirchen, Neukirchener Verlag, 1960.

NÖTSCHER, F. (editor). *Echter Bibel,* Würzburg, Echter, 1955-1959.

RAD, G. VON, *Das erste Buch Mose,* "Das Alte Testament Deutsch" 2/4, Göttingen, Vandenhoeck & Ruprecht, 1953; ET *Genesis,* Philadelphia, Westminster, 1961.

RUDOLPH, W. *Jeremia,* "Handbuch zum Alten Testament" 12, Tübingen, Mohr, 1958².

ZIMMERLI, W. *Prediger,* "Das Alte Testament Deutsch" 16/1, Göttingen, Vandenhoeck & Ruprecht, 1962.

OLD TESTAMENT THEOLOGY

BARR, J. *The Semantics of Biblical Language*, New York, Oxford University Press, 1961.

BOMAN, T. *Hebrew Thought Compared with Greek*, Philadelphia, Westminster, 1960.

DUBARLE, A. M. *Le péché originel dans l'Ecriture*, "Lectio Divina" 20, Paris, Cerf, 1958, ET *The Biblical Doctrine of Original Sin*, New York, Herder and Herder, 1964.

EBELING, G. *Word and Faith*, Philadelphia, Fortress, 1963.

EICHRODT, W. *Theologie des Alten Testaments*, Göttingen, Vandenhoeck & Ruprecht, 1, 1957[5]; 2-3, 1961[4]; ET of volume 1: *Theology of the Old Testament* 1, Philadelphia, Westminster, 1961.

GUILLET, J. *Themes of the Bible*, Notre Dame, Fides, 1960.

IMSCHOOT, P. VAN. *Théologie de l'Ancien Testament* 1-2, Tournai, Desclée et Cie., 1954-1956.

JACOB, E. *Theology of the Old Testament*, New York, Harper, 1958.

JOHNSON, A. R. *The Vitality of the Individual in the Thought of Ancient Israel*, Cardiff, University of Wales, 1949.

————. *The One and the Many in the Israelite Conception of God*, Cardiff, University of Wales, 1961[2].

KNIGHT, G. A. F. *A Christian Theology of the Old Testament*, Richmond, John Knox, 1959.

McKENZIE, J. L. *The Two-Edged Sword*, Milwaukee, Bruce, 1956.

————. *Myths and Realities*, Milwaukee, Bruce, 1963.

MURPHY, R. E. "A New Theology of the Old Testament," *Catholic Biblical Quarterly* 23, 1961, 217-233.

PLOEG, J. VAN DER. "Une théologie de l'Ancien Testament, est-elle possible?" *Ephemerides Theologicae Lovanienses* 38, 1962, 417-434.

RAD, G. VON. *Theologie des Alten Testaments* 1-2, Munich, Kaiser, 1958-1960; ET *Old Testament Theology* 1, New York, Harper, 1962.

RAHNER, K. *Theological Investigations* 1 (Baltimore, Helicon, 1961), 79-118.

RAMLOT, M. L. "Une décade de théologie biblique," *Revue thomiste* 64, 1964, 65-96, à suivre.

RENCKENS, H. *Israel's Concept of the Beginning. The Theology of Genesis I-III*, New York, Herder and Herder, 1964.

RENDTORFF, R. "Die Offenbarungsvorstellungen im alten Israel," in

W. Pannenberg, *Offenbarung als Geschichte*, Göttingen, Vandenhoeck & Ruprecht, 1961, 1963[2].

STENDAHL, K. "Biblical Theology," *Interpreter's Dictionary of the Bible* 1 (Nashville, Abingdon, 1962), 1, 418-432.

VAUX, R. DE. "A propos de théologie biblique," *Zeitschrift für die alttestamentliche Wissenschaft* 68, 1956, 225-227.

VAWTER, B. A *Path Through Genesis*, New York, Sheed & Ward, 1956.

VRIEZEN, TH. C. An *Outline of Old Testament Theology*, Oxford, Blackwell, 1958.

THE RELATION OF THE TESTAMENTS

ANDERSON, B. W. (editor). *The Old Testament and Christian Faith. A Theological Discussion*, New York, Harper, 1963.

BROWN, R. E. *The Sensus Plenior of Sacred Scripture*, Baltimore, St. Mary's, 1955.

———. "The *Sensus Plenior* in the Last Ten Years," *Catholic Biblical Quarterly* 25, 1963, 262-285.

COPPENS, J. *Les Harmonies des deux Testaments*, Tournai, Casterman, 1949[2].

GRELOT, P. *Sens chrétien de l'Ancien Testament*, Tournai, Desclée et Cie., 1962.

LARCHER, C. *L'actualité chrétienne de l'Ancien Testament*, "Lectio Divina" 34, Paris, Cerf, 1962.

McCARTHY, D. J. "Personality, Society and Inspiration," *Theological Studies* 24, 1963, 553-576.

MURPHY, R. E. "The Relationship between the Testaments," *Catholic Biblical Quarterly* 26, 1964, 349-359.

RAD, G. VON. *Theologie des Alten Testaments* 1-2, Munich, Kaiser, 1958-1960; ET *Old Testament Theology* 1, New York, Harper, 1962.

ROBINSON, J. M. "Interpretation of Scripture in Biblical Studies Today," in S. H. Miller and G. E. Wright, *Ecumenical Dialogue at Harvard. The Roman Catholic-Protestant Colloquium*, Cambridge (Mass.), Harvard University Press, 1964.

DE VAUX, R. "A propos de théologie biblique," *Zeitschrift für die alttestamentliche Wissenschaft* 68, 1956, 225-227.

VAWTER, B. "The Fuller Sense: Some Considerations," *Catholic Biblical Quarterly* 26, 1964, 85-96.

VRIEZEN, TH. C. An *Outline of Old Testament Theology*, Oxford, Blackwell, 1958.

WESTERMANN, C. (editor). *Essays on Old Testament Hermeneutics,* Richmond, John Knox, 1963.

THE HISTORY OF ISRAEL

ALBRIGHT, W. F. *The Biblical Period from Abraham to Ezra,* revised edition, New York, Harper, 1963.

ALT, A. *Kleine Schriften zur Geschichte des Volkes Israel* 1-3, Munich, Beck, 1953-59.

BALTZER, K. *Das Bundesformular,* "Wissenschaftliche Monographien zum Alten und Neuen Testament" 4. Neukirchen, Neukirchener Verlag, 1960.

BEYERLIN, W. *Herkunft und Geschichte der ältesten Sinaitraditionen,* Tübingen, Mohr, 1961.

BRIGHT, J. *Early Israel in Recent History Writing,* "Studies in Biblical Theology" 19, Naperville, Allenson, 1956.

————. *A History of Israel,* Philadelphia, Westminster, 1959.

BRUNET, A. "Le Chroniste et ses sources," *Revue biblique* 60, 1953, 481-508; 61, 1954, 349-386.

FREEDMAN, D. N. "The Babylonian Chronicle," *The Biblical Archaeologist Reader,* New York, Doubleday, 1961.

————. "The Chronicler's Purpose," *Catholic Biblical Quarterly* 23, 1961, 436-442.

JENNI, E. "Zwei Jahrzehnte Forschung an den Büchern Josua bis Könige," *Theologische Rundschau* 27, 1961, 1-32; 97-146.

MENDENHALL, G. *Law and Covenant in Israel and the Ancient Near East,* Pittsburgh, Biblical Colloquium, 1955. Reprinted from "Law and Covenant in Israel and the Ancient Near East," *The Biblical Archaeologist* 17, 1954, 26-46, 49-76.

NOTH, M. *Ueberlieferungsgeschichte des Pentateuch,* Stuttgart, Kohlhammer, 1948[2].

————. *Ueberlieferungsgeschichtliche Studien,* Tübingen, Niemeyer, 1957[2].

————. *The History of Israel,* London, Black, 1960[2].

————. "Der Beitrag der Archäologie zur Geschichte Israels," *Vetus Testamentum Supplements* 7 (Leiden, Brill, 1960), 262-282.

VAUX, R. DE. "Israel," *Dictionnaire de la Bible Supplément* 4, Paris, Letouzey, 1949.

————. *Ancient Israel,* New York, McGraw-Hill, 1961.

WRIGHT, G. E. *Biblical Archaeology,* Philadelphia, Westminster, 1957, 1962[2].

MISCELLANEOUS AREAS
Exegesis and Dogma

ALONSO SCHÖKEL, LUIS. "Argument d'Ecriture et théologie biblique dans l'enseignement théologique," *Nouvelle revue theologique* 81, 1959, 337-354.

HAAG, H. "Zum Verhältnis Exegese-Dogmatik," *Tübinger Theologische Quartalschrift* 142, 1962, 1-22.

RAHNER, K. "Exegese und Dogmatik," in H. Vorgrimler, *Exegese und Dogmatik*, Mainz, Matthias-Grünewald, 1962.

SCHILLEBEECKX, E. H. "Exegese, Dogmatik und Dogmenentwicklung," in H. Vorgrimler, *Exegese und Dogmatik*, Mainz, Matthias-Grünewald, 1962.

Messianism

COPPENS, J. (editor). *L'Attente du Messie*, Bruges, Desclée de Brouwer, 1954.

GELIN, A. "Messianisme," *Dictionnaire de la Bible Supplément* 5, Paris, Letouzey, 1957.

GRELOT, P. "L'accomplissement des Ecritures en Jésus-Christ," *Le Christ, envoyé de Dieu*, Bulletin du Comité des Etudes, Compagnie de Saint-Sulpice 35; Paris, 1961.

MCKENZIE, J. L. *Myths and Realities*, pp. 203-231, Milwaukee, Bruce, 1963. Reprinted from "Royal Messianism," *Catholic Biblical Quarterly* 19, 1957, 25-52.

MOWINCKEL, S. *He That Cometh*, Oxford, Blackwell, 1956.

MURPHY, R. E. "Notes on Old Testament Messianism and Apologetics," *Catholic Biblical Quarterly* 19, 1957, 5-15.

RINGGREN, H. *The Messiah in the Old Testament*, "Studies in Biblical Theology" 18, Naperville, Allenson, 1956.

Literary Genres

ALBRIGHT, W. F. *From the Stone Age to Christianity*, New York, Doubleday, 1957[2].

ALONSO SCHÖKEL, LUIS. *Estudios de Poética Hebrea*, Barcelona, Flors, 1963.

CAZELLES, H. "Le mythe et l'Ancien Testament," *Dictionnaire de la Bible Supplément*, Paris, Letouzey, 1959.

CHILDS, B. S. *Myth and Reality in the Old Testament,"* Studies in Biblical Theology" 27, Naperville, Allenson, 1960.

DAHOOD, M. J. "Ugaritic Studies and the Bible," *Gregorianum* 43, 1962, 55-79.

FEUILLET, A. "Jonas," *Dictionnaire de la Bible Supplément* 4, Paris, Letouzey, 1949.

HOOKE, S. H. (editor). *Myth, Ritual and Kingship*, Oxford, Clarendon, 1958².

MCKENZIE, J. L. *Myths and Realities*, pp. 182-200, Milwaukee, Bruce, 1963. Reprinted from "Myth in the Old Testament," *Catholic Biblical Quarterly* 21, 1959, 265-282.

MENDENHALL, G. *Law and Covenant in Israel and the Ancient Near East*, Pittsburgh, Biblical Colloquium, 1955. Reprinted from "Law and Covenant in Israel and the Ancient Near East," *The Biblical Archaeologist* 17, 1954, 26-46, 49-76.

MILIK, J. T. " 'Prière de Nabonide' et autres écrits d'un cycle de Daniel," *Revue biblique* 63, 1956, 407-415.

MORAN, W. "The Ancient Near Eastern Background of the Love of God in Deuteronomy," *Catholic Biblical Quarterly* 25, 1963, 77-87.

SKEHAN, P. W. "The Hand of Judith," *Catholic Biblical Quarterly* 25, 1963, 94-110.

VERGOTE, J. *Joseph en Egypte*, Louvain, Publications Universitaires, 1959.

Psalms and Canticle of Canticles

AUDET, J. P. "Le sens du Cantique des Cantiques," *Revue biblique* 62, 1955, 197-221

DUBARLE, A. M. "L'amour humain dans le Cantique des Cantiques," *Revue biblique* 61, 1954, 67-86.

GERLEMANN, G. *Das Hohelied*, "Biblischer Kommentar" 18/2, Neukirchen, Neukirchener Verlag, 1963.

KRAUS, H. J. *Psalmen* 1-2, "Biblischer Kommentar" 15, 1-2, Neukirchen, Neukirchener Verlag, 1960.

LANGHE, R. DE (editor). *Le Psautier*, Louvain, 1962.

MOWINCKEL, S. *The Psalms in Israel's Worship* 1-2, Nashville, Abingdon, 1962.

MURPHY, R. E. "Recent Literature on the Canticle of Canticles," *Catholic Biblical Quarterly* 16, 1954, 1-11.

OUDENRIJN, M. A. VAN DEN. "Vom Sinne des Hohen Liedes," *Divus Thomas* 31, 1953, 257-280.

ROBERT, A., FEUILLET, A. AND TOURNAY, R. *Le Cantique des Cantiques*, "Etudes bibliques," Paris, Gabalda, 1963.

RUDOLPH, W. *Das Hohelied*, "Kommentar zum Alten Testament" 17/2, Gütersloh, Mohn, 1962.

The Prophets

FOHRER, G. "Zehn Jahre Literatur zur alttestamentlichen Prophetie (1951-1960)," *Theologische Rundschau* 28, 1962, 1-75, 235-297, 301-374.

GUNNEWEG, A. H. J. *Mündliche und schriftliche Tradition der vorexilischen Prophetenbücher*, Göttingen, Vandenhoeck & Ruprecht, 1959.

HESCHEL, A. J. *The Prophets*, New York, Harper, 1962.

LINDBLOM, J. *Prophecy in Ancient Israel*, Philadelphia, Muhlenberg, 1962.

RAD, G. VON. *Theologie des Alten Testaments* 2, Munich, Kaiser, 1960.

VAWTER, B. *The Conscience of Israel*, New York, Sheed & Ward, 1961.

Wisdom Literature

COUTURIER, G. "Sagesse babylonienne et Sagesse israélite," *Sciences ecclésiastiques* 14, 1962, 265-309.

LAMBERT, W. G. *Babylonian Wisdom Literature*, Oxford, Clarendon, 1960.

MURPHY, R. E. "The Concept of Wisdom Literature," in J. L. McKenzie, *The Bible in Current Catholic Thought*, New York, Herder and Herder, 1962, 46-54.

NOTH, M., AND THOMAS, D. W. (editors). *Wisdom in Israel and in the Ancient Near East* [*Festschrift* in honor of H. H. Rowley, *Vetus Testamentum Supplements* 3], Leiden, Brill, 1955.

Les Sagesses du proche-orient ancien, Paris, Presses Universitaires, 1964.

WRIGHT, G. E. *God Who Acts*, "Studies in Biblical Theology" 8, Naperville, Allenson, 1952.

WÜRTHWEIN, E. *Die Weisheit Aegyptens und das Alte Testament*, Marburg, Elwert, 1960.

The Dead Sea Scrolls

BENOIT, P. "Qumran et le Nouveau Testament," *New Testament Studies* 7, 1960-1961, 276-296.

BRAUN, H. "Qumran und das Neue Testament," *Theologische Rund-*

schau 28, 1962, 97-234; 29, 1963, 142-176, 189-260, and to be continued.

BURCHARD, C. *Bibliographie zu den Handschriften vom Toten Meer,* "Beihefte zur Zeitschrift für die Alttestamentliche Wissenschaft" 76, Berlin, Töpelmann, 1957.

CHARLES, R. H. *The Apocrypha and Pseudepigrapha of the Old Testament,* 2 volumes, New York, Oxford University Press, 1913, reprinted 1963.

CROSS, F. M., JR. *The Ancient Library of Qumran and Modern Biblical Studies,* New York, Doubleday, 1961².

————. "The Development of the Jewish Scripts," in G. E. Wright, *The Bible and the Ancient Near East,* New York, Doubleday, 1961, 133-202.

Discoveries in the Judean Desert 1-3, New York, Oxford University Press, 1955, 1961, 1962.

DUPONT-SOMMER, A. *The Essene Writings from Qumran,* New York, Meridian, 1962.

FITZMYER, J. A. "The Use of Explicit Old Testament Quotations in Qumran Literature and in the New Testament," *New Testament Studies* 7, 1960-1961, 297-333.

————. "Qumran and the Interpolated Paragraph in 2 Cor 6,14— 7,1," *Catholic Biblical Quarterly* 23, 1961, 271-280.

GASTER, T. H. *The Dead Sea Scriptures,* New York, Doubleday, 1956, 1964².

MILIK, J. T. *Ten Years of Discovery in the Wilderness of Judaea,* Naperville, Allenson, 1959.

MURPHY, R. E. "The Dead Sea Scrolls and New Testament Comparisons," *Catholic Biblical Quarterly* 18, 1956, 263-272.

NÖTSCHER, F. *Zur theologischen Terminologie der Qumran-Texte,* "Bonner Biblische Beiträge" 10, Bonn, Hanstein, 1956.

Revue de Qumran, edited by J. CARMIGNAC, Paris, Gabalda, 1958-.

VAUX, R. DE. *L'archéologie et les manuscrits de la Mer Morte,* New York, Oxford University Press, 1961.

VERMÈS, G. *The Dead Sea Scrolls in English,* Baltimore, Penguin, 1962.

New Testament Studies

JOHN J. COLLINS, S.J.

It is no exaggeration to say that the past ten years have been memorable for New Testament scholarship. In 1954 the first issue of *New Testament Studies* appeared, and that same year witnessed the publication of the article generally considered the beginning of the "new quest" of the historical Jesus. Meanwhile, books and articles have appeared in abundance. Kittel's theological dictionary is nearing completion, and the first volume has been translated into English. The resurrected Catholic *Biblische Zeitschrift* is now in its eighth year. *The Interpreter's Bible* and *The Interpreter's Dictionary of the Bible* and a second edition of *Peake's Commentary on the Bible* have been published. Besides commentaries on individual books, whole new series have been undertaken, such as the Oxford "New Clarendon Bible," the "Cambridge Greek New Testament," and "Harper's New Testament Commentary." Congresses on the Gospels have been held at Oxford; Louvain and Rome have been the sites of international congresses of Catholic exegetes, and the papers read at these meetings have been published. In fact, so great has been the amount of scholarly writing that Peter Nober's bibliography has overflowed from *Biblica* into *Verbum Domini* with an *elenchus suppletorius*. And, best of all, in the field of Scripture there has been a marked *rapprochement* between Catholics and Protestants which was exemplified by the presence and addresses of Augustin Cardinal Bea at the Harvard University Roman Catholic-Protestant Colloquium of March 27-30, 1963. Any attempt to survey so vast a field means difficulty, and even if one draws up a list of important books, he finds that daily he wishes to add more titles. For that reason, I intend to touch only on certain points that seem of some relevance for Catholics today, but which also have an ecumenical value, because these points may help Catholics to understand and to profit from the work of Protestants, and, on the other hand, because Protestants may be assisted in seeing the reasons behind some Catholic positions.[1]

Scripture and Tradition

First let us consider the question of Scripture and tradition. Until recent years, Scripture alone was considered the fundamental principle of Protestantism, while Catholics arguing from the Council of Trent decree proclaimed Scripture *and* tradition as the rule of faith. J. R. Geiselmann of Tübingen challenged this interpretation of Trent's decree.[2] According to him, all revelation is contained in Scripture, and the majority of recent Catholic writers tend to accept this view. Jacques Dupont expresses the matter thus: The Gospel message is contained in written books and in unwritten traditions. Some Catholics today maintain that there are certain truths found only in tradition. However, the Church in her teaching does not appeal to tradition alone, but to Scripture as clarified by tradition. As an ecumenical gesture, many are hoping that the Vatican Council will adopt this position.[3] However, the problem arises in connection with dogmas such as the Immaculate Conception and the Assumption of the Blessed Virgin. Protestants do not think these doctrines are revealed. Some Catholics derive them from tradition, while others find them implicit in Scripture which is clarified by tradition.

[1] For further information, the reader is referred to the book notices, reviews, and articles in *New Testament Abstracts* to which frequently a reference is inserted below in brackets. [8-100] means volume 8, abstract number 100. [8 p. 100] means volume 8, page 100.

[2] *Die Heilige Schrift und die Tradition,* "Quaestiones Disputatae" 18, Freiburg, Herder, 1962.

[3] J. Dupont, O.S.B., "Ecriture et tradition," *Nouvelle revue théologique* 85, 1963, 337-356, 449-468 [8-25].

INSPIRATION

Another area, in which the debate is domestic, is the nature of inspiration. Until recent times, many, when thinking of inspiration, conceived of a man who collected his material and then composed a book under the influence of the Holy Ghost. Recent studies, however, show that most of the biblical books are the fruit of the labor of many persons, and even of many years. For that reason, modern scholars stress the social character of inspiration, the influence of God on various, perhaps numerous, persons whose activity contributed to the production of a scriptural book.[4] Karl Rahner, S.J., has indicated the social character of inspiration and pointed out how it includes the traditional view of inspiration. In willing the Church, God willed that these books should be a constitutive element of the Church, and this concept includes and clarifies the traditional idea of inspiration. If God wills the books of the New Testament as the objectivization of the definitive and exact expression of the early Church's consciousness of her faith, then he must be in truth the author of Scripture. How God influences the intellect and the will of the individuals concerned is a matter that can be left to the schools for discussion.[5]

Besides Rahner, P. Benoit, O.P., is perhaps the most influential writer on this topic. His latest article on this matter considers recent discussions and St. Thomas' idea of revelation and inspiration. He states that, unlike Thomas, some modern Thomist writers reduce revelation to a passive acceptance of ideas or images and speak as if inspiration were not a form of revelation. Actually, all revelation (perception of divine truth) demands an "inspiration," that is, an elevation of the spirit; and every supernatural elevation of the spirit, in illuminating the judgment with a divine light, ends in a certain perception of divine truth, that is, in a "revelation." St. Thomas's analysis of prophetic knowledge was affected by the

[4] See J. L. McKenzie, S.J., "The Social Character of Inspiration," *Catholic Biblical Quarterly* 24, 1962, 115-124 [7-32].

[5] K. Rahner, S.J., "Ueber die Inspiration der Schrift," in L. Klein, ed., *Diskussion über die Bibel*, Mainz, Grünewald, 1964[2], 7-16; especially 13. See also L. J. Topel, S.J., "Rahner and McKenzie on the Social Theory of Inspiration," *Scripture* 16, 1964, 33-44.

Greek tradition which took "knowledge" in a speculative sense. Today, Thomas would modify his position and would accept the now generally recognized primacy of affectivity and action in the Semitic idea of knowledge. Revelation in the Bible is not primarily communication of supernatural knowledge; it is the disclosing of God's will for the guidance of his people's action. As regards the relation between revelation and inspiration, it seems good to include the speculative judgment under revelation. Revelation, therefore, includes the speculative knowledge of divine truth (attained by natural reflection or by infusion of ideas and images). Inspiration includes practical judgment (about the communication of knowledge obtained by "revelation").[6]

TEXTS AND VERSIONS

The most important discoveries in the field of textual criticism have been the Bodmer Papyri, so called because of their owner, Martin Bodmer, and are housed in his library at Cologny, Switzerland. The oldest complete codices of the New Testament are from the fourth century, the Vatican and the Sinaticus codices. The Chester Beatty Papyri on St. Paul and on the Gospels date from the third century at the earliest. The Bodmer Papyri include in Greek parts of St. Luke, St. John, the Acts, and the Catholic Epistles. There are Coptic fragments of St. Matthew and Romans. But the most exciting find was the manuscript of John (P^{66}) and the manuscript of Luke-John (P^{75}). These writings are dated by K. Aland as second-third century. The readings are still being studied. Thus far, there has been no major departure from the customarily accepted text.[7]

[6] P. Benoit, O.P., "Révélation et inspiration selon la Bible, chez Saint-Thomas et dans les discussions modernes," *Revue biblique* 70, 1963, 321-370 [8-826].

[7] See J. J. C., "Papyrus Bodmer II," *New Testament Abstracts* 2, 1958, 129-132; K. Aland, "Neue Neutestamentliche Papyri," *New Testament Studies* 3, 1957, 261-286 [2-235]; 9, 1963, 303-316 [8-40]; K. Aland, *Synopsis Quattuor Evangeliorum*, Stuttgart, Württembergische Bibelanstalt, 1964, p. xv.

The New English Bible

The most important event in biblical translation was the appearance of the New English Bible[8] which appeared in 1961 and was the fruit of thirteen years' labor by a team of scholars working under the direction of C. H. Dodd. The success of the version is evident from its sales of over five million copies and from the number of reviews, synopsized in *New Testament Abstracts*, that it received. The rendition is a complete break with the traditional Authorized Version. The language is modern, and the rendition free. Almost from the beginning, there has been a debate whether the freedom used verged on paraphrase. On the one hand are those persons who prefer a translation which remains rather close to the text. To their mind, the translator should give what the original said and let the reader find the full meaning, since often part of the meaning is only implied. Others maintain that any good translation is an interpretation, and therefore interpretation and to a certain extent commentary are part of the translation. "A good translation is the best commentary" aptly summarizes this position.

Whether the New English Bible is a good study tool is also a matter of debate. A reviewer in the *Times Literary Supplement* (63, 1964, 460, "New Testament Commentaries"), observes that the new Oxford and Cambridge series both have chosen the New English Bible as their basis. The choice, he writes,

is readily intelligible. But is it wise? As soon as the NEB appeared it was evident that, whatever its merits for public or private reading, it suffered from serious disadvantages as a tool for any exact study of the biblical text—its renderings are far too free and inconsistent. And time has served only to reinforce the initial impression. It is doubtful, therefore, whether the NEB can ever become the standard translation for academic purposes such as the RV is at present and has been for years.

And another *Times* reviewer praises the use of the Revised Standard Version for the Pelican Gospel Commentaries as a much

[8] *The New English Bible. New Testament*, New York, Oxford and Cambridge university presses, 1961 [5, p. 351]. For the general background, see B. M. Metzger, *The Text of the New Testament. Its Transmission, Corruption and Restoration*, New York, Oxford, 1964 [8, p. 459].

sounder choice for this type of commentary than the New English Bible.[9]

One of the complaints made against the New English Bible was that the reader did not know what Greek text was being followed. The text was clearly not always that of Nestle. Meanwhile the underlying Greek New Testament text has appeared.[10]

A Common Bible

A common English Bible for Protestants and Catholics has been a topic of discussion for quite a while.[11] Among scholars, the subject seemed rather academic, since they all use the same tools without adverting to the religious orientation of the person or persons who did the work. But for the general public, a common Bible has great ecumenical meaning. Foremost among the early advocates of such a project were W. M. Abbott, S.J., and Bernard Orchard, O.S.B. It was the latter who finally brought the plan to completion, and now an edition of the Revised Standard Version has been published with the *imprimatur*. The principal obstacles to be overcome were these: First, the Protestant canon omits several Old Testament books which are part of the Catholic Bible. Secondly, Catholic editions are required to have explanatory notes. Also, on a few texts Catholics would differ from the Revised Standard translation. Fortunately, the Protestant owners of the Version allowed these changes to be made and the Catholic edition is now available.

The Revised Standard is quite modern; an excellent study tool, and should be widely used. Perhaps an augury of future events may be seen in Alexander Jones's 1964 commentary on St. Mark which uses its text.[12]

An observation on a minor point of textual criticism is relevant

[9] *Times Literary Supplement* 63, 1964, 360.

[10] *The Greek New Testament. Being the Text Translated in the New English Bible,* introduction by R. V. G. Tasker, New York, Oxford and Cambridge university presses, 1964.

[11] W. M. Abbott, S.J., "The Laity, Scripture and Christian Unity," *Religion in Life* 33, 1964, 268-274 [8-838]; Anon., "Common Bible Projects," *Herder Correspondence* 1, 1964, 35-37 [8-840]; Anon., "The Common Bible," Bulletin no. 26, *The Dialogue,* October, 1963, 1-8.

[12] *The Gospel According to St. Mark. A Text and Commentary for Students,* New York, Sheed & Ward, 1964 [8, p. 466].

here: The meaning of the term *anthrōpois eudokias* in the angels' song on Christmas (Lk 2:14) has been clarified by readings in the Dead Sea Scrolls. The sense of the term is not that men have good will, but that men are the object of God's good will or his love. The Revised Standard puts it thus: "Men with whom he is pleased." But the objection was raised that there was no instance of the genitive of the expression which refers to God's good pleasure. J. A. Fitzmyer, S.J., has pointed out that the Qumran literature has two instances of the phrase "sons of his [God's] good pleasure." And because "sons" and "men" are frequently interchanged in these writings, the phrase can mean "men of good will." Furthermore, there was discovered at Qumran an Aramaic fragment with the same expression. Thus we now have both an Aramaic and a Hebrew equivalent for St. Luke's expression, and the occurrence of the same phrase in both languages indicates its common and frequent usage.[13]

FORM CRITICISM

Shortly after World War I there arose a method of interpretation for the Synoptic Gospels which has influenced all Gospel study to the present day. The method is called form criticism, and at the risk of oversimplification its principles can be summarized thus: 1) The framework of the Gospels is not historical but artificial. 2) Once this framework is broken, we are left with a number of individual units which resemble beads that have been unstrung. These individual units are then classified according to different forms, such as narratives, miracle stories, pronouncement stories, legends, etc. 3) The rules that characterize the development of these forms are studied and applied to the material. One could, it is said, speak of the biology of the saga. A passage containing a highly developed doctrine would be judged to be the result of considerable evolution, and the same would be said of a form which aptly met the needs of the early Church.

The two great names connected with the movement have been

[13] Joseph A. Fitzmyer, S.J., " 'Peace upon Earth among Men of His Good Will' (Lk 2:14)," *Theological Studies* 19, 1958, 225-227 [3-92].

Rudolf Bultmann and Martin Dibelius.[14] Unfortunately for form criticism, certain philosophical principles were early associated with the method, principles which many scholars challenged. Among Catholics, some condemned the method outright; others pointed out that the excesses were not necessarily part of the method. Nevertheless, no scientific commentary today can afford to neglect the method of form criticism.

The positive and the negative aspects of form criticism are taken into account in the letter of the Pontifical Biblical Commission of April 24th, 1964.[15] The letter states that the Catholic exegete can use the sound (*sana*) elements of form criticism, but then warns against certain philosophical and theological errors often connected with this method. These errors are then enunciated and can be grouped under four headings: 1) Some form critics deny the existence of the supernatural order, the personal intervention of God in the world by means of revelation, and the possibility of miracles and prophecies. 2) Others proceed from a false concept of faith, as if faith had no relation to historical truth and in fact cannot be reconciled with it. 3) Others almost *a priori* deny the historical nature and worth of the documents of revelation. 4) Finally, others, minimizing the Apostles' authority as witnesses of Christ and their office and influence in the primitive community, magnify the creative power of this community.

A Protestant scholar who recognizes that form criticism has made an abiding contribution to Synoptic studies makes this remark on the history of the method:

It is now generally agreed that the form critics overstated their case and unduly disregarded the accepted results of earlier scholarship. They ignored the presence of eyewitnesses of the ministry of Jesus among

[14] R. Bultmann, *Die Geschichte der synoptischen Tradition*, revised edition, Göttingen, Vandenhoeck & Ruprecht, 1958[3]; ET *The History of the Synoptic Tradition*, New York, Harper, 1963 [8, p. 286]; M. Dibelius, *Die Formgeschichte des Evangeliums*, edited by G. Bornkamm, Tübingen, Mohr-Siebeck, 1961[4] [6, p. 413].

[15] *L'Osservatore Romano* 110, May 14th, 1964, 3. See also Joseph A. Fitzmyer, S.J., "The Gospel Truth. What the Recent Vatican Statement Means to Modern Catholic Biblical Scholars," *America* 110, 1964, 844-846; R. E. Murphy, O. Carm., "The Biblical Instruction," *Commonweal* 80, 1964, 418-420.

the first generation of Christians. They drew questionable parallels between oral tradition in other cultures, where the period of transmission is reckoned in centuries, and oral tradition in the primitive Church, where the period is reckoned in decades. They attributed incredible powers to the community, not recognizing that creative work is rarely produced by committees. They forgot that Jesus cast much of his teaching into poetic form and, as a rabbi, expected his disciples to memorize it. They assumed that the early Church could not distinguish its own teaching from that of Jesus, when in fact we know that Paul was meticulously careful to do so (1 Cor 7:10, 25). They underestimated the historical value of the outline of Jesus' ministry preserved by Mark. And they failed to notice that many of the questions which, on the evidence of the Epistles, were hotly disputed in the apostolic age are not dealt with in the recorded teaching of Jesus, so that the Church cannot be accused of reading its own concerns back into the gospel tradition.[16]

THREE STAGES OF TRADITION

Another important statement in the Biblical Commission's letter concerns the period of oral tradition that preceded the writing of the Gospels. The exegete in studying the life and teaching of Jesus should carefully distinguish three stages of tradition (*tria tempora traditionis*). These stages are, first, the life and teaching of Our Lord himself; secondly, the preaching of the Apostles; thirdly, the writing of the Evangelists. There is no reason to deny, we are told, that the Apostles gave to their audience the words and deeds of the Lord with that fuller understanding which they enjoyed when instructed by the events of the risen Christ and taught by the light of the Holy Spirit. For just as he interpreted to them both the Old Testament and his own words, so they also interpreted his words and deeds according to the needs of the hearers in various ways. In this sentence of the letter may be heard an echo of form criticism: "These different ways of speaking in which the preachers proclaimed Christ are to be distinguished and carefully pondered: catecheses, narratives, testimonies, hymns, doxologies, prayers and other literary genres which were customary in Scripture and at that

[16] G. B. Caird, *The Gospel of St. Luke*, "Pelican Gospel Commentaries," Baltimore, Penguin, 1963, 22 [8, p. 291].

period." The third step in tradition is the way in which the Evangelist employs a pericope. By putting a passage in this or that context, the sacred writer explains the meaning for the benefit of his readers. And the exegete should determine what the Evangelist's purpose was in placing the passage where he did.

THE OUR FATHER

The examination of the Lord's Prayer affords a very clear illustration of how his words might be modified between the time they were spoken and when they were incorporated into the inspired written text. The Gospels contain two editions of the Our Father —one in Matthew 6:9-12, the other in Luke 11:2-4. Both forms are alike except that Matthew has phrases not found in Luke, phrases which contain ideas Our Lord expressed on other occasions, and expands phrases already contained in both Matthew and Luke.

Now, it is hardly possible that Our Lord taught the Our Father on two occasions and in two different forms. Instead, it appears that one or both of the Evangelists recorded the prayer as it was recited at their time in some local Christian community.

Probably, Luke's shorter form is closer to the authentic words of Jesus. For who would have wished or dared to shorten so venerable a prayer? It is much more likely that certain parts were made more explicit and some developments added. Traces of liturgical evolution can be detected in Matthew, for some manuscripts add "Amen," while others append the beautiful doxology, "For thine is the kingdom and the power and the glory forever. Amen." [17] This doxology, incidentally (which all modern versions omit from the prayer) is in no way Protestant. It is part of the liturgy for Eastern Rite Catholics, and is found as early as the Didache.

[17] H. van den Bussche, *Understanding the Lord's Prayer*, New York, Sheed & Ward, 1963, 19-22 [7, p. 392]. See also J. Jeremias, *The Lord's Prayer*, Philadelphia, Fortress, 1964 [8, p. 477]; H. Schürmann, *Praying with Christ. The "Our Father" for Today*, New York, Herder and Herder, 1964 [8, p. 469]; E. Lohmeyer, *Das Vaterunser*, Göttingen, Vandenhoeck & Ruprecht, 1961⁴ [6, p. 141]; R. E. Brown, S.S., "The *Pater Noster* as an Eschatological Prayer," *Theological Studies* 22, 1961, 175-208 [6-288].

NORMS FOR INTERPRETATION

Both for his scholarly background and for his skill in reaching a wider audience, Alexander Jones is deservedly renowned. His long awaited translation of the *Bible de Jérusalem*, the famous commentary edited by the Dominican Fathers, is still in preparation. Meanwhile, he has given us a brief commentary on Mark, intended for students, which contains a rather extended introduction. The concluding section is as follows. After recalling that the Gospels are the echo of a living preaching which sought to touch the heart and not to satisfy curiosity, he draws from this principle these conclusions: The Gospels do not give a complete account of Our Lord's earthly life. Rigid historical sequence is not to be expected. In the conflict section (Mk 2:1—3:6), Mark has assembled incidents of the same kind from different periods. Time phrases should not be stressed. One should not try to force the Gospels into artificial agreement on these temporal indications. Luke used Mark but does not hesitate to invert Mark's order for his own purpose. Word-for-word agreement is not to be expected. In Mark Our Lord is quoted, "Take only a staff." In Matthew we have "Take no staff." Both have the meaning: Take only the bare necessities. Another instance is that of the blind man who is healed as Jesus is leaving Jericho (Mark) or entering it (Luke). It is evident that Luke who used Mark attached no importance to a mile one way or the other.[18]

As regards the time indications in the Gospels, a similar attitude is found in A *Harmony of the Gospels in the Knox Translation* (New York, Sheed & Ward, 1963). The editors, L. Johnston and A. Pickering, assert: "No attempt has been made to harmonize the date of each evangelist, to try to decide which order is 'correct,' and then to force the others into that pattern. As far as possible, each gospel has been left in its own order" (p. vi).

DEMYTHOLOGIZING

With consequences more far-reaching than his contribution to form criticism has been Rudolf Bultmann's attitude on another topic. During the dark days of the last war, seeking to make the

18 A. Jones, *The Gospel According to St. Mark*, 23-25.

New Testament more meaningful for modern man, Bultmann wrote a famous pamphlet entitled *New Testament and Mythology. The Problem of Eliminating the Mythological Elements from the Proclamation of the New Testament.* Since then, many books and numerous articles have been written—enough to fill six volumes—supporting or challenging Bultmann's position.[19] A judicious survey of the present state of the question is provided by two articles which appeared in the January and April 1964 issues of the *Catholic Biblical Quarterly.*[20] In the first article Raymond E. Brown observes that many Catholics confuse demythologizing (which is what they really object to) with form criticism, which is not peculiar to Bultmann at all, and the confusion is compounded when technical form criticism is identified with the principle of literary form or genre, "a principle *mandatory* in Catholic exegesis since *Divino afflante Spiritu.*" [21]

There is, he points out, danger of misunderstanding Bultmann's use of the term "myth," for he does not in fact define the word exactly. But "myth" for him is not a fairy tale, and demythologizing does not signify the expurgation of myth; it means the interpretation of myth in existential terms.[22] Brown thus outlines Bultmann's sense of the practical value of the Gospels and his apparent unconcern for the historical Jesus: Once scholars had agreed on the kerygmatic nature of the Gospels and that they had originated in isolated units of material, the possibility of a biographical approach to Jesus seemed ruled out. According to Barthian theology, seeking a historical basis for faith would be to seek false security, but for Bultmann the preached word offered the possibility of authentic existence (the existential expression for something akin to salva-

[19] See *Kerygma and Myth,* edited by H. W. Bartsch, volume 1, revised edition, New York, Harper, 1961; volume 2, Greenwich (Conn.), Seabury, 1962 [7, p. 146]; S. Neill, *The Interpretation of the New Testament 1861-1961,* New York, Oxford, 1964, 222-235, especially 225.

[20] Volume 26; R. E. Brown, S.S., "After Bultmann, What?—An Introduction to the Post-Bultmannians," 1-30; P. J. Cahill, S.J., "Rudolf Bultmann and Post-Bultmann Tendencies," 153-178. They review the work of E. Käsemann, James Robinson, E. Fuchs, G. Ebeling, H. Conzelmann and especially of G. Bornkamm whose 1956 *Jesus of Nazareth* was the first study of the historical Jesus to issue from the Bultmannian school since Bultmann's own *Jesus and the Word* appeared thirty years earlier.

[21] Brown, *art. cit.,* 1.

[22] *Art. cit.,* 2, n. 5.

tion or life in grace) as long as it was rooted, however vaguely, in the action of God in Jesus Christ. Any detailed verification of the deeds or words of Jesus seemed irrelevant. Bultmann insisted that the kerygma should be based on Jesus of Nazareth, even if the Incarnation, atonement, and Resurrection be mythological expressions through which one interprets life rather than objective statements about Jesus of Nazareth.[23] This detached attitude was the occasion for some to accuse Bultmann of taking away the entire historical foundation of Christianity.

THE POST-BULTMANNIANS AND THE NEW QUEST

Brown reminds Catholics that they should recognize that the hermeneutical discussion has moved beyond Bultmann. The past decade has been called the post-Bultmannian era and is dominated by Bultmann's pupils who are responsible for the "new quest of the historical Jesus." Ernst Käsemann's 1953 address to Bultmann's former students at Marburg[24] is considered the commencement of the "new quest."

The new quest has a concept of history different from that of the old quest. The latter thought of history as facts, as something external, almost coldly objective. The new concept of history treats indeed of facts and causes and of the externals of events, but is even more interested in what R. G. Collingwood calls the "inside" of events. Thus history gains meaning only when the historian himself stands within history and takes part in it. This type of historical research can view the kerygma (what Jesus meant to the primitive Church) and its appeal (what Jesus should mean for us) much more sympathetically than could the scientific historiography of the nineteenth century.

The new quest asks to what extent the kerygma continues Jesus' understanding of himself. (For the post-Bultmannians, Jesus' understanding of himself is not a question of inner feelings, but an understanding that overflowed into actions and words.) If the acceptance of the kerygma of the primitive Church through faith

[23] Art. cit., 5.
[24] "Das Problem des historischen Jesus," Zeitschrift für Theologie und Kirche 51, 1954, 125-153.

brought salvation (or "authentic self-existence"), did Jesus himself issue a salvific proclamation? Did he offer the possibility of authentic self-existence to those who heard him?

The new quest claims to have established that Jesus intended to confront the hearer inescapably with the God who is near, that is to say, that Jesus intended an historical encounter with himself to be an eschatological encounter with God, and that consequently he understood his existence as that of bringer of eschatological salvation. Thus the new quest claims to have proved all that it can: not necessarily that the kerygma is true (which lies beyond proof and is in the realm of faith), but that the kerygma is faithful to Jesus.

Some of the reservations expressed concerning the new quest are these: The modern "inner" history should be combined with the older "external" history of the nineteenth century, which should be cleansed of its imperfections and not completely discarded.[25] Furthermore, Robinson's approach might suggest that there could be a divine faith in Jesus independent of the Church's proclamation.[26] Also, the results of the new quest are meager and disappointing; there is a too one-sided existentialist preoccupation, and the methodology used seems defective.[27]

THE CHRONOLOGY OF THE PASSION

One perennial problem seemed for a time to have found a definite solution, the problem of the length of the Passion and the day of the Last Supper. There has always been the question of the relation of the Synoptic narrative to that of St. John. According to the latter, the Pharisees would not enter the praetorium of Pilate lest they be defiled and unable to eat the Passover that Friday evening. The Synoptics, however, seem to indicate that the Last Supper was on Thursday. Was it, then, a Passover meal? Various solutions have been given—that the Last Supper was not a Passover meal, that Our Lord by his authority anticipated the day of the Passover, that because of the large number of lambs to be slaughtered in

[25] Cahill, *art. cit.*, 164.
[26] Brown, *art. cit.*, 21.
[27] *Art. cit.*, 24-30.

the Temple, the custom arose that some would eat the Passover a day earlier; but there is no evidence to confirm such a custom.

In 1957, Mlle. Annie Jaubert argued that at the time of the New Testament there were two liturgical calendars, one official in Jerusalem, the other unofficial. The latter was followed by the Qumran community of the Dead Sea Scrolls, and according to this calendar the Passover would be eaten on Tuesday evening. Therefore, the Synoptics would be correct in speaking of the Passover which was on Tuesday evening for Jesus and the disciples. And John correctly indicates that the Pharisees followed the official Jerusalem Temple calendar and were eating the Passover on Friday.[28]

Few books have received so many notices and reviews as has *La date de la Cène*. At first, reception of its thesis was favorable, especially in Catholic circles, but lately opinion seems to be changing.[29] X. Léon-Dufour, S.J., has formulated the objections thus: The existence of the sectarian calendar is undeniable, but there is no proof that Christ conformed to Qumran's paschal ritual, and even if he did, how can one reconcile that assumption with the respect he showed for the Temple ritual (Mt 5:23f.; 23:2f.)? Moreover, the desire to space the Passion events over a longer period of time misunderstands the thought of the Evangelists, who unanimously emphasize the haste of the proceedings. The real value of the book is that it shows the existence of the Jewish sacerdotal calendar.[30]

Other scholars who find the Jaubert Passion chronology unsatisfactory are P. Benoit,[31] J. Blinzler,[32] P. Gaechter,[33] and J. Jeremias.[34]

---

[28] *La date de la Cène. Calendrier biblique et liturgie chrétienne*, "Etudes bibliques," Paris, Gabalda, 1957 [4-856r—862r]; see S. Smith, S.J., "The Holy Week Chronology. A New Approach," *Irish Ecclesiastical Record* 93, 1960, 223-236. See also the articles referred to in *New Testament Abstracts* [5-65].

[29] R. E. Brown, S.S., "The Date of the Last Supper," *The Bible Today* 1, 1964, 727-733 [8-888 = 5-54].

[30] *Recherches de science religieuse* 48, 1960, 489-495 [5-594r].

[31] *Revue biblique* 64, 1958, 590-594 [4-860r].

[32] "Qumran-Kalender und Passionschronologie," *Zeitschrift für die Neutestamentliche Wissenschaft* 49, 1958, 238-251 [4-45].

[33] "Eine neue Chronologie der Leidenswoche," *Zeitschrift für katholische Theologie* 80, 1958, 555-561 [3-556].

[34] *Journal of Theological Studies* 10, 1959, 131-133 [4-861r].

"Except for Fornication"

A text that has caused endless controversy is the statement in Matthew which can be translated literally, "whoever puts away his wife, except for fornication [*porneia*], and marries another, commits adultery" (Mt 19:9; cf. 5:32). The term *"porneia"* can have an extended meaning and include immorality of any kind; commonly, it has been understood as adultery. Some assert that in the case of adultery, Christ allowed divorce and remarriage. Others, noting that Mark, Luke, and Paul do not mention the case of adultery, thought that the Church introduced the exception. Among Catholics, the traditional interpretation has been that the passage allowed separation, but not a new marriage, in the case of adultery.

Another interpretation of the term *"porneia"* was espoused by Joseph Bonsirven, S.J.[35] He believed that the term meant incest and referred to a marriage null and void because contracted within the forbidden degrees of relationship as set forth in the Mosaic Law. When speaking of the incestuous man at Corinth, Paul uses the term *"porneia"* (1 Cor 5:1), and the word could have that sense in the decree of the Council of Jerusalem (Acts 15:28). According to this interpretation, Matthew 19:9 would mean that in case of an incestuous marriage, divorce would be permitted, in fact would be mandatory, because the union was invalid from the beginning.

Bonsirven's opinion won many adherents. But Jacques Dupont has latterly returned to the traditional Catholic interpretation.[36] And a most unusual opinion has been proposed by A. M. Dubarle, O.P.[37] He believes that the Matthean sayings should be interpreted in the light of Matthew 5:17-19, where Christ says he has not come to destroy the Law: Because Mosaic legislation allowed the innocent party in a divorce to remarry, the passages in Matthew allow divorce and a new marriage in the case not of a single act of adultery, but of grave and continued infidelity. He concludes that the

[35] *Le divorce dans le Nouveau Testament*, Paris, Desclée, 1948.
[36] J. Dupont, O.S.B., *Mariage et divorce dans l'Evangile. Matthieu 19, 3-12 et parallèles*, Bruges, Abbaye de Saint-André, Desclée de Brouwer, 1959 [5, p. 111].
[37] "Mariage et divorce dans l'Evangile," *Orient syrien* 9, 1964, 61-73 [8-938].

New Testament contains two accounts of Christ's teaching on divorce—one which permits no exception (Mark, Luke, Paul), another which allows an exception (Matthew). By forbidding divorce in the case of adultery, the Church has somewhat extended Jesus' teaching, but her purpose has been to prevent abuses in a matter where great danger resides. The following issue of the same journal carried an article opposing Dubarle's stand,[38] and the editor announced that the controversy was closed.

An interesting refinement on the theory of Bonsirven is evident in the writings of P. Benoit,[39] H. J. Richards,[40] and P. Gaechter.[41] Instead of understanding that Our Lord spoke of the case of *porneia*, it is thought that the phrase was inserted by Matthew or by the editor of the Greek Gospel of Matthew. Writing for a predominantly Jewish Christian audience, he would have spelled out the fuller meaning of the Lord's teaching and indicated that the regulation of Acts 15 still holds for them, that marriage within the forbidden Mosaic degrees is illicit. Thus the phrase would refer to an ecclesiastical decision of local and temporary import.

Today the weight of Catholic authorities seems to have moved towards this last interpretation, but the question has remained sufficiently debatable; P. Benoit changed his opinion within a few years, as Brendan McGrath points out.[42]

So many other tempting books and articles have appeared on the Gospels that we can hardly hope to list them and much less to discuss them. One great work, however, must be mentioned: C. H. Dodd on the history of the Fourth Gospel.[43] He finds that the Gospel has a tradition independent of the Synoptics, a tradition which dates from before A.D. 66, and the author, he holds, is not the Apostle.

[38] J. Dauvillier, "L'Indissolubilité du mariage," *Orient syrien* 9, 1964, 265-289.

[39] *L'Evangile selon Saint-Matthieu*, Paris, Cerf, 1961[3], 121-122.

[40] "Christ on Divorce," *Scripture* 11, 1959, 22-32 [3-581].

[41] *Das Matthäus-Evangelium. Ein Kommentar*, Innsbruck, Tyrolia, 1964, 183-184 [8, p. 464].

[42] *Catholic Biblical Quarterly* 24, 1962, 322-323.

[43] *Historical Tradition in the Fourth Gospel*, New York, Cambridge, 1963 [8, p. 287].

PAUL AND THE SALVATION OF THE NATIONS

Let us pass over Acts and discuss some aspects of Paul's life. Two major works on the Apostle have appeared in the past decade, one by a Protestant, the other by a Jewish, professor.

The first is Johannes Munck's *Paul and the Salvation of Mankind*,[44] which can be summarized as follows: Paul regarded himself as a figure in salvation history, as the apostle of the Gentiles on whom the consummation of the world depended. As proof of this statement, three key texts are invoked, 2 Thessalonians 2:6-7, Romans 9—11, and Romans 15:14f. We shall delay only on the first passage. Here Paul speaks of a person and a power that restrains the lawlessness of the last days. He is not speaking of the Roman state and the Roman emperor, but of himself and of his preaching. Paul must preach, his preaching to the Gentiles must be completed; only then will the end of all come to pass.

Even today, Munck asserts, scholars are unconsciously affected by the outlook of the last-century Tübingen school that contrasted Petrinism and Paulinism. Even now, scholars hold that there was hostility between Paul and the primitive community. In actual fact, there was no opposition. The difference concerned only the time when the mission to the Gentiles should begin. The Jerusalem group wished first to convert the Jews and then proceed to the Gentiles. But Paul was determined to preach at once to the Gentiles, and through them he would provoke the Jews to jealousy and thus occasion the conversion of his own people.

In the conviction that the end would take place in Jerusalem, Paul went up to that city with the money collected from his churches and with certain converts who represented the fullness of the Gentiles. The presence of these Gentile Christians and the rich gifts brought by the nations to Zion, Paul hoped, would bring about the conversion of Israel. Instead, the mission failed, and the Apostle was cast into prison. Undismayed, the prisoner of Jesus Christ looked forward confidently to his coming defense before the

---

[44] Richmond, John Knox, 1960 [4, p. 308; 6, p. 244], ET of *Paulus und die Heilsgeschichte*, Acta Jutlandica, Publications of the University of Aarhus, 26, 1, Copenhagen, 1954. See W. D. Davies, *New Testament Studies* 2, 1955/56, 60-72.

Emperor, and he conceived that this defense would be a symbolic witness to all the nations. Thus his preaching would be consummated, and the end of all would be at hand.

There is something most attractive in this grand-scale interpretation of such diverse elements. However, as often happens in a brilliant and simple explanation, the thesis may at times interpret the evidence. Thus the words "of those who have believed" are eliminated from Acts 21:20, and the Jewish Christian adversaries of Paul become simply Jews.

Two general criticisms can be offered. First, if the original community were as close to Paul's outlook as Munck claims, it would be hard to explain the rise of Jewish Christianity and of the Judaizing movement that caused Paul so much anguish. Secondly, the interpretation of Paul is determined entirely by the eschatological conviction that he was the Apostle to the Gentiles on whom the end of all depended. The Epistles, however, reveal a decrease in strictly eschatological interest, and Acts indicates that Paul's missionary work was governed not by the eschatological drama, but by the leading of the Spirit. These and other criticisms may be found in W. D. Davies' lengthy review of Munck's thesis, which meanwhile has not won many followers.

PAUL AND JUDAISM

The second major work on Paul is that of H. J. Schoeps, *Paul, The Theology of the Apostle in the Light of Jewish Religious History*.[45] Davies, whose *Paul and Rabbinic Judaism* is a classic, devoted a lengthy review to the volume.[46] He praised the author for his encyclopedic learning and termed the volume an education in the world of Paul. Its thesis is exceedingly complex and is presented at length by Davies. In his summation, Davies finds, first, that Schoeps postulates too rigid categories of Palestinian and Hellenistic Judaism in the first century. Secondly, no adequate attempt has been made

---

[45] Philadelphia, Westminster, 1961, ET (slightly revised) of *Paulus. Die Theologie des Apostels im Lichte der jüdischen Religionsgeschichte*, Tübingen, Mohr-Siebeck, 1959 [4, p. 100].

[46] *New Testament Studies* 10, 1964, 295-304 [8-1208r].

to explain Paul's conversion; yet, without some explanation, justice cannot be done to the significance of the historical Jesus for Paul and to the role of the Church in Paul's conversion. Thirdly, Paul is placed in a strait-jacket of eschatological speculation. And the intensity of Paul's devotion to Christ, whom he imitated (and imitation implies knowledge of and devotion to Jesus), is not felt. Fourthly, at crucial points such as Christology, the sacraments and the Law, Schoeps appeals to Hellenism for the explanation of peculiarities more explicable in terms of Judaism. Finally, the Paul here presented is a split personality: Judaistic and Hellenistic concepts jostle each other in his mind and never come to terms.

Tarsus or Jerusalem?

It is generally assumed that Paul spent his early years in Tarsus and went to Jerusalem when perhaps eight to fifteen years old. These early years spent in the Greek city of Tarsus are said to explain Paul's knowledge of Greek and his understanding of the Greek mind.

Professor W. C. van Unnik has challenged this view and maintains that all Paul's training was received in Jerusalem.[47] He favors the New English Bible punctuation of Acts 22:3: " 'I am a true-born Jew,' he said, 'a native of Tarsus in Cilicia. I was brought up in this city, and as a pupil of Gamaliel I was thoroughly trained in every point of our ancestral law.' " On the other hand, by its punctuation the Revised Standard Version makes "bringing up" and "being educated" synonyms, both the work of Gamaliel: "I am a Jew, born at Tarsus in Cilicia, but brought up in this city at the feet of Gamaliel, educated according to the strict manner of the law of our fathers." Following the New English Bible punctuation, van Unnik affirms that Paul states he was brought up (*anatethrammenos*) in Jerusalem and [later], as a pupil of Gamaliel, was thoroughly trained (*pepaideumenos*) in the Law. The two Greek terms are not synonyms. *Trophē* and *paideia* refer to quite different periods in the life of a young person. *Trophē* signifies the ear-

[47] *Tarsus or Jerusalem. The City of Paul's Youth*, London, Epworth, 1962 [8, p. 156].

lier, informal training given by the parents or others within the home and not by a distinguished rabbi such as Gamaliel to whom pupils of undergraduate age would come for *paideia*.

Important consequences would follow from this new interpretation. Aramaic would be the Apostle's native tongue, and his knowledge of Hellenism would come chiefly from the period following his conversion. The weakness of the evidence for the theory is that it all comes from Luke (Acts 22:3; 26:4) and not from the Epistles. But Paul's writings contain nothing that contradicts this view, and the Apostle's most precise reference to his early days (Phil 3:5) is quite consistent with the opinion that he lived in Jerusalem almost from the beginning.

PAUL AND THE COMPUTER

A century ago, Ferdinand Christian Baur and his colleagues of the Tübingen school claimed that only four of the fourteen Epistles ascribed to Paul—Romans, 1 and 2 Corinthians and Galatians—are certainly his. The same conclusion was reached in 1964, by employing the help of the electronic computer.[48] Not a few biblical scholars who professed incredulity were perhaps considered deplorably unscientific, but they could take comfort from the protest of a scientist who said that "we should stand firm and tell the machines to mind their own business and go back to deciding for ourselves what we want to think is important." [49]

In the case of the Pauline letters, the computer was fed materials on the frequency and distribution of certain conjunctions. The computer indicated that on this basis the letters fell into four groups marked by four distinct patterns of usage. The next step is to interpret the findings, and here the human interpreter and the subjective factor enter in. Certainly, account should be taken of the thought content of a writing. Should there be a clash between content and style, what is said is ultimately more decisive than the way in which it is said.

We need to remember that a writer's style does not always re-

[48] See F. F. Bruce, "St. Paul in Rome," *Bulletin of the John Rylands Library* 46, 1964, 326-345, especially 326-331.
[49] Bruce, *art. cit.*, 327.

main the same. A reviewer of a professor's book once remarked that the professor had two quite distinct styles, but it was not suggested that the professor had written only half of what appeared under his name. Furthermore, when a writer discovers, or is told, that he uses a particular expression to excess, he is inclined to go to the opposite extreme and to avoid it entirely.

It is argued that the computer analysis of works ascribed to Plato and to any of the Attic orators reveals no such diversity of patterns as appear in the Pauline writings. Here, however, we should remember that these classical authors were conscious literary stylists who polished and repolished their work before publication. Obviously, Paul did not do so. Besides, the consistency of Plato's style and the diversity of Paul's have long been recognized. Here the computer has simply exhibited in more precise statistical form what we already knew. Even without the aid of a computer, we can distinguish the impassioned, argumentative, and fractured style of Galatians from the calm, meditative style of Ephesians with its piled-up genitival phrases and lengthy sentences.

Another factor to remember is Paul's use of scribes. But some cry out, Why should the letters of Isocrates or Demosthenes or Plato or any other writer of Greek epistles have been unchanged in this process and only the letters of Paul have been extensively altered? For one thing, to repeat, these classical writers were stylists who were greatly concerned with the literary form of their writings. Paul was not. Moreover, Paul apparently left the secretary largely responsible for the form and composition of some of his letters, and it is precisely in the use of particles and the length of sentences that the idiosyncrasies of the amanuensis are most apparent. F. F. Bruce, to whom much of the preceding is indebted, remarks that any interpretation which denies Philippians to Paul supplies its own *reductio ad absurdum*.

Though a computer was not used, statistical analysis has been employed by others in testing the authorship of the Pastorals and of John's Gospel. K. Grayston and G. Herdan examined the letters to Timothy and to Titus in the light of statistical linguistics.[50] Using an improved technique compared to the method previously

[50] "The Authorship of the Pastorals in the Light of Statistical Linguistics," *New Testament Studies* 6, 1959, 1-15 [4-470].

employed by P. N. Harrison, the authors study the use of vocabulary in all the Pauline corpus and in the Catholic Epistles. For nine of the Pauline Epistles, a constant ratio is obtained, but the ratio becomes variable when applied to the Catholic Epistles and to the Pastorals. The authors conclude that the linguistic evidence justifies the belief that the Pastorals have a different style from the other Pauline Epistles. They add: "Whether this implies a difference in authorship depends upon one's conception of what style means" (p. 15).

A similar statistical method was applied to the Gospel of John by G. H. C. MacGregor and A. Q. Morton.[51] From a study of sentence and paragraph lengths in the Fourth Gospel, the authors conclude that there are two sources in the Gospel which they term J₁ and J₂. The argument is based on Morton's belief that all early Christian books were codices, not rolls, for Morton's theory of dislocations and transpositions is more easily established if the original was a codex. Yet, as S. V. McCasland observes, it is hard to believe that all the New Testament writers used not only codices but codices with pages of such regularity in size as postulated here.[52] Originally, MacGregor was skeptical about Morton's statistical analysis. He became persuaded when he saw that the statistics confirmed his own previously held hypothesis of two sources, a hypothesis based solely on critical grounds. In brief, scholars regard the statistical argument as of secondary value and demanding careful scrutiny.

DECREES OF THE BIBLICAL COMMISSION ON AUTHORSHIP

Today the question of the authorship of a biblical book does not have the same importance it did a generation or two ago. At that time the denial of authorship frequently contained a challenge to the authority of the writing. At present, there is more general recognition that the authority of the work is guaranteed by the Church.

Just ten years ago, the second edition of the *Enchiridion Bibli-*

[51] *The Structure of the Fourth Gospel*, Edinburgh, Oliver & Boyd, 1961 [6, p. 141].

[52] *Journal of Biblical Literature* 80, 1961, 283-284 [6-620r].

cum was published.[53] Among the documents is a decree of the Biblical Commission dated June 12th, 1913 (n. 412) which affirms that Paul wrote the Pastorals. Another decree, of June 24th, 1914 (n. 416), favors the Pauline authorship of Hebrews. Naturally, the question arose: Are these decrees still binding on Catholics? An answer to the question appeared in two reviews of the *Enchiridion*, one by the Secretary of the Commission[54] and the other by the Assistant Secretary.[55] Both of them stated in the same words that some of the decrees have an historical value and are no longer binding. The key passage reads thus:

As long as these decrees propose views which are neither immediately nor mediately connected with truths of faith and morals, it goes without saying that the scholar may pursue his research with complete freedom and may utilize the results of his research, provided always that he defers to the supreme teaching authority of the Church.

J. Dupont interprets the intent of the decree when he asserts that questions of authorship, date of composition, and integrity no longer have the crucial importance attached to them fifty years ago.[56] Today it is clearly seen that these questions are independent of the inspiration and inerrancy of the text. The entire matter is summarized with full documentation by E. F. Siegman, C.PP.S.[57]

We have here presented only a few examples of New Testament studies that have appeared during the past ten years. Much more could be written, especially on biblical theology,[58] but the preced-

[53] Rome, Arnodo, 1954.

[54] A[thanasius] M[iller], "Das neue biblische Handbuch," *Benediktinische Monatschrift* 31, 1955, 49-50.

[55] Arduinus Kleinhaus, "De nova Enchiridii Biblici editione," *Antonianum* 30, 1955, 63-65.

[56] "A propos du nouvel *Enchiridion Biblicum*," *Revue biblique* 62, 1955, 414-419, especially 418.

[57] "The Decrees of the Pontifical Biblical Commission. A Recent Clarification," *Catholic Biblical Quarterly* 18, 1956, 23-29. See also B. Ahern, C.P., "Who Wrote the Pauline Epistles?" *The Bible Today* 1, 1964, 754-760, especially 760: "Few hold the authenticity of *Hebrews;* the authorship of *Ephesians* and the pastoral letters is still under debate."

[58] The principal books are noticed in *New Testament Abstracts*, and summaries of reviews are given in the section entitled "Books and Opinions." A survey and recent bibliography can be found in R. Schnackenburg, *Neutestamentliche Theologie. Der Stand der Forschung*, Munich, Kösel, 1963 [8, p.

ing items will illustrate some of the activity that has characterized a decisive decade.

Bibliography

For further information, the reader is referred to the book notices, reviews and articles in *New Testament Abstracts* to which frequently a reference is inserted below in brackets. [8-100] means volume 8, abstract number 100. [8, p. 100] means volume 8, page 100.

INTRODUCTORY

CROWNFIELD, F. R. *A Historical Approach to the New Testament*, New York, Harper, 1961 [5, p. 349].

FEINE, P., and BEHM, J. *Einleitung in das Neue Testament*, edited by W. G. Kümmel, revised edition. Heidelberg, Quelle & Myer, 1963^{12} [8, p. 458].

GRANT, R. M. *A Historical Introduction to the New Testament*, New York, Harper, 1963 [8, p. 145].

KEE, H. C., and YOUNG, F. W. *Understanding the New Testament*, Englewood Cliffs, Prentice-Hall, 1957 [2, p. 200].

ROBERT, A., and FEUILLET, A. *Introduction à la Bible* 2. *Nouveau Testament*, Tournai, Desclée et Cie., 1959.

ROWLINGSON, D. T. *Introduction to New Testament Study*, New York, Macmillan, 1956.

WIKENHAUSER, A. *New Testament Introduction*, New York, Herder and Herder, 1960 [8, p. 284].

INSPIRATION

BENOIT, P. "Inspiration," in A. Robert and A. Tricot, *Guide to the Bible* 1. New York, Desclée, 1960.

481]. His *New Testament Theology Today*, New York, Herder and Herder, 1963, is a translation of the 1961 French edition [8, p. 161]. An excellent presentation of the most recent effort to bridge the gap between exegesis and theology is *The New Hermeneutic*, "New Frontiers in Theology" 2, edited by J. M. Robinson and J. B. Cobb, New York, Harper, 1964 [8, p. 460]. Among Catholic works, see Q. Quesnell, S.J., *This Good News. An Introduction to the Catholic Theology of the New Testament*, Milwaukee, Bruce, 1964 [8, p. 480].

FORESTELL, J. T. "The Limitation of Inerrancy," *Catholic Biblical Quarterly* 20, 1958, 9-18 [2-488].

JONES, A. "Biblical Inspiration. A Christian Rendezvous?" *Scripture* 10, 1958, 97-109 [3-302].

LÉON-DUFOUR, X. *Les évangiles et l'histoire de Jésus,* "Parole de Dieu," Paris, Seuil, 1963 [8, p. 290].

MACKENZIE, R. A. F. "Some Problems in the Field of Inspiration," *Catholic Biblical Quarterly* 20, 1958, 1-8 [2-490].

RAHNER, KARL. *Ueber die Schriftinspiration,* "Quaestiones Disputatae" 1, Freiburg, Herder, 1957 [3, p. 114]. ET *Inspiration in the Bible,* New York, Herder and Herder, 1961 [6, p. 276].

REID, J. K. S. *The Authority of Scripture,* London, Methuen, 1957.

STANLEY, D. M. "Balaam's Ass, or a Problem in New Testament Hermeneutics," *Catholic Biblical Quarterly* 20, 1958, 50-56 [2-493].

————. "The Concept of Biblical Inspiration," *The Catholic Theological Society of America, Proceedings of the Thirteenth Annual Convention,* 1958, 65-89 [4-16].

SCRIPTURE AND TRADITION

BEUMER, J. *Die mündliche Ueberlieferung als Glaubensquelle,* New York-Freiburg, Herder 1962 [8, p. 456].

DUPONT, J. "Ecriture et tradition," *Nouvelle revue théologique* 85, 1963, 337-356, 449-468 [8-25].

GEISELMANN, J. R. *Die Heilige Schrift und die Tradition,* "Quaestiones Disputatae" 18, Freiburg, Herder, 1962.

HANSON, R. P. C. *Tradition in the Early Church,* "The Library of History and Doctrine," Philadelphia, Westminster, 1963 [8, p. 164].

MORAN, G. *Scripture and Tradition. A Survey of the Controversy,* New York, Herder and Herder, 1963 [8, p. 146].

TAVARD, G. H. *Holy Writ or Holy Church. The Crisis of the Protestant Reformation,* New York, Harper, 1959 [4, p. 303].

DEMYTHOLOGIZING

BORNKAMM, G. "Die Theologie Rudolf Bultmanns in der neueren Diskussion. Zum Problem der Entmythologiserung und Hermeneutik," *Theologische Rundschau* 29, 1963, 33-141 [8-814].

BROWN, R. E. "After Bultmann, What? —An Introduction to the Post-Bultmannians," *Catholic Biblical Quarterly* 26, 1964, 1-30 [8-815].

BULTMANN, R. "On the Problem of Demythologizing," *Journal of Religion* 42, 1962, 96-102 [7-17].

CAHILL, P. J. "Rudolf Bultmann's Concept of Revelation," *Catholic Biblical Quarterly* 24, 1962, 297-306 [7-410].

FRIES, H. *Bultmann, Barth und die katholische Theologie,* Stuttgart, Schwaben, 1957.

MACQUARRIE, J. *The Scope of Demythologizing. Bultmann and His Critics,* "The Library of Philosophy and Theology," New York, Harper, 1961 [5, p. 362].

MALEVEZ, L. *Le message chrétien et le mythe. La théologie de R. Bultmann.* Bruges, Desclée de Brouwer, 1954. ET *The Christian Message and Myth. The Theology of Rudolf Bultmann.* Westminster, Newman, 1960 [4, p. 310].

MARLÉ, R. *Rudolf Bultmann et l'interprétation du Nouveau Testament,* Paris, Aubier, 1956.

OGDEN, S. M. *Christ Without Myth. A Study Based on the Theology of Rudolf Bultmann,* New York, Harper, 1961 [6, p. 268].

THROCKMORTON, B. H., JR. *The New Testament and Mythology,* Philadelphia, Westminster, 1959 [, p. 199].

TEXTS AND VERSIONS

ALAND, K. (editor). *Synopsis Quattuor Evangeliorum locis parallelis evangeliorum apocryphorum et patrum adhibitis,* Stuttgart, Württembergische Bibelanstalt, 1964.

COLLINS, J. J. "Papyrus Bodmer II," *New Testament Abstracts* 2, 1958, 129-132 [2-322].

The Greek New Testament. Being the Text Translated in the New English Bible, Introduction by R. V. G. TASKER, New York, Oxford and Cambridge university presses, 1964.

METZGER, B. M. "Four English Translations of the New Testament," *Christianity Today* 8, 1963, 168-172 [8-511].

————. *The Text of the New Testament. Its Transmission, Corruption, and Restoration,* New York, Oxford University Press, 1964 [8, p. 459].

A COMMON BIBLE

ABBOTT, W. M. "The Laity, Scripture and Christian Unity," *Religion in Life* 33, 1964, 268-274 [8-838].

ANONYMOUS. "The Common Bible," Bulletin No. 26, *The Dialogue,* October, 1963, 1-8.

ANONYMOUS. "Common Bible Projects," *Herder Correspondence* 1, 1964, 35-37 [8-840].

NEW TESTAMENT (GENERAL)

DAUBE, D. *The New Testament and Rabbinic Judaism,* London, Athlone, 1955.

DAVIES, W. D., and DAUBE, D. (editors). *The Background of the New Testament and Its Eschatology,* New York, Cambridge University Press, 1956.

DODD, C. H. *New Testament Studies,* Manchester, Manchester University Press, 1954.

GAECHTER, P. *Petrus und seine Zeit. Neutestamentliche Studien,* Innsbruck, Tyrolia, 1958 [3, p. 209].

KÜMMEL, W. G. *Das Neue Testament. Geschichte der Erforschung seiner Probleme,* "Orbis Academicus," Freiburg-Munich, Alber, 1958 [4, p. 94].

NEILL, S. *The Interpretation of the New Testament 1861-1961,* The Firth Lectures, 1962, New York, Oxford University Press, 1964.

Nelson's Bible Commentary Based on the Revised Standard Version, edited by F. C. GRANT, New York, Nelson, 1962. Volume 6: F. C. Grant, *New Testament. Matthew—Acts.* Volume 7: F. C. Grant, *New Testament. Romans—Revelation* [8, p. 281].

Peake's Commentary on the Bible, revised edition, edited by M. BLACK AND H. H. ROWLEY, New York, Nelson, 1962 [7, p. 262].

GOSPELS (GENERAL)

BLACK, M. *An Aramaic Approach to the Gospels and Acts,* Oxford, Clarendon, 1954².

CERFAUX, L. *The Four Gospels. An Historical Introduction,* Introduction by L. Johnston, Westminster, Newman, 1960 [5, p. 243].

Faith, Reason and the Gospels. A Selection of Modern Thought on Faith and the Gospels, edited by J. J. HEANEY, Westminster, Newman, 1961 [6, p. 414].

The Gospel Story, Based on the translation of the Four Gospels by RONALD KNOX, arranged in a continuous narrative with explanations by RONALD COX, New York, Sheed & Ward, 1958 [3, p. 210].

The Gospels Reconsidered. A Selection of Papers Read at the International Congress on the Four Gospels in 1957, Oxford, Blackwell, 1960 [6, p. 140].

HARRINGTON, W. J. *Explaining the Gospels*, New York, Paulist Press, 1963 [8, p. 465].

LÉON-DUFOUR, X. *Les évangiles et l'histoire de Jésus*, "Parole de Dieu," Paris, Seuil, 1963 [8, p. 290].

RIESENFELD, H. *The Gospel Tradition and Its Beginnings. A Study in the Limits of "Formgeschichte,"* London, Mowbray, 1957 [4, p. 284].

STANLEY, D. M. "Liturgical Influences on the Formation of the Four Gospels," *Catholic Biblical Quarterly* 21, 1959, 24-38 [3-567].

Studia Evangelica. Papers Presented to the International Congress on "The Four Gospels in 1957," edited by K. ALAND AND F. L. CROSS, Berlin, Akademie, 1959.

Studies in the Gospels in Memory of R. H. Lightfoot, edited by D. E. NINEHAM, Oxford, Blackwell, 1955.

VAWTER, B. *A Popular Explanation of the Four Gospels* 1-2, Huntington, Our Sunday Visitor Press, 1955.

SYNOPTIC GOSPELS

BEARE, F. W. *The Earliest Records of Jesus*. Nashville, Abingdon, 1962. [7, p. 265].

BULTMANN, R. *Die Geschichte der synoptischen Tradition*, revised edition, Göttingen, Vandenhoeck & Ruprecht, 1958[3]. ET *The History of the Synoptic Tradition*, New York, Harper, 1963 [8, p. 286].

BUNDY, W. E. *Jesus and the First Three Gospels. An Introduction to the Synoptic Tradition*, Cambridge (Mass.), Harvard University Press, 1954.

CAMBIER, J., CERFAUX, L., et al. *La formation des Evangiles. Problème synoptique et Formgeschichte*, "Recherches bibliques" 2, Bruges, Desclée de Brouwer, 1957 [4, p. 283].

DIBELIUS, M. *Die Formgeschichte des Evangeliums*, edited by G. BORNKAMM, Tübingen, Mohr-Siebeck, 1961[4] [6, p. 413].

DOEVE, J. W. *Jewish Hermeneutics in the Synoptic Gospels and Acts*, Assen, van Gorcum, 1954.

GRÄSSER, E. *Das Problem der Parusieverzögerung in der synoptischen Evangelien und in der Apostelgeschichte*, Berlin, Töpelmann, 1957.

A Harmony of the Gospels in the Knox Translation, edited by L. JOHNSTON AND A. PICKERING, New York, Sheed & Ward, 1963 [8, p. 288].

McCool, F. J. "Revival of Synoptic Source-Criticism," *Theological Studies* 17, 1956, 459-493 [1-185].

Schmid, J. *Synopse der drei ersten Evangelien mit Beifügung der Johannes-Parallelen*, revised edition, Regensburg, Pustet, 1960³ [5, p. 356].

Solaces, Bruno de. *A Greek Synopsis of the Gospels. A New Way of Solving the Synoptic Problem*, Leiden, Brill; Toulouse, Institut Catholique, 1959 [4, p. 306].

Vaganay, L. *Le Problème Synoptique. Une hypothèse de travail*, Tournai, Desclée et Cie., 1954 [1, p. 152].

THE HISTORICAL JESUS

The Historical Jesus and the Kerygmatic Christ. Essays on the New Quest of the Historical Jesus, translated and edited by C. E. Braaten and R. A. Harrisville, Nashville, Abingdon, 1964 [8, p. 466].

Der historische Jesus und der Christus unseres Glaubens. Eine katholische Auseinandersetzung mit den Folgen der Entmythologisierungstheorie, edited by K. Schubert. Vienna-Freiburg, Herder, 1962 [8, p. 145].

Robinson, J. M. *A New Quest of the Historical Jesus*, "Studies in Biblical Theology" 25, Naperville, Allenson, 1959 [5, p. 326].

See also *New Testament Abstracts*, which frequently has a heading "Jesus of History" which includes abstracts of recent articles, for example 8-925—930.

JESUS (GENERAL)

Bornkamm, G. *Jesus of Nazareth*, New York, Harper, 1960 [5, p. 353].

Colwell, F. C. *Jesus and the Gospel*, New York, Oxford University Press, 1963 [7, p. 391].

Dibelius, M. *Jesus*, Appendixes added by W. G. Kümmel, Berlin, de Gruyter, 1960³ [5, p. 353].

Enslin, M. S. *The Prophet from Nazareth*, New York, McGraw-Hill, 1961 [5, p. 354].

Léon-Dufour, X. *Les évangiles et l'histoire de Jésus*, "Parole de Dieu," Paris, Seuil, 1963 [8, p. 290].

Taylor, V. *The Life and Ministry of Jesus*, Nashville, Abingdon, 1955.

MATTHEW

BENOIT, P. *L'Evangile selon Saint Matthieu*, "La Sainte Bible," Paris, Cerf, 1961[3] [6, p. 268].

FENTON, J. C. *The Gospel of St. Matthew*, Baltimore, Penguin, 1963 [8, p. 291].

FILSON, F. V. *The Gospel According to St. Matthew*, "Black's New Testament Commentaries," London, A. & C. Black, 1960 [7, p. 108].

GAECHTER, P. *Das Matthäus-Evangelium. Ein Kommentar*, Innsbruck, Tyrolia, 1964 [8, p. 464].

GOODSPEED, E. J. *Matthew Apostle and Evangelist*, Philadelphia, John C. Winston, 1959 [4, p. 97].

LOHR, C. H. "Oral Techniques in the Gospel of Matthew," *Catholic Biblical Quarterly* 23, 1961, 403-435 [6-448].

STANLEY, D. M. *The Gospel of St. Matthew*, "New Testament Reading Guide," Collegeville, Liturgical Press, 1963[2].

STENDAHL, KRISTER. *The School of St. Matthew and the Use of the Old Testament*, Uppsala, Almqvist, 1954.

MATTHEW 1-2

BOURKE, M. M. "The Literary Genus of Matthew 1-2," *Catholic Biblical Quarterly* 22, 1960, 160-175 [5-73].

GALBIATI, E. "Esegesi degli Evangeli festivi: L'Adorazione dei Magi (*Matt*. 2, 1-12)," *Bibbia e Oriente* 4, 1962, 20-29 [6-761].

LEANEY, R. "The Birth Narratives in St. Luke and St. Matthew," *New Testament Studies* 8, 1962, 158-166 [6-759].

MUÑOZ IGLESIAS, S. "El género literario del Evangelio de la Infancia en San Mateo," *Estudios Bíblicos* 17, 1958, 243-273 [3-576].

STENDAHL, KRISTER. "Quis et Unde? An Analysis of Mt 1-2," *Judentum, Urchristentum, Kirche*, 1960, 94-105 [5-707].

SERMON ON THE MOUNT (MATTHEW 5-7)

DAVIES, W. D. *The Setting of the Sermon on the Mount*, New York, Cambridge University Press, 1964 [8, p. 464].

DUPONT, J. *Les Béatitudes. Le Problème littéraire. Les deux versions du Sermon sur la montagne et des Béatitudes*, new edition, Bruges, Abbaye de Saint-André; Louvain, Nauwelaerts, 1958 [6, p. 122].

JEREMIAS, JOACHIM. *The Sermon on the Mount*, Philadelphia, Fortress, 1963 [8, p. 298].

Manson, T. W. *Ethics and the Gospel,* New York, Scribner, 1960 [5, p. 355].

The Our Father (Matthew 6:9-13)

Brown, R. E. "The *Pater Noster* as an Eschatological Prayer," *Theological Studies* 22, 1961, 175-208 [6-288].

Bussche, H. van den. *Understanding the Lord's Prayer,* New York, Sheed & Ward, 1963 [7, p. 392].

Jeremias, Joachim. *The Lord's Prayer.* Philadelphia, Fortress, 1964 [8, p. 477].

Lohmeyer, E. *Das Vaterunser,* Göttingen, Vandenhoeck & Ruprecht, 1961⁴ [6, p. 141].

Schürmann, H. *Praying with Christ. The "Our Father" for Today,* New York, Herder and Herder, 1964 [8, p. 469].

Parables

Dodd, C. H. *The Parables of the Kingdom,* revised edition, New York, Scribner, 1961 [6, p. 139].

Jeremias, Joachim. *The Parables of Jesus,* revised edition, New York, Scribner, 1963 [8, p. 289].

Mullins, A. *A Guide to the Kingdom. A Simple Handbook on the Parables,* Westminster, Newman, 1963 [8, p. 290].

Peter's Confession (Matthew 16:13-23)

Vögtle, A. "Messiasbekenntnis und Petrusverheissung. Zur Komposition Mt 16:13-23 Par.," *Biblische Zeitschrift* 1, 1957, 252-272 [2-533]; 2, 1958, 85-103 [3-76].

Divorce

Dauvillier, J. "L'Indissolubilité du mariage," *Orient syrien* 9, 1964, 265-289 [Reply to Dubarle].

Dubarle, A. M. "Mariage et divorce dans l'Evangile," *Orient syrien* 9, 1964, 61-73 [8-938].

Dupont, J. *Mariage et divorce dans l'Evangile. Matthieu* 19, 3-12 *et parallèles,* Bruges, Abbaye de Saint-André, Desclée de Brouwer, 1959. Pp. 239 [5, p. 111].

Leeming, B., and Dyson, R. " 'Except it be for fornication' (Mt 5:32; 19:9)," *Scripture* 8, 1956, 75-82.

Richards, H. J. "Christ on Divorce," *Scripture* 11, 1959, 22-32.

THE PASSION

BROWN, R. E. "The Date of the Last Supper," *The Bible Today* 1, 1964, 727-733 [8-888 = 5-54].

JAUBERT, A. *La date de la Cène. Calendrier biblique et liturgie chrétienne,* "Etudes bibliques," Paris, Gabalda, 1957. Pp. 159 [4-856r —862r].

LEAL, J. "Feria quinta: dies Ultimae Coenae," *Verbum Domini* 41, 1963, 229-237 [8-891].

SMITH, S. "The Holy Week Chronology. A New Approach," *Irish Ecclesiastical Record* 93, 1960, 223-236 [5-65].

THE TRIAL

BLINZLER, J. *Der Prozess Jesu. Das jüdische und das römische Gerichtsverfahren gegen Jesus Christus auf Grund der ältesten Zeugnisse dargestellt und beurteilt,* revised edition, Regensburg, Pustet, 1960³ [5, p. 243]. ET *The Trial of Jesus. The Jewish and Roman Proceedings against Jesus Christ Described and Assessed from the Oldest Accounts,* Westminster, Newman, 1959 [4, p. 96].

WINTER, P. *On the Trial of Jesus,* "Studia Judaica. Forschungen zur Wissenschaft des Judentums" 1, Berlin, de Gruyter, 1961 [5, p. 356].

MARK

BEASLEY-MURRAY, G. R. *Jesus and the Future. An Examination of the Eschatological Discourse Mark 13 with Special Reference to the Little Apocalypse,* London, Macmillan, 1954.

BURKILL, T. A. *Mysterious Revelation. An Examination of the Philosophy of St. Mark's Gospel,* Ithaca, Cornell University Press, 1963 [7, p. 390].

CARRINGTON, P. *According to Mark. A Running Commentary on the Oldest Gospel,* New York, Cambridge University Press, 1960 [5, p. 243].

CRANFIELD, C. E. B. *The Gospel according to Saint Mark,* "Cambridge Greek Testament Commentary," New York, Cambridge University Press, 1963 [8, p. 287].

DAVIES, W. D. "Reflections on Archbishop Carrington's 'The Primitive Christian Calendar'," in W. D. Davies and D. Daube, *The Background of the New Testament and Its Eschatology,* New York, Cambridge University Press, 1956.

JOHNSON, S. E. *The Gospel According to St. Mark,* "Harper's New

Testament Commentaries," New York, Harper, 1961 [5, p. 355].

JONES, A. *The Gospel According to St. Mark. A Text and Commentary for Students,* New York, Sheed & Ward, 1964 [8, p. 466].

LIGHTFOOT, R. H. *The Gospel Message of St. Mark,* New York, Oxford University Press, 1950, 1962 [7, p. 138].

MARXSEN, W. *Der Evangelist Markus. Studien zur Redaktionsgeschichte des Evangeliums,* Göttingen, Vandenhoeck & Ruprecht, 1959².

MITTON, C. L. *The Gospel According to St. Mark,* London, Epworth, 1957.

NINEHAM, D. E. *The Gospel of St. Mark,* "Pelican Gospel Commentaries," Baltimore, Penguin, 1963 [8, p. 291].

TROCMÉ, E. *La Formation de l'évangile selon Marc,* "Etudes d'histoire et de philosophic religieuses" 57, Paris, Presses Universitaires, 1963 [8, p. 469].

LUKE

BARRETT, C. K. *Luke the Historian in Recent Study,* London, Epworth, 1961 [6, p. 413].

CADBURY, H. J. *The Making of Luke-Acts,* Naperville, Allenson, 1958 [4, p. 97].

CONZELMANN, H. *Die Mitte der Zeit. Studien zur Theologie des Lukas,* revised edition, "Beiträge zur historischen Theologie" 17, Tübingen, Mohr-Siebeck, 1962⁴ [6, p. 413]. ET of second edition: *The Theology of St. Luke,* New York, Harper 1960 [5, p. 360].

FITZMYER, J. A. " 'Peace upon Earth among Men of His Good Will' (Lk 2:14)," *Theological Studies* 19, 1958, 225-227 [3-92].

HASTINGS, A. *Prophet and Witness in Jerusalem. A Study of the Teaching of Saint Luke,* Baltimore, Helicon, 1958 [3, p. 326].

JEREMIAS, JOACHIM. *The Eucharistic Words of Jesus,* New York, Macmillan, 1955.

JONES, A. "Background of the Annunciation," *Scripture* 11, 1959, 65-81 [4-665].

LAURENTIN, R. *Structure et théologie de Luc I-II,* "Etudes bibliques," Paris, Gabalda, 1957 [3-505r].

LEANEY, A. R. C. *A Commentary on the Gospel According to St. Luke,* "Harper's New Testament Commentaries," New York, Harper, 1958.

LOHSE, E. *Die Auferstehung Jesu Christi im Zeugnis des Lukasevan-*

gelium, "Biblische Studien" 31, Neukirchen, Neukirchener Verlag, 1961 [6, p. 141].

SCHMID, J. *Das Evangelium nach Lukas. Uebersetzt und erklärt*, revised edition, "Regensburger Neues Testament" 3, Regensburg, Pustet, 1960⁴ [6, p. 142].

SCHÜRMANN, H. *Quellenkritische Untersuchung des lukanischen Abendmahlsberichtes Lk 22, 7-38 1-3*, "Neutestamentliche Abhandlungen, Münster, Aschendorff, 1953, 1955, 1957, [5-591r].

————. *Der Abendmahlsbericht Lucas 22, 7-38 als Gottesdienstordnung, Gemeindeordnung, Lebensordnung*, Paderborn, Schöningh, 1957; Leipzig, St. Benno, 1960 [5-591r; 5, p. 356].

John

BARRETT, C. K. *The Gospel According to St. John*, London, S.P.C.K., 1955.

BOISMARD, M. E. *St. John's Prologue*, Westminster, Newman, 1957 [2, p. 198].

BOUYER, L. *The Fourth Gospel*, Westminster, Newman, 1964 [8, p. 463].

BRAUN, F. M. *Jean le théologien. Les grandes traditions d'Israël et l'accord des Ecritures selon le Quatrième Evangile*, "Etudes bibliques," Paris, Gabalda, 1964 [8, p. 463].

DODD, C. H. *The Interpretation of the Fourth Gospel*, New York, Cambridge University Press, 1953.

————. *Historical Tradition in the Fourth Gospel*, New York, Cambridge University Press, 1963 [8, p. 287].

GÄRTNER, B. *John 6 and the Jewish Passover*, "Coniectanea Neotestamentica" 17, Lund, Gleerup; Copenhagen, Munksgaard, 1959 [4, p. 97].

GROSSOUW, W. *Revelation and Redemption. A Sketch of the Theology of St. John*, Westminster, Newman, 1955.

HIGGINS, A. J. B. *The Historicity of the Fourth Gospel*, London, Lutterworth, 1960 [5, p. 244].

HOWARD, W. F. *The Fourth Gospel in Recent Criticism*, revised by C. K. Barrett, London, Epworth, 1955⁴.

KILMARTIN, E. J. "The Formation of the Bread of Life Discourse [John 6]," *Scripture* 12, 1960, 75-78 [5-121].

————. "Liturgical Influence on John 6," *Catholic Biblical Quarterly* 22, 1960, 183-191 [5-120].

MacGREGOR, G. H. C., and MORTON, A. Q. *The Structure of the Fourth Gospel*, Edinburgh, Oliver & Boyd, 1961 [6, p. 141].

RICHARDSON, A. *The Gospel according to Saint John. Introduction and Commentary,* "Torch Bible Commentaries," Naperville, Allenson, 1959 [3, p. 326].

SCHNACKENBURG, R. "Neuere englische Literatur zum Johannesevangelium," *Biblische Zeitschrift* 2, 1958, 144-154 [3-102].

SIDEBOTTOM, E. M. *The Christ of the Fourth Gospel,* London, S.P.C.K., 1961 [6-622r].

VAWTER, B. "The Johannine Sacramentary," *Theological Studies* 17, 1956, 151-166 [1-64].

VIRGULIN, S. "Recent Discussion of the Title 'Lamb of God'," *Scripture* 13, 1961, 74-80 [6-166].

ACTS

BRUCE, F. F. *The Acts of the Apostles. The Greek Text with Introduction and Commentary,* Grand Rapids, Eerdmans, 1960² [7, p. 390].

CADBURY, H. J. *The Book of Acts in History,* New York, Harper, 1955.

DIBELIUS, M. *Studies in the Acts of the Apostles,* edited by H. H. Greeven, London, SCM, 1956.

HAENCHEN, E. *Die Apostelgeschichte,* Göttingen, Vandenhoeck & Ruprecht, 1958¹¹.

MOULE, C. F. D. *Christ's Messengers. Studies in the Acts of the Apostles,* New York, Association, 1957 [2, p. 296].

O'NEILL, J. C. *The Theology of Acts in its Historical Setting,* Greenwich (Conn.), Seabury, 1961 [6, p. 416].

RICCIOTTI, G. *The Acts of the Apostles,* Milwaukee, Bruce, 1958 [2, p. 201].

La Sainte Bible. Les Actes des Apôtres, Introduction by L. CERFAUX, translation and notes by J. DUPONT, Paris, Cerf. 1958 ² [4, p. 95].

TROCMÉ, E. *Le "Livre des Actes" et l'Histoire,* Paris, Presses Universitaires, 1957.

WIKENHAUSER, A. *Die Apostelgeschichte,* Regensburg, Pustet, 1956⁴.

WILLIAMS, C. S. C. *The Acts of the Apostles,* "Harper's New Testament Commentaries," New York, Harper, 1958.

PAUL (GENERAL)

ALLMEN, J. J. VON. *Pauline Teaching on Marriage,* "Studies in Christian Faith and Practice" 6, London, Faith Press, 1963 [8, p. 156].

AMIOT, F. *The Key Concepts of St. Paul,* New York, Herder and Herder, 1962 [7, p. 274].

BRUCE, F. F. "St. Paul in Rome," *Bulletin of the John Rylands Library* 46, 1964, 326-345.

BRUNOT, A. *Le génie littéraire de Saint Paul*, Paris, Cerf, 1955.

――――. *Saint Paul and His Message.* "Twentieth Century Encyclopedia of Catholicism" 70, New York, Hawthorn, 1959 [4, p. 196].

CANTINAT, J. *Les Epîtres de Saint Paul expliquées*, Paris, Gabalda, 1960 [5, p. 357].

CERFAUX, L. *Christ in the Theology of St. Paul*, New York, Herder and Herder, 1958 [5, p. 93].

――――. *The Church in the Theology of St. Paul*, New York, Herder and Herder, 1959 [5, p. 93].

――――. *Le Chrétien dans la théologie paulinienne*, "Lectio Divina" 33, Paris, Cerf, 1962 [7, p. 275].

DAVIES, W. D. *Paul and Rabbinic Judaism. Some Rabbinic Elements in Pauline Theology*, London, S.P.C.K., 1955, 1964 [8, p. 471].

DEISSMANN, A. *Paul. A Study in Social and Religious History*, New York, Harper, 1957.

ELLIS, E. E. *Paul's Use of the Old Testament*, Edinburgh, Oliver & Boyd, 1957.

――――. *Paul and His Recent Interpreters*, Grand Rapids, Eerdmans, 1961 [6, p. 144].

GROSSOUW, W. *In Christ. A Sketch of the Theology of St. Paul*, Westminster, Newman, 1959 [4, p. 307].

HEATHCOTE, A. W. *An Introduction to the Letters of St. Paul*, London, Darton, Longman and Todd, 1963 [8, p. 154].

HERMANN, I. *Kyrios und Pneuma. Studien zur Christologie der Paulinischen Hauptbriefe*, "Studien zum Alten und Neuen Testament" 2, Munich, Kösel, 1961 [6, p. 149].

HUNTER, A. M. *Interpreting Paul's Gospel*, London, SCM, 1954.

It is Paul Who Writes, based on the translation of the Epistles of Saint Paul and of the Acts of the Apostles by RONALD KNOX, arranged in a continuous narrative with explanations by RONALD COX, New York, Sheed & Ward, 1959 [4, p. 196].

KNOX, J. *Chapters in a Life of Paul*, Nashville, Abingdon, 1964 [8, p. 473].

MITTON, C. L. *The Formation of the Pauline Corpus Letters*, London, Epworth, 1955.

MUNCK, J. *Paul and the Salvation of Mankind*, Richmond, John Knox, 1960 [4, p. 308; 6, p. 244].

NOCK, A. D. *St. Paul*, New York, Harper, 1938, 1963 [8, p. 295].

Rigaux, B. *Saint Paul et ses Lettres. Etat de la question,* "Studia Neotestamentica, Subsidia" 2, Bruges, Desclée de Brouwer, 1962 [7, p. 394].

Schoeps, H. J. *Paul. The Theology of the Apostle in the Light of Jewish Religious History,* Philadelphia, Westminster, 1961 [6, p. 272].

Stanley, D. M. *Christ's Resurrection in Pauline Soteriology,* "Analecta Biblica" 13, Rome, Pontificio Istituto Biblico, 1961 [6, p. 277].

Studiorum Paulinorum Congressus Internationalis Catholicus 1961. Simul Secundus Congressus Internationalis Catholicus de Re Biblica: Completo Undevicesimo Saeculo post S. Pauli in Urbem Adventum 1-2. "Analecta Biblica" 17-18, Rome, Pontificio Istituto Biblico, 1963 [8, p. 148].

Tresmontant, C. *Saint Paul and the Mystery of Christ,* New York, Harper, 1957 [2, p. 297].

Unnik, W. C. van. *Tarsus or Jerusalem. The City of Paul's Youth,* London, Epworth, 1962 [8, p. 156].

Wikenhauser, A. *Pauline Mysticism. Christ in the Mystical Teaching of St. Paul,* New York, Herder and Herder, 1960 [5, p. 248].

ROMANS

Barrett, C. K. *A Commentary on the Epistle to the Romans,* "Harper's New Testament Commentaries," New York, Harper, 1957 [4, p. 288].

————. *Reading Through Romans,* London, Epworth, 1963 [8, p. 471].

Bruce, F. F. *The Epistle of Paul to the Romans,* "Tyndale New Testament Commentaries" 6, Grand Rapids, Eerdmans, 1963 [8, p. 474].

Dodd, C. H. *The Epistle of Paul to the Romans,* London, Collins, 1959 [5, p. 113].

Huby, J. *Saint Paul. Epître aux Romains. Traduction et commentaire,* edited by S. Lyonnet, "Verbum Salutis" 10, Paris, Beauchesne, 1957 [3, p. 106].

Leenhardt, F. J. *The Epistle to the Romans. A Commentary,* London, Lutterworth, 1961 [see 3, p. 106].

La Sainte Bible. Les Epîtres de Saint Paul aux Galates, aux Romains, translated by S. Lyonnet, Paris, Cerf, 1959² [4, p. 95].

Taylor, V. *The Epistle to the Romans,* London, Epworth, 1956.

1 CORINTHIANS

ALLO, E. B. *Saint Paul. Première Epître aux Corinthiens*, Paris, Gabalda, 1956 [2].

HÉRING, J. *La première épître de Saint Paul aux Corinthiens*, "Commentaire du Nouveau Testament" 7, Neuchâtel, Delachaux et Niestlé, 1959[2] [5, p. 247].

SCHMITHALS, W. *Die Gnosis in Korinth. Eine Untersuchung zu den Korintherbriefen*, Göttingen, Vandenhoeck & Ruprecht, 1956 [7, p. 244].

2 CORINTHIANS

ALLO, E. B., *Saint Paul. Seconde Epître aux Corinthiens*, Paris, Gabalda, 1956[2].

HÉRING, J. *La seconde Epître aux Corinthiens*, "Commentaire du Nouveau Testament" 8, Neuchâtel, Delachaux et Niestlé, 1958 [3, p. 105].

PRÜMM, K. *Diakonia Pneumatos. Der zweite Korintherbrief als Zugang zur apostolischen Botschaft* 2/1 [2 Cor 1-7], Freiburg, Herder, 1960 [6, p. 419].

GALATIANS

SCHLIER, H. *Der Brief an die Galater*, "Kritisch-exegetischer Kommentar über das Neue Testament, Meyers Kommentar" 7, Göttingen, Vandenhoeck & Ruprecht, 1962[12] [7, p. 142].

EPHESIANS

CROSS, F. L. *Studies in Ephesians*, London, Mowbray, 1956.

GOODSPEED, E. J. *The Key to Ephesians*, Chicago, University of Chicago Press, 1956.

MUSSNER, F. *Christus das All und die Kirche*, "Studien zur Theologie des Epheserbriefes: Trier Theologische Studien" 5, Trier, Paulinus, 1955.

La Sainte Bible. Les Epîtres de Saint Paul aux Philippiens, à Philémon, aux Colossiens, aux Ephesiens, translated by P. BENOIT, Paris, Cerf, 1959[3] [4, p. 303].

SCHLIER, H. *Der Brief an die Epheser. Ein Kommentar*, Düsseldorf, Patmos, 1958[2] [4, p. 100].

PHILIPPIANS

BEARE, F. W. A *Commentary on the Epistle to the Philippians*, "Harper's New Testament Commentaries," New York, Harper, 1959 [4, p. 196].

PHILEMON

KNOX, J. *Philemon Among the Letters of Paul. A New View of Its Place and Importance*, Nashville, Abingdon, 1959[2] [4, p. 100].

1-2 THESSALONIANS

DEWAILLY, L. M. *La jeune église de Thessalonique. Les deux premières Epîtres de Saint Paul*, "Lectio Divina" 37, Paris, Cerf, 1963 [8, p. 154].

MASSON, C. *Les deux Epîtres de Saint Paul aux Thessaloniciens*, "Commentaire du Nouveau Testament" 11a, Neuchâtel, Delachaux et Niestlé, 1957 [4, p. 289].

RIGAUX, B. *Saint Paul. Les Epîtres aux Thessaloniciens*, Paris, Gabalda, 1956.

PASTORAL EPISTLES

BARRETT, C. K. *The Pastoral Epistles in the New English Bible*, "New Clarendon Bible," New York, Oxford University Press, 1963 [7, p. 393].

DIBELIUS, M., and CONZELMANN, H. *Die Pastoralbriefe*, Tübingen, 1955[3].

GRAYSTON, K., and HERDAN, G. "The Authorship of the Pastorals in the Light of Statistical Linguistics," *New Testament Studies* 6, 1959, 1-15 [4-470].

KELLY, J. N. D. *The Pastoral Epistles: I Timothy, II Timothy, Titus*, "Harper's New Testament Commentaries," New York, Harper, 1964 [8, p. 294].

HEBREWS

CODY, A. *Heavenly Sanctuary and Liturgy in the Epistle to the Hebrews. The Achievement of Salvation in the Epistle's Perspective*, St. Meinrad, Grail, 1960 [6, p. 144].

HÉRING, J. *L'Epître aux Hébreux*, "Commentaire du Nouveau Testament," Neuchâtel, Delachaux et Niestlé, 1954.

KÄSEMANN, E. *Das wandernde Gottesvolk. Eine Untersuchung zum Hebräerbrief*, Göttingen, Vandenhoeck & Ruprecht, 1957[2].

MICHEL, O. *Der Brief an die Hebräer*, Göttingen, Vandenhoeck & Ruprecht, 1957[10].

VANHOYE, A. *La Structure littéraire de l'Epître aux Hébreux*, "Studia Neotestamentica, Studia" 1, Bruges, Desclée de Brouwer, 1963 [8, p. 156].

————. *Traduction structurée de l'Epître aux Hébreux*, Rome, Pontificio Istituto Biblico, 1963 [8, p. 474].

CATHOLIC EPISTLES

BONSIRVEN, J. *Les Epîtres de Saint Jean*, "Verbum Salutis" 9, Paris, Beauchesne, 1954.

SCHELKLE, K. H. *Die Petrusbriefe—Der Judasbrief*, "Herders theologischer Kommentar zum Neuen Testament," edited by A. Wikenhauser and A. Vögtle, 13/2, Freiburg, Herder, 1961 [7, p. 116].

SCHNACKENBURG, R. *Die Johannesbriefe*, "Herders theologischer Kommentar zum Neuen Testament" 13/3, Freiburg, Herder, 1953.

James

BLACKMAN, E. C. *The Epistle of James*, Naperville, Allenson, 1958.

DIBELIUS, M., and GREEVEN, H. *Der Brief des Jakobus*, Göttingen, Vandenhoeck & Ruprecht, 1957[8].

1 Peter

BOISMARD, M. E. *Quatre hymnes baptismales dans la première épître de Pierre*, "Lectio Divina" 30, Paris, Cerf, 1961 [6, p. 144].

CROSS, F. L. *1 Peter. A Paschal Liturgy*, London, Mowbray, 1954.

APOCALYPSE

CERFAUX, L., and CAMBIER, J. *L'Apocalypse de Saint-Jean lue aux chrétiens*, "Lectio Divina," Paris, Cerf, 1955.

FEUILLET, A. *L'Apocalypse. Etat de la question*, "Studia Neotestamentica, Subsidia" 3, Bruges, Desclée de Brouwer, 1963 [8, p. 154].

LeFROIS, B. J. *The Woman Clothed with the Sun (Apoc 12). Individual or Collective: An Exegetical Study*, Rome, Herder, 1954.

BIBLICAL THEOLOGY

ALAND, K. *Did the Early Church Baptize Infants?* "Library of History and Doctrine," Philadelphia, Westminster, 1963 [8, p. 162].

BULTMANN, R. *Theology of the New Testament* 1-2, London, SCM, 1952, 1955.

COLLINS, J. J. "Chiasmus, the 'ABA' Pattern and the Text of Paul," extractum ex *Studiorum Paulinorum Congressus Internationalis Catholicus*, 1961, Rome, Pontificio Istituto Biblico, 1963.

CULLMANN, O. *Immortality of the Soul or Resurrection of the Dead? The Witness of the New Testament*, New York, Macmillan, 1958 [3, p. 113].

————. *Christologie du Nouveau Testament*, "Bibliothèque théologique," Neuchâtel, Delachaux et Niestlé, 1958 [6, p. 128]; ET of the 1957 German edition: *The Christology of the New Testament*, London, SCM, 1959.

DURRWELL, F. X. *The Resurrection. A Biblical Study*, New York, Sheed & Ward, 1960 [6, p. 129].

HUNTER, A. M. *Introducing New Testament Theology*, Philadelphia, Westminster, 1957 [2, p. 294].

JEREMIAS, JOACHIM. *The Origins of Infant Baptism. A Further Study in Reply to Kurt Aland*, "Studies in Historical Theology" 1, Naperville, Allenson, 1963 [8, p. 305].

QUESNELL, Q. *This Good News. An Introduction to the Catholic Theology of the New Testament*, Milwaukee, Bruce, 1964 [8, p. 480].

RICHARDSON, A. *An Introduction to the Theology of the New Testament*, New York, Harper, 1959 [3, p. 330].

ROBINSON, J. M., and COBB, J. B., JR. (eds.). *The New Hermeneutic*, "New Frontiers in Theology" 2, New York, Harper, 1964 [8, p. 460].

SCHNACKENBURG, R. *God's Rule and Kingdom*, New York, Herder & Herder, 1963 [8, p. 302].

————. *Neutestamentliche Theologie. Der Stand der Forschung*, Munich, Kösel, 1963 [8, p. 481]. ET of the 1961 French edition: *New Testament Theology Today*, New York, Herder and Herder, 1963 [8, p. 161].

————. *Die sittliche Botschaft des Neuen Testamentes*, Munich, Max Hueber, 1962[2]; ET of the second German edition: *The Moral Teaching of the New Testament*, New York, Herder and Herder, 1965.

STAUFFER, E. *New Testament Theology*, London, SCM, 1955.

Patristic Studies

WALTER J. BURGHARDT, S.J.

In a single paper rather circumscribed in length it is impossible to present, even to suggest, all the significant advances that patristic study has made in the decade 1954-1964. Outstanding contributions have appeared on scores of individual writers from the Apostolic Fathers to John Damascene; simply to list these would be to lengthen this essay beyond legitimate bounds. The bibliography on Augustine for 1950-1960 has recently appeared, and it counts more than a thousand pages;[1] to appraise this formidable material would require separate treatment by an Augustine expert. Individual problems, patristic themes from Trinitarian theology to eschatology, have also been researched in impressive depth and with gratifying results; to analyze or synthesize all this surpasses any one scholar's competence. In such circumstances, the compass of this paper must be quite modest: I shall evaluate certain general or reference works of unusual significance in the field of the Fathers, and then concentrate on a small number of patristic themes that have captivated me in the past decade. The net result will be an incomplete survey, but it may prove more useful and stimulating than an exhaustive catalogue that could only turn into another manual of patrology.

1. GENERAL WORKS

In this first category, I shall deal with 1) manuals of patrology and histories of Christian literature, 2) histories of dogma and doc-

---

[1] T. van Bavel, *Répertoire bibliographique de s. Augustin 1950-1960*, The Hague, Nijhoff, 1963.

trine, 3) histories of philosophy, 4) editions, 5) translations, 6) encyclopedias and dictionaries, 7) lexicons, and 8) periodicals and bibliographical aids.

MANUALS OF PATROLOGY AND
HISTORIES OF CHRISTIAN LITERATURE

Among the manualists, Altaner and Quasten are outstanding. Berthold Altaner's *Patrologie. Leben, Schriften und Lehre der Kirchenväter*[2] is indisputably the best one-volume presentation in the field, the ideal handbook for terse, precise information. Altaner, who died in early 1954, had a genius for accurate compression; his bibliographies are discouragingly rich; his critical temper is serene and sure. The success of his manual is attested by the many translations and adaptations in Italian (four editions, 1940-1952), Spanish (four editions, 1945-1956), French (two editions, 1941, 1961), Polish and Hungarian, (1947), and English (1958).[3] Perhaps the major deficiency of the fifth German edition is that the enormous strides taken by patristic research, combined with Altaner's advancing age and poor health, kept him from consistently utilizing in his doctrinal syntheses (for example, Gregory of Nyssa and Cyril of Alexandria) the contemporary discoveries and discussions which his bibliographies suggest. The so-called "sixth edition," [4] the work of Albert Stuiber, to whom Altaner entrusted the continuation of his *Patrologie* in 1959, is a reprint of the fifth, save for the removal of errors and the addition of the latest literature, as far as this was possible without change of pagination or typography.

The most remarkable of the manuals is that of Johannes Quasten, Professor of Ancient Church History and Christian Archeology in the Catholic University of America. Three of the projected five volumes have appeared.[5] These are the fruit of three decades

---

[2] Freiburg, Herder, 1958[5].

[3] Berthold Altaner, *Patrology*, New York, Herder and Herder, 1960.

[4] Berthold Altaner, *Patrologie. Leben, Schriften und Lehre der Kirchenväter*, corrected and supplemented by Alfred Stuiber, Freiburg, Herder, 1960[6].

[5] Johannes Quasten, *Patrology* 1. *The Beginnings of Patristic Literature*; 2. *The Ante-Nicene Literature after Irenaeus*; 3. *The Golden Age of Greek Patristic Literature: From the Council of Nicaea to the Council of Chalcedon*, Westminster, Newman, 1950, 1953, 1960.

of exacting research and productive activity by one whose firsthand mastery of early Christian literature, liturgy, and archeology is equaled by few contemporary scholars. The methodology is familiar enough: an author's life story is recapitulated, his literary productivity outlined, his significance for Christian thought synthesized and illustrated—all with the orderliness, clarity, and synthetic compression essential to a manual. But Quasten is not content with compilation; he controls his materials—ancient texts and contemporary research—with a practiced ease. He outstrips Cayré[6] in his possession and utilization of the last quarter century of research, and is more detailed than Steidle[7] and Mannucci-Casamassa.[8] For the period and personalities covered, he has the most comprehensive, well-rounded, up-to-date bibliographies available in any manual. Unlike Altaner, Quasten writes to be read, not merely consulted; rarely does a manualist wear his learning so lightly. An uncommon, delightful feature of this *Patrology* is the generous number of excerpts (almost two hundred in volume 1; two hundred and fifty in volume 2; one hundred and sixty-eight smaller-type quotations in volume 3) from early Christian literature quoted in attractive English dress—selections designed to entice the reader with significant patristic passages, to indicate the

[6] The first volume, and the early section of the second volume, in F. Cayré's *Précis de patrologie et d'histoire de la théologie* (3 volumes, Paris, 1927-1944; second edition of volume 1, 1931) did splendid service for a quarter century as an eminently readable handbook, and was translated into English by H. Howitt, *Manual of Patrology and History of Theology* (Paris, 1936-1940); but the bibliographies should be supplemented from Altaner and Quasten; and even the "édition refondue" of the first two volumes, *Patrologie et histoire de la théologie* (Paris, 1953-1955), does not do justice to the gigantic progress of patristic scholarship in the intervening years.

[7] Basilius Steidle's *Patrologia seu Historia antiquae litteraturae christianae* (Freiburg, 1937) is very precise and fairly rich in detailed information, but, as Joseph de Ghellinck once remarked, it has unhappily pruned from its program the entire element of the history of doctrine, so important to Cayré and one of Altaner's precious features.

[8] Ubaldo Mannucci's *Istituzioni di patrologia* (2 volumes, revised edition by Antonio Casamassa, Rome, 1948-1950[6]) is intended for students of theology; hence the emphasis on the theological content of patristic productions. It is useful, too, for its Italian-language bibliography. As "una vera e propria Patrologia," it expressly excludes the New Testament, biblical apocrypha, symbols of faith, liturgical texts, canonical sources, martyr acts, epigraphy, etc.

unfolding of theology in its infancy and adolescence, and to illustrate the approach of the Fathers to the deposit of faith.

An important observation: Quasten is being translated. What commends these translations to student and scholar is that they are not simply translation; they mark progression. In both the French version[9] and the Spanish,[10] Quasten has made it his effort to keep abreast of patristic research and to put to profit the suggestions made by competent critics in reviews of the English edition; the improvements touch bibliography and text. *Initiation* and *Patrología* are themselves, therefore, indispensable manuals, either as replacements for the corresponding English volumes or at least as supplements thereto. Within the inescapable limits of a manual, Quasten's *Patrology* is scholarship at its finest.

F. L. Cross, well-known editor of *The Oxford Dictionary of the Christian Church*, has given us the first of three projected volumes on the Church Fathers.[11] This initial volume is a rapid survey of Christian literature from the Apostolic Fathers to the beginning of the fourth century. Cross's primary gift is his ability to link compression with accuracy; he has put out a manual designed not for continuous reading but for use in conjunction with the texts. Cross is a splendid guide, knowledgeable and judicious, for one who would walk with the Fathers, one who is ready to read them in text or translation. This purpose must be kept in mind, else the reader is confronted with dry bones: summaries of works, manuscript tradition, etc. He will not find here Quasten's extracts, Altaner's bibliographies, the engaging qualities of Swete's ageless *Patristic Study*.[12] This sort of manual can only come alive in the reader's hand if his other hand holds the works of a Church Father. Then will its richness be revealed; then will he second Daniélou's pithy

[9] Johannes Quasten, *Initiation aux Pères de l'église*, 3 volumes, Paris, Cerf, 1955, 1957, 1963.

[10] Johannes Quasten, *Patrología*, 2 volumes, Madrid, La Editorial Católica, 1961, 1962. Note that the first Spanish volume presents the first two of Quasten's English volumes in one.

[11] *The Early Christian Fathers*, London, Duckworth, 1960.

[12] Two thirds of Henry Barclay Swete's *Patristic Study* (New York, 1904, new impression, 1909) is a stimulating résumé of patristic works of the first five centuries; the rest deals with the value of such study, and with courses, methods, and bibliography for beginners.

assertion that "this little book, whose sound scholarship is expressed in such limpid language, is more substantial than many volumes that are more ponderous, more pedantic, less learned." [13]

For a more comprehensive survey of the Syriac literature, Altaner and Quasten should be supplemented by Ortiz de Urbina.[14] Extending to the death of Damascene and including, besides the orthodox writers, the Nestorian and Monophysite theologians as well, this compendium has profited from its predecessors, Duval, Wright, and especially Baumstark; it adds the literature that has appeared in the thirty-six years since Baumstark; and it incorporates with critical selectivity the research of recent decades. The special qualities of this manual are its clear, concise, yet sufficiently detailed sketches of the individual writers and its rich bibliographies.

As for histories of ancient Christian literature, we have not yet supplanted a number of remarkable works that are decades old. I mean, for general histories, Bardenhewer, Harnack, Jordan, Krüger, Lietzmann, and Goodspeed; for Latin literature, Moricca and Labriolle, Bardy and de Ghellinck, and Section 8 of the *Handbuch der Altertumswissenschaft*; for Christian Africa, the seven-volume *Histoire* of Monceaux; for Latin poetry, Raby, Weyman, and Manitius; for Greek literature, Puech, Stählin, and Bardy. Still, I would stress four more recent works of genuine significance: Dekkers, Beck, Graf, and Campenhausen.

An indispensable tool of patristic research is the *Clavis patrum latinorum*, which E. Dekkers published in collaboration with Aem. Gaar,[15] as introductory to the Latin section of the so-called New Migne, the *Corpus christianorum* edition of the Fathers. It enumerates, substantially in the order which they are to take in *Corpus christianorum*, all the extant Latin texts from Tertullian to Bede, and lists the best editions available today, the pertinent manuscripts, and whatever works, notes, or reviews are of significance for the critical determination of the texts.

[13] *Recherches de science religieuse* 49, 1961, 569.

[14] Ignatius Ortiz de Urbina, *Patrologia syriaca*, Rome, Istituto Orientale, 1958.

[15] Eligius Dekkers, *Clavis patrum latinorum*. Bruges, Beyaert, 1961[2]. This is volume 3 of the annual *Sacris erudiri*, published by the Benedictines of St. Peter's Abbey, Steenbrugge, Belgium.

Karl Krumbacher's magisterial history of Byzantine literature[16] has been supplanted (without being rendered useless) by Hans-Georg Beck's *Kirche und theologische Literatur im byzantinischen Reich.*[17] Beck's is a remarkable achievement. For the first time, we have a historical and thematic synthesis of our knowledge of the Byzantine Church, its organization, the development and expansion of Byzantine monasticism, the ecclesiastical geography of the Christian East, the sources of Church law, liturgy, and hagiography; also, the most significant points of controversy between the churches from the sixth century on.[18]

A sure guide, heretofore lacking, to early Arabic literature is to be found in the first two volumes of Georg Graf's monumental *Geschichte der christlichen arabischen Literatur.*[19] This is essentially a repertory of texts and authors, with indication of manuscripts, editions, and bibliography; the criterion of division is confessional, coinciding often with the geographical.

In 1956, Hans von Campenhausen gave us the second edition of his superb little book on the Greek Fathers.[20] There he painted twelve portraits—some quite charming—from Justin to Cyril of Alexandria, with the deceptive ease and rich insight that stem from decades of research and contemplation. In 1959, a good English translation came from the pen of Stanley Godman.[21] In 1960, Campenhausen produced a companion volume on the Latin litera-

---

[16] *Geschichte der byzantinischen Literatur*, Munich, 1897².

[17] Munich, Beck, 1959.

[18] In Krumbacher's volume, the patristic section was authored by Albert Ehrhard; his exposition was an attractive ideal and a powerful stimulus to philology. A basic tool of research is Ehrhard's monumental work on the sources of Byzantine hagiography, *Ueberlieferung und Bestand der hagiographischen und homiletischen Literatur der griechischen Kirche von den Anfängen bis zum Ende des 16. Jahrhunderts* ("Texte und Untersuchungen" 50-52, Leipzig, Hinrichs, 1937-1952), a vast repertory based on forty years of investigation, at once analysis and synthesis, rich, methodical, reliable. Publication was temporarily arrested by Ehrhard's death in 1940, but was resumed by Peter Heseler (died 1948) and then by Johannes M. Hoeck as editors. *Ueberlieferung*, the question of transmission, still lacks the final part of volume 3: retrospective study, addenda and corrigenda, indexes; the whole of *Bestand*, inventory, actual state of the literature, remains to be published.

[19] Five volumes, Vatican City, Bibliotheca Apostolica Vaticana, 1944-1953.

[20] *Die griechischen Kirchenväter*, Stuttgart, Kohlhammer, 1956².

[21] Hans von Campenhausen, *The Fathers of the Greek Church*, New York, Pantheon, 1959.

ture of the early Church.[22] It is a portrait gallery of the more significant Latin Fathers and ecclesiastical writers: Tertullian, Cyprian, Lactantius, Ambrose, Jerome, Augustine, and Boethius. The merits of Campenhausen's twin works are several and striking. He sees the Fathers as they saw themselves: authorized interpreters of the Bible and of Christian tradition. He has the uncommon power of revealing the relevance of the Fathers for contemporary man. Vast erudition and balanced judgment are wed to a faculty of suggestion which Daniélou sees as one of the conspicuous qualities of the German genius. It is true, some of Campenhausen's positions are contestable—for example, his understanding of Cyril of Alexandria as man and theologian, or his conclusion that Origen "had no feeling for the deeper, objective problems of a truly Christian theology," that his solutions were "the solutions of a theorist of genius who constructed reality from the idea, without being moved at a deeper level by doubt and suffering." [23] But the fact remains, Campenhausen is knowledgeable, readable, intelligently provocative—more likely to be appreciated by the initiate than by the novice.

HISTORIES OF DOGMA AND DOCTRINE

Among Protestant histories of dogma, the classical triad, for achievement and continuing influence, is Harnack-Loofs-Seeberg. Adolf Harnack's *Lehrbuch der Dogmengeschichte*[24] was "a brilliant exposition, on broad lines, which makes of dogma a Greek harvest on the soil of the Gospel." [25] Friedrich Loofs's *Leitfaden zum Studium der Dogmengeschichte,*[26] concise, systematically conceived, rigidly constructed, and clearly presented, suffered from nineteenth-century rationalistic historicism. Reinhold Seeberg's greatest

[22] *Lateinische Kirchenväter*, Stuttgart, Kohlhammer, 1960; ET *The Fathers of the Latin Church*, London, A. & C. Black, 1964.

[23] *The Fathers of the Greek Church*, 56.

[24] Three volumes, Freiburg, 1909-1910[4], new impression, 1931-1932.

[25] J. de Ghellinck, *Patristique et moyen âge* 2, Gembloux, 1947, 53. De Ghellinck's third volume (Gembloux, 1948, 1-102) carries a penetrating evaluation of Harnack and his work.

[26] Fourth edition, Halle, 1906; sixth edition, Parts 1 and 2, by Kurt Aland, Tübingen, 1959.

achievement, his *Lehrbuch der Dogmengeschichte*,[27] revealed a genuine effort at objectivity, showed an unusual awareness of Catholic literature, and was precious for its Protestant exposition of Protestant thought. In a genuine sense, these three classics mark the end of the comprehensive histories of dogma in Evangelical theology.[28] The contemporary stress within Protestantism is on the individual monograph, and a characteristic feature of today's history of dogma is the new edition, or more frequently the reprinting, of Harnack-Loofs-Seeberg.[29]

On the Anglican scene, the judicious but dated work of Bethune-Baker[30] has been superseded, after a half century of service, by J. N. D. Kelly's *Early Christian Doctrines*.[31] Kelly traces the development of the principal Christian doctrines (Trinity, Christology, soteriology, ecclesiology, sacraments, eschatology) from the close of the first century to the middle of the fifth, evinces wide and discriminating reading, is balanced in judgment (though criticized as perhaps too analytic), and, though I have some reservations on several of his interpretations, I do not hesitate to recommend it as required reading for the student in quest of a synoptic view of early

[27] Four volumes, third and fourth editions, Leipzig, 1920-1933, reprinted, 1954-1955.

[28] Walther Köhler's *Dogmengeschichte als Geschichte des christlichen Selbstbewusstseins* (Volume 1, Zurich, Niehans, 1951[3]; volume 2 [posthumous], 1951) and Martin Werner's *Die Entstehung des christlichen Dogmas problematisch dargestellt* (Tübingen, Katzmann, 1954[2]) represent a lower level of achievement. Kurt Aland has pointed out ("Dogmengeschichte," *Die Religion in Geschichte und Gegenwart* 2, Tübingen, 1958[3], 231) that Werner begins with a strong critique of Harnack, but is unable to sustain it and ultimately remains within Harnack's sphere of influence.

[29] Thus, we have a reprint (7 volumes, New York, Russell & Russell, 1958) of the English translation of the Harnack *Lehrbuch* which N. Buchanan and others made on the third German edition (1886-1890) under the title *History of Dogma* (7 volumes, Boston, 1895-1900), and this is now available in paperback (7 volumes in 4, New York, Dover). The English translation of Seeberg which Charles E. Hay made (*Textbook of the History of Doctrines*, 2 volumes, Philadelphia, 1905) on the first German edition (1895-1898) has been republished in a double volume (Grand Rapids, Baker, 1956).

[30] James Franklin Bethune-Baker, *An Introduction to the Early History of Christian Doctrine to the Time of the Council of Chalcedon*, London, 1903, 1951[9].

[31] London, A. & C. Black, 1958.

127

theology. It is the best single volume for a total vision of doctrinal development in the patristic age.[32]

Roman Catholic contributions on the level of wide-ranging histories have not been singularly impressive. A word of commendation is due to the seventeenth-century Jesuit Denys Petau (Dionysius Petavius), who gave to positive theology its rightful place in sacred science and has left a storehouse of patristic arguments in his *Dogmata theologica*.[33] Schwane, Otten, and de Groot left much to be desired.[34] Perhaps the best over-all presentation has been Tixeront's *Histoire*,[35] not an analytic treatment of the history of separate dogmas, but a synthetic exposition of the complete doctrine of a definite period in the Church's life. In these circumstances, it is gratifying to see the gradual publication of what promises to be the most complete of the multivolumed manuals, the *Handbuch der Dogmengeschichte* edited by Michael Schmaus and Alois Grillmeier with the cooperation of many specialists and published by Herder of Freiburg. The five volumes, in twenty-nine fascicles, deal with 1) fundamental theology, that is, revelation, faith, Scripture and tradition, dogma and its development, and historical method; 2) the Trinity, creation, and sin; 3) Christology, soteriology, Mariology, and ecclesiology; 4) sacramental doctrine; 5) grace and eschatology. At the present writing, five fascicles have

[32] The second edition (1960) corrects several misprints, modifies about a dozen passages, inserts a new paragraph at the end of Chapter 12, and improves the bibliographies.

[33] Eight volumes, Vives edition, Paris, 1865-1867.

[34] Joseph Schwane's *Dogmengeschichte* (4 volumes, Freiburg, 1862-1890; second edition of volumes 1 and 2, 1892-1895) was rather a dogmatic theology in historical form than a genuine history of dogmas. The first true handbook in English, Bernard J. Otten's *A Manual of the History of Dogmas* (2 volumes, St. Louis, 1917-1918; second edition of volume 2, 1925), is regrettably weak on the significant point of progress in the understanding of a dogma and on its historical evolution. J. F. de Groot's *Conspectus historiae dogmatum ab detate PP. apostolicorum usque ad saec. 13* (2 volumes, Rome, 1931) is orientated to students of theology; its method is preferably analytic; its order is at once chronological and topical; its post-1920 bibliography is inadequate.

[35] Joseph Tixeront, *Histoire des dogmes dans l'antiquité chrétienne*, 3 volumes: volume 1, Paris, 1930[11]; volume 2, 1931[9]; volume 3, 1928[8]. An English version was fashioned from the fifth French edition (1905-1912) by H. L. Brianceau: *History of Dogmas*, 3 volumes: volume 1, St. Louis, 1930[3]; volume 2, 1923[2]; volume 3, 1926[2].

appeared: Beumer on oral tradition,[36] Scheffczyk on creation and providence,[37] Neunheuser on Baptism and Confirmation,[38] Poschmann on Penance and the Last Anointing,[39] and Neunheuser on the Eucharist in the Middle Ages and the modern era.[40] The great merit of this new history of dogmas is its detailed presentation of Christian doctrine in its evolution, by a corps of acknowledged authorities. The most obvious drawback is the delay in publication: only five of the twenty-nine fascicles through more than a decade (though three of these appeared in 1962-1963). The enterprise is in danger of being somewhat dated before completion.

Two observations are pertinent here. The first observation: A summary of *Dogmengeschichte* such as the above can be misleading. It deals with comprehensive works. The fact is, every research article or book on patristic thought is a contribution to the history of dogmas and doctrines. Some of these, if only a small fraction of the whole, will be mentioned in the second principal section of this paper, where I shall deal with significant work on specialized patristic themes.

The second observation is kin to the first. If the historians of dogma and doctrine in the past decade seem fewer than their fathers and less competent, the impression is born of illusion. The progress of patristics in the last generation has stemmed from specialized monographs rather than *études d'ensemble*. And the reason is not far to seek. In the present state of patristic research, no single scholar—not even a Kelly or a Cross, a Quasten or a Grillmeier—is capable of controlling either the primary source-material in its entirety or the collectivity of current literature based on that material. The genius of the immediate past has been the monograph; the task of the future will be the intensification of such

[36] Johannes Beumer, *Die mündliche Ueberlieferung als Glaubensquelle*, Freiburg, Herder, 1962. Chapter 2 (pp. 15-44) deals with the Fathers, stressing the first three centuries.

[37] Leo Scheffczyk, *Schöpfung und Vorsehung*, Freiburg, Herder, 1963. Chapter 2 (pp. 30-70) covers the patristic period.

[38] Burkhard Neunheuser, *Taufe und Firmung*, Freiburg, Herder, 1956. Sections 3-7 (pp. 24-79) deal with the patristic era.

[39] Bernhard Poschmann, *Busse und Letzte Oelung*, Freiburg, Herder, 1951. Chapter 1 is mostly (pp. 10-64) devoted to the patristic age.

[40] Burkhard Neunheuser, *Eucharistie in Mittelalter und Neuzeit*, Freiburg, Herder, 1963.

specialized research, but with sterner stress on planned collaboration and a keener eye on the ensemble to which specialization contributes. And, most importantly, what is needed is the scholar competent not only in the factual evidence, the sheer data of doctrinal development, but also in the theological interpretation of the data, after the fashion of Karl Rahner and Bernard Lonergan. Otherwise we are in danger of degenerating into sheer antiquarians.

HISTORIES OF PHILOSOPHY

Comparatively few general studies have been devoted to the philosophy of the Fathers. Emile Bréhier even disputed its existence. Probably the best manual is still Geyer's indispensable survey of patristic and Scholastic philosophy,[41] though a generation of research should be incorporated; for the so-called "twelfth edition" (1951) leaves the eleventh (1928) unchanged. Geyer is objective, exact, erudite, critical, rich in information, with exceptionally extensive (if now quite dated) bibliographies.

For the years 1950 on, I would single out three comprehensive works in this area; the authors are Copleston, Gilson, and Wolfson. The second volume of Frederick Copleston's far-famed *History of Philosophy* moves from Augustine to Scotus.[42] The synthetic chapter on the patristic period has been called by a competent historian of philosophy "a masterpiece of selectivity and compression," and Copleston's "exposition and evaluation of St. Augustine's contribution to Christian wisdom . . . one of the best introductions to the philosophic thought of the Bishop of Hippo which we have ever read." [43]

Etienne Gilson's *History of Christian Philosophy in the Middle*

---

[41] Bernhard Geyer, *Die patristische und scholastische Philosophie*, Basel, Schwabe, 1928[11]. This is volume 2 of the famous Ueberweg *Grundriss der Geschichte der Philosophie*. The English translation by G. Morris and N. Porter, *History of Philosophy from Thales to the Present Time* (volume 1, New York, 1885), is unserviceable, because made on the fourth German edition.

[42] Frederick Copleston, *Mediaeval Philosophy. Augustine to Scotus*, Westminster, Newman, 1950.

[43] James I. Conway, *Theological Studies* 12, 1951, 281.

Ages,[44] which begins with the Greek apologists of the second century, has been lauded for its honesty in the reading of sources and for its restraint in selection, comparison, and criticism.

A bold venture is Harry Austryn Wolfson's *The Philosophy of the Church Fathers,* the first volume of which appeared eight years ago.[45] As its subtitle indicates, Wolfson's concerns in volume 1 are properly theological. His subject is the utilization of the technical categories of Greek philosophy for the elaboration of patristic theology—an interesting topic, as Daniélou has pointed out,[46] and quite well handled, but a history of scientific theology rather than of patristic philosophy. (The second volume may prove more genuinely philosophical, for it will deal with the knowledge of God and with anthropology.) An able critic[47] has expressed admiration for the breadth of Wolfson's enterprise, his staggering yet easy erudition, his hypothetico-deductive method, his judicious use of patristic sources, his serene and unimpassioned tone; but he laments Wolfson's interpretation of certain early texts on the Trinity, his consistent neglect of Neoplatonism and its role in the later patristic period, his total lack of concern for the "form" of the works studied, his merciless dissection of patristic works to the loss of their blood and life, and his sweeping assertion (p. vi) that the work of the Fathers consisted in "recasting . . . Christian beliefs in the form of a philosophy, . . . thereby producing . . . a Christian version of Greek philosophy." [48]

EDITIONS

Of the many collections of patristic texts, four merit special mention in "the decisive decade," 1954-1964: *Corpus christianorum,*

[44] New York, Random House, 1955.

[45] Cambridge (Mass.), Harvard University Press, 1956. It is subtitled *Faith, Trinity, Incarnation.*

[46] See his review in *Theological Studies* 17, 1956, 594-598.

[47] E. Fortin, *The Bridge* 4, 1962, 371-378.

[48] Worth more than passing mention, though I have not been able to consult it personally, is Guillermo Fraile's *El judaísmo y la filosofía. El cristianismo y la filosofía: El islamismo y la filosofía* (Madrid, La Editorial Católica, 1959), the second volume of his *Historia de la filosofía.* A bibliography, *Patristische Philosophie,* by Othmar Perler (= *Bibliographische Einführungen in das Studium der Philosophie* 18, Bern, Francke, 1950), is still valuable, though somewhat dated.

Hamman's Supplement to Migne, *Sources chrétiennes,* and *Corpus scriptorum christianorum orientalium.*

The 1950s inaugurated a New Migne. The Benedictine monks of St. Peter's Abbey, Steenbrugge, Belgium, propose to do for our century what the remarkable Abbé did for his: to put within everyone's reach, in a single collection, the best extant editions of all the ancient Christian writings down to the dawn of the Carolingian Renaissance—not only works specifically patristic, but also conciliar, hagiographical, and liturgical texts, burial inscriptions, diplomas, etc. The text printed in *Corpus christianorum* depends on varying factors. 1) Wherever a modern edition exists which is thoroughly satisfactory, it is reprinted, with additions or corrections as warranted. 2) Some editions result from a collation of different good editions among themselves and with the manuscripts. 3) Where a good critical edition neither exists nor can be anticipated, *Corpus christianorum* either reproduces, with up-to-date apparatus, an old edition (such as the Maurist) which is satisfactory enough, or else provides a new critical text. The individual volumes are published in limited editions, to make possible the eventual utilization of subsequently disclosed information, manuscripts, and texts, and in this way to keep constantly abreast of current research. Of the three series contemplated—Latin, Greek, and Oriental—it is the Latin that is the exclusive field of concentration now: an estimated one hundred and eighty volumes, six to eight hundred pages each, ten volumes to appear each year. In point of fact, publication began in 1953; at the present writing, thirty-four volumes have appeared, nine of them on Augustine.[49] Despite an initial suspicion of certain scholars that such a program cannot maintain a uniform standard of professional excellence, *Corpus christianorum* will recommend itself to librarians and even to experts as, in seed at least, the most complete critical collection of patristic literature.

But since Migne remains indispensable as a collection and even for some individual writings, the Franciscan Adalbert Hamman is editing a Supplement to *Patrologia Latina* 1-96 (Tertullian to Bede) in four volumes. The program envisaged, though highly scholarly, is essentially utilitarian, and speed is admittedly of the essence of the enterprise. To render more useful what is already in

[49] *Corpus christianorum, Series latina,* Turnhout, Brepols, 1953-.

Migne, Hamman corrects erroneous attributions of authorship, regroups works unjustifiably separated, and furnishes the latest results of scholarly criticism for writings whose origin is warmly disputed. To complete and enrich the *Patrologia Latina,* several hundred patristic works are being added (that is, published in their proper places in the Supplement) which were forgotten by the original editors or were discovered later, and are now scattered in periodicals or scientific tomes not always easy of access. The first two volumes have appeared (each in four separate fascicles) and the first fascicle of volume 3.[50] Volume 1 covers *Patrologia Latina* 1-21; volume 2, *Patrologia Latina* 22-48, primarily Jerome and Augustine. Volume 3 (= *Patrologia Latina* 49-65) will run from Cassian to Fulgentius of Ruspe, and volume 4 (= *Patrologia Latina* 66-96) from Benedict to Bede.

A successful French effort to encourage a more vital possession of our intellectual and spiritual heritage through profound and extensive study of entire patristic works is the series of texts and translations entitled *Sources chrétiennes,* under the direction of Henri de Lubac, Jean Daniélou, and Claude Mondésert.[51] As I write, ninety-eight volumes have appeared (sixty-two of them since 1954, plus several new editions of older volumes) in six series: Latin, Greek, Byzantine, Oriental, para-Christian, and Western monastic. Many of the texts, such as Musurillo's presentation of Methodius' *Banquet,* are new critical editions; a number of the lengthier introductions, such as de Lubac's studies of Origen's exegesis, and some of the commentaries, such as Hadot's four hundred pages on Marius Victorinus, are precious contributions to patristic study and the history of theology.

Corpus scriptorum christianorum orientalium, originally edited by Jean-Baptiste Chabot, Ignazio Guidi, Henri Hyvernat, and Bernard Carra de Vaux, taken in hand shortly before World War I by the Catholic University of America and the Catholic University of Louvain, and presently under the secretary-generalship of René Draguet,[52] comprises six series of texts (Arabic, Armenian, Coptic,

---

[50] *Patrologiae cursus completus, Series latina, Supplementum* 1, 2, and 3/1, edited by Adalbert Hamman, O.F.M., Paris, Garnier, 1958-.
[51] Paris, Cerf, 1942-.
[52] Louvain (originally Paris), Secrétariat du CorpusSCO, 1903-.

Ethiopic, Georgian, and Syriac) and translations (usually Latin, sometimes a modern language). A special section, *Subsidia*, includes commentaries on those texts, and other editions and contributions intended to set them in their proper historical context, as well as various other aids to their full understanding. To date, two hundred and forty-two volumes have been published, one hundred and two of them since 1954.

TRANSLATIONS

Of the many series of translations of patristic literature in many languages, I shall call attention to three that have attracted increasing attention in the past decade. *Ancient Christian Writers*, inaugurated by Johannes Quasten and Joseph C. Plumpe (died 1957),[53] has evoked consistent commendation from reviewers because it normally provides not merely adequate introductions and accurate, even at times felicitous, translations by recognized authorities in the field, but generous explanatory notes (theological, philological, exegetical, historical, etc.) without which that elusive "man in the street" is helpless in the face of the Fathers. At this writing, thirty-three volumes have appeared and a score more are ready for editing.

The Fathers of the Church, founded by Ludwig Schopp and now under the editorial direction of Roy J. Deferrari,[54] is appearing at a faster rate than *Ancient Christian Writers*—a speed that occasioned legitimate scholarly concern in *The Fathers of the Church's* infancy; the individual volumes are frequently larger; notes are normally kept to a minimum; and the emphasis thus far has been on Augustine (eighteen of the forty-nine volumes to date).

The French translations in the *Sources chrétiennes* series (see above, under "Editions") have come out with sufficient frequency and expertise to make feasible the aim of this splendid collection:

---

[53] Now edited by Quasten and Walter J. Burghardt, Westminster, Newman, 1946-.

[54] Washington, D.C. (originally New York), Catholic University of America Press, 1947-.

a living, dynamic possession of our Christian heritage through broad and deep study of entire patristic texts.

ENCYCLOPEDIAS AND DICTIONARIES

If I may omit, for spatial considerations, the updating of the *Dictionnaire de théologie catholique* and the slow but solid continuation of the *Dictionnaire d'histoire et de géographie ecclésiastiques*, the *Dictionnaire de spiritualité ascétique et mystique*, the *Dictionnaire de droit canonique*, and *Paulys Realencyclopädie der classischen Altertumswissenschaft*, five important encyclopedias or dictionaries have come to us from the fifties and early sixties.

Indispensable for an understanding of the relations between early Christianity and its environment is the *Reallexikon für Antike und Christentum*, founded by Franz Joseph Dölger, Theodor Klauser, Helmut Kruse, Hans Lietzmann, and Jan Hendrik Waszink, and edited by Klauser.[55] Its program is clear-cut: to describe how early Christianity came to terms with the heritage of the ancient world. The area envisioned is the Hellenistic Mediterranean civilization, with inclusion of the Near East, Persia, and Egypt; the time in question embraces the first six centuries of the Christian era. The *Reallexikon* presents its subject matter in the form of a dictionary, in articles appearing under key words ("Alexandria," "Basilika," "Christenverfolgung," etc.) arranged in alphabetical order. Thus far, five complete volumes have been published, taking us down to "Erfinder."

A realistic appreciation of exploding knowledge seems to lie at the root of the revised *Lexikon für Theologie und Kirche*, edited by Josef Höfer and Karl Rahner,[56] only a quarter century after the first edition under Konrad Hofmann. The special consultant for patrology is Hugo Rahner, and the pertinent notices by various patristic scholars are models of compression, with select bibliographies. Eight of the projected ten volumes are in print. The vision that produced the *Lexikon* recalls the courageous words of Hermann Herder which inspired the earlier edition in the dark days after World War I: *"Wir brauchen das Werk, also schaffen wir es."*

[55] Stuttgart, Hiersemann, 1950-.
[56] Freiburg, Herder, 1957²-.

The Protestant approach and viewpoint, even on matters patristic, was long represented in Johann Herzog's *Realencyclopädie für protestantische Theologie und Kirche*,[57] which was particularly rich in biographical material and valuable for its surveys of movements and parties through the Christian centuries. Based on the *Realencyclopädie*, condensation of it in great part, was *The New Schaff-Herzog Encyclopedia of Religious Knowledge*, edited by Samuel Macauley Jackson and others,[58] though supplementary material was often added to adapt the work to the needs of English and American readers. Names that appear regularly and are a guarantee of patristic scholarship are Krüger, Loofs, Harnack, Bonwetsch, Seeberg, and Preuschen. An "extension" of the *New Schaff-Herzog* is the *Twentieth Century Encyclopedia of Religious Knowledge*, edited by Lefferts A. Loetscher.[59] It endeavors to present, among other things, "the results of the most important recent scholarship in the patristic" period. Happily, articles by Robert M. Grant are more frequent than any other contribution in this area.

The directive principle of the third edition of *Die Religion in Geschichte und Gegenwart*, edited by Kurt Galling,[60] is "the Christian faith as understood by Evangelical Protestantism." It contains brief articles on individual Fathers and longer articles on key topics (for example, "Altchristliche Literaturgeschichte," "Christologie: II. Dogmengeschichtlich") by recognized scholars like Molland and Aland, Schneemelcher and Campenhausen, H. Chadwick, W. Jaeger, and Andresen.

For ready reference even in patristics, *The Oxford Dictionary of the Christian Church*, edited by F. L. Cross,[61] offers brief, objective, scholarly notices, with bibliographies which, while restricted, are generally excellent, critical, up-to-date.

[57] Edited by Johann J. Herzog; third edition by Albert Hauck, 24 volumes, Leipzig, 1896-1913.
[58] Thirteen volumes, New York, 1908-1914.
[59] Two volumes, Grand Rapids, Baker, 1955.
[60] Third edition by Kurt Galling, 6 volumes (index volume to follow), Tübingen, Mohr, 1957-1962.
[61] New York, Oxford University Press, 1957.

LEXICONS

For all too long, the patristic scholar has been chained to lexicons which, apart from Suicer's ancient *Thesaurus ecclesiasticus*,[62] are not professedly patristic. Particularly frustrating, because the urgency is so evident and the promise so rich, has been our restless waiting for the Lexicon of Patristic Greek, first suggested in 1906, in preparation for more than half a century, often announced, just as often slowed by financial and professional problems.[63] But in 1961 the first of five fascicles appeared, in 1962 the second, taking us down almost to the end of "epsilon," [64] and the third fascicle is expected very soon. The *Patristic Greek Lexicon* proposes 1) to analyze and illustrate the language of Christian theology and institutions in their formative period, that is, from the last years of the first century to the early years of the ninth; and 2) to remedy the inadequate treatment of the everyday vocabulary of the Greek Fathers in other lexicons. Despite legitimate complaints on the general program and on specific details,[65] the *Patristic Greek Lexicon* is a landmark in patristic scholarship.

For primitive Greek patristic literature, the fifth edition of Bauer's *Wörterbuch*[66] is a precious mine. Bauer's radical effort is an attempt 1) to evaluate the results realized by the scientific investigation of Hellenistic Greek and especially of the language of the Septuagint, so as to make early Christian literature intelligible; and 2) to appraise the progress effected by theologians and historians with reference to this literature and to the history that speaks with its voice. To facilitate personal judgments and stimulate more profound effort, Bauer presents the reader with the very material issuing from ancient sources and contemporary research, with the principal interpretations on controverted issues, and with copious references to publications of divergent tendencies. Fortunately, we

[62] Johann Kaspar Suicer, *Thesaurus ecclesiasticus e patribus graecis ordine alphabetico*, 2 volumes, Amsterdam, 1682, 1728².

[63] See *Theological Studies* 11, 1950, 265-268; 17, 1956, 92.

[64] A *Patristic Greek Lexicon*, edited by G. W. H. Lampe, Oxford, Clarendon.

[65] See *Theological Studies* 24, 1963, 462-463.

[66] Walter Bauer, *Griechisch-deutsches Wörterbuch zu den Schriften des Neuen Testaments und der übrigen urchristlichen Literatur*, Berlin, Töpelmann, 1958⁵.

have a translation and adaptation of Bauer's fourth edition (1952) by William F. Arndt and F. Wilbur Gingrich.[67] Besides some more or less significant adaptations and additions in the treatment of words, the references to scholarly periodical literature in Bauer's fourth edition were brought up to the latter part of 1954 in Arndt-Gingrich, and a number of other bibliographical items were added. Despite all its richness, however, Arndt-Gingrich must be supplemented by the fifth German edition.[68]

The most thorough, detailed, and important of the Latin lexicons is undoubtedly the *Thesaurus linguae latinae*, begun under the editorial direction of the Academies of Berlin, Göttingen, Leipzig, Munich, and Vienna, to which other academies and societies have been added through the years.[69] It covers antiquity down to 600 A.D. To date, six gigantic volumes are complete, volumes 7 and 8 are incomplete and in progress, approximately half the alphabet has been covered, and since 1954 fascicles have been published at an average of about one a year.

A valuable lexical aid is Albert Blaise's *Dictionnaire latin-français des auteurs chrétiens*,[70] whose limits are the period of Tertullian and the end of the Merovingian era. Revised for its theological vocabulary by Henri Chirat, of the faculty of Catholic theology at Strasbourg, it gives nonclassical terms, classical terms with new meanings, archaic or poetic terms taken up by prose writers, and classical meanings which call for historical, grammatical, or stylistic comment.

[67] A *Greek-English Lexicon of the New Testament and Other Early Christian Literature*, Chicago, University of Chicago Press, 1957.

[68] Worth noting here—if only because it forms a parallel tool with Bauer for the study of the language of the primitive Church—is F. Blass and A. Debrunner, A *Greek Grammar of the New Testament and Other Early Christian Literature*, translated (from German edition 9-10) and revised by Robert W. Funk, incorporating supplementary notes of Debrunner (Chicago, University of Chicago Press, 1961). Concerned primarily with the language of the Greek New Testament, Blass-Debrunner examines also the other early Christian literature (Apostolic Fathers, New Testament apocrypha, and the pseudo-Clementine literature), in order to place the New Testament within the development of Greek as the language of the Church. Like the Bauer *Lexicon*, the Blass-Debrunner *Grammar* "is henceforth indispensable" (Edgar R. Smothers, *Theological Studies* 23, 1962, 272).

[69] Leipzig, Teubner, 1904–. A revised Supplement to TLL's invaluable *Index librorum, scriptorum, inscriptionum* (1904) appeared in 1958.

[70] Strasbourg, "Le Latin Chrétien," 1954.

On the later edge of our period is J. F. Niermeyer's French-English *Mediae latinitatis lexicon minus*,[71] with ten fascicles to date, reaching to "sequipeda." A compendious lexicon for rapid information, its Latin quotations are taken in the main from 550-1150.

PERIODICALS AND BIBLIOGRAPHICAL AIDS

To the scores of periodicals that can be of service to the student of patristics we must now add especially the *Jahrbuch für Antike und Christentum*,[72] an annual which succeeds to the journal *Antike und Christentum* founded by Franz Joseph Dölger[73] and has for function to keep the *Reallexikon für Antike und Christentum* (see above, under "Encyclopedias and Dictionaries") abreast of contemporary research. Add, too, *Augustinus*,[74] *Oriens christianus*,[75] *L'Orient syrien*,[76] and *Revue des études augustiniennes*.[77]

To keep up with the discouragingly massive productivity in patristics, we have a highly useful instrument now in the *Bibliographia patristica*, an annual edited by Wilhelm Schneemelcher, with an international corps of collaborators.[78] Thus far, six volumes have appeared, covering the literature from 1956 to 1961—a single year in each volume. With the 1959 titles (volume 4, 1961), the *Bibliographia* became a project of the Patristic Commission of the Academies of Sciences at Göttingen, Heidelberg, Mainz, and Munich.[79]

[71] Leiden, Brill, 1954-.
[72] Münster, Aschendorff, 1958-.
[73] Six volumes, Münster, 1929-1950.
[74] Madrid, 1956-.
[75] Leipzig, 1901-1941; Wiesbaden, 1953-.
[76] Paris, 1956-.
[77] Paris, 1955-. This is a continuation of *L'Année théologique augustinienne*, Paris, 1952-1954.
[78] Berlin, de Gruyter, 1959-.
[79] H. Chirat, in his French adaptation of Altaner's fifth German edition, *Précis de patrologie* (Mulhouse, Salvator, 1961), observes (p. 11) that he has not included in his bibliographical additions all the references furnished by the available volumes (1-3) of *BP*, "because these compilations, over and above the inaccuracies and omissions for which they can be criticized, incorporate publications that are hardly scientific in quality or are more difficult to obtain than their significance warrants."

2. THEOLOGICAL THEMES

In this second category I shall deal with 1) Judaism, Gnosticism, and Hellenism, 2) spirituality, 3) the image of God in man, 4) Mariology, 5) Christology, 6) Origen, and 7) doctrinal development.

JUDAISM, GNOSTICISM, HELLENISM

In the second century, nascent Christianity had to confront three powerful forces: Judaism, Gnosticism, and Hellenism. In each of these areas, scholarship has made remarkable progress through the past decade.

The rediscovery of Judeo-Christianity, that is, a Christianity expressing itself through the thought-forms and life-forms of Late Judaism, promises to effect a revolution in our understanding of early Christianity's history. This has been made possible by some handsome discoveries: The manuscripts of Qumran are giving us a better insight into the Judaism that was contemporaneous with the beginnings of Christianity, and the Nag Hammadi finds offer a number of documents with close ties to Judeo-Christianity, be they heterodox alterations of orthodox texts, or the heterodox expression of Judeo-Christianity that goes by the name of Gnosticism.

In a remarkably complete, uncommonly well-documented picture of primitive Christianity and Judaism, Leonhard Goppelt distinguishes clearly the various aspects or phases of Judaism that forced from Christianity a variety of attitudes, and gives a fascinating description of Christianity in different regions at the beginning of the second century, when it had broken with Judaism but had not yet found its place in the Greek milieu.[80] Goppelt's research supplements and completes the distinguished work of Simon, Schoeps, Dix, Brandon, and Reicke.

In this same area, many more works of the decade could and should be listed, simply because they are mines of information on the phenomenon of Judeo-Christianity. Such would be, for example, the volume that Erik Peterson put together from past arti-

[80] *Christentum und Judentum im ersten und zweiten Jahrhundert. Ein Aufriss der Urgeschichte der Kirche,* Gütersloh, Bertelsmann, 1954.

cles, all of them reworked and enriched with new notes;[81] or the twelve volumes of Goodenough on the evolution of Jewish symbolism in the Greco-Roman period;[82] or Testa's striking confirmation of much of the literary evidence from the data of recent Palestinian archeology.[83] But I suggest that for the patrologist and theologian the best single work is the first volume of Daniélou's projected three-volume history of Christian doctrines before Nicaea. Two volumes of the trilogy are already in print.[84] Volume 1 is an effort to recapture in detail the Semitically structured theology which preceded the Christian utilization of Greek philosophy—a theology unnoticed by Harnack, until recently hardly recognized—a theology expressed in the framework of contemporary Jewish thought, that is, the categories of apocalyptic. The four main sections of this volume present the sources, the intellectual milieu, the doctrines, and the institutions. Volume 2 deals with the significance of Hellenism for the Gospel. Besides the impact of Greek scholastic method on the exegesis of the second and third centuries and the growth in the understanding of tradition from the primitive catechesis, the principal themes which Daniélou sees as developing under Hellenistic influence are the transcendence of God, the Person of the Word, the nature of man, and the theology of the devil. As Joseph Crehan pointed out, in his history "Daniélou is following with a difference the old Tübingen dialectic: first a Jewish thesis, now a Hellenistic antithesis, and presumably in the third volume the higher synthesis of these two movements." [85] Daniélou's *Histoire* may well prove his most distinctive and abiding contribution to our understanding of early Christian theology.

For some years now, the study of Gnosticism has made decisive progress, and this for two reasons. First, there are new sources of

[81] *Frühkirche, Judentum und Gnosis. Studien und Untersuchungen*, Rome, Herder, 1959.

[82] Erwin R. Goodenough, *Jewish Symbols in the Greco-Roman Period*, 11 volumes, New York, Pantheon, 1953-1964. Volume 12 is scheduled for publication in 1965.

[83] P. E. Testa, *Il simbolismo dei Giudeo-Cristiani*, Jerusalem, Tipografia dei PP. Francescani, 1962.

[84] Jean Daniélou, *Histoire des doctrines chrétiennes avant Nicée* 1. *Théologie du judéo-christianisme*; 2. *Message évangélique et culture hellénistique aux IIe et IIIe siècles*, Tournai, Desclée et Cie., 1958, 1961.

[85] *Theological Studies* 23, 1962, 661.

information, thanks to the manuscript discoveries at Nag Hammadi. Second, there is progress in method. It is becoming increasingly clear that the Gnostic texts contain two elements: on the one hand, a dualistic doctrine radically opposed to Christianity—Gnosticism properly so called; on the other hand, a wealth of theological, exegetical, and ritual data borrowed from the Christianity of the second century.[86] In consequence, the Gnostic texts have become a primary source for the interpretation of second-century Christianity and may well compel radical revision of cherished conclusions in this area.

One of the most distinguished students of Gnosticism is the Gregorian Professor Antonio Orbe. His series, "Valentinian Studies," planned for five volumes, is a landmark in Gnostic research. Unsuspected riches have come to us from the four volumes thus far published: his investigation of John 1:3;[87] his research into the first heresies before the persecution of the Church—really a treatise on martyrdom, on the sacrament of the dying and "purgatory," and on the theology of the cross;[88] his study of the Word's procession within the Trinity;[89] and his work on Valentinian Christology with its antecedents and parallels.[90] Volume 4 (untitled) has yet to appear. What we have in this splendid enterprise is not merely a description of the system of Valentinus and his disciples, but a reconsideration of second- and third-century theology based on mastery of the source material and detailed exploration of the texts. The series is indispensable, of capital importance for an intimate understanding of early Christianity.

From among other major contributions I select three. There is the second volume of Hans Jonas's *Gnosis und spätantiker Geist*, twenty years after the first.[91] Though the context is the same as

---

[86] See Daniélou, *Recherches de science religieuse* 44, 1956, 585.

[87] *En los albores de la exegesis Iohannea (Ioh. I, 3)*, "Estudios Valentinianos" 2, Rome, Università Gregoriana, 1955.

[88] *Los primeros herejes ante la persecución*, "Estudios Valentinianos" 5, Rome, Università Gregoriana, 1956.

[89] *Hacia la primera teología de la procesión del Verbo*, "Estudios Valentinianos" 1/1 and 1/2, Rome, Università Gregoriana, 1958.

[90] *La unción del Verbo*, "Estudios Valentinianos" 3, Rome, Università Gregoriana, 1961.

[91] 2/1. *Von der Mythologie zur mystischen Philosophie*, Göttingen, Vandenhoeck & Ruprecht, 1954. A third volume (= 2/2) is still to come. Jonas's

Orbe's, the method is strikingly different, for Jonas is a philosopher, nourished by Cassirer and Heidegger, and eager to uncover the phenomenology of Gnosticism. It is an admirable effort, with fine insights and results, though its essential thesis has been sharply challenged.[92] Then there is Houssiau's presentation of Irenaeus's Christology within Irenaeus's own perspective: Gnostic dualism confronted by Christian unity[93]—unity of the two Testaments, of the Son and the Savior, of Adam's human nature and Christ's.[94] Finally, Robert M. Grant underscores Gnosticism's Jewish atavisms and demonstrates, more exactly than any of his predecessors, its link with Jewish apocalyptic.[95]

As for Christianity's confrontation with Hellenism, here, too, the past decade has been decisive and suggestive. Carl Andresen, for example, has recaptured, perhaps for the first time in definitive fashion, the true face of Celsus and his importance.[96] He reveals how the unity of Celsus' thought is not to be sought in a philosophical argument, but in history—an argument from tradition.

---

later work, *The Gnostic Religion. The Message of the Alien God and the Beginnings of Christianity* (Boston, Beacon, 1958), "while retaining the point of view of the larger work and restating many of its arguments, is different in scope, in organization, and in literary intention. For one thing, it keeps to the area which is by general consent termed gnostic and refrains from striking out into the wider and more controversial ground where the other work, by an extension of meaning, attempts to uncover the presence of a metamorphized 'gnostic principle' in manifestations quite different from the primary ones (as in the systems of Origen and Plotinus). . . . Then, much of the more difficult philosophical elaboration, with its too technical language—the cause for much complaint in the German volumes—has been excluded from this treatment, which strives to reach the general educated reader as well as the scholar. . . . On the other hand, in some respects the present volume goes beyond the earlier presentation: certain texts are more fully interpreted . . . and it has been possible to include new material of recent discovery. Inevitably, although this is a new book and not a translation, it does duplicate, with some rephrasing, certain parts of the German work" (xvii-xviii).

[92] See Daniélou, *Recherches de science religieuse* 43, 1955, 576-581.

[93] Albert Houssiau, *La christologie de saint Irénée*, Louvain, Publications Universitaires, 1955.

[94] For a good presentation of the various facets of Irenaeus's theology, see Quasten, *Patrology* 1, 294-313.

[95] *Gnosticism and Early Christianity*, New York, Columbia University Press, 1959. See also Grant's work in collaboration with David Noel Freedman, *The Secret Sayings of Jesus* (Garden City, Doubleday, 1960).

[96] *Logos und Nomos. Die Polemik des Kelsos wider das Christentum*, Berlin, de Gruyter, 1955.

What Celsus defends is Hellenism as a whole. His originality lies in the philosophical use he makes of the historical argument; here his philosophy of history is a reply to Justin Martyr, to his philosophy of history.

In the matter of Hellenism, however, as in the area of Judeo-Christianity, it is Daniélou's *Histoire des doctrines chrétiennes avant Nicée*, specifically the second volume (see above), that is normative for our grasp of the problem as a whole. Even so, I would suggest that perhaps the most promising, stimulating, and suggestive of the decade's works is an extensive book that has not yet received the attention it merits. I mean the pioneering work of Claude Tresmontant. His fine effort to uncover the philosophy underlying biblical thought[97] is now followed by a similar but far more detailed approach to early Christianity.[98] Bréhier's thesis—early Christianity had no properly Christian philosophy; Christianity had not and has not a philosophic content of its own—Tresmontant finds contradicted by the evidence. He finds in the early centuries of our era an independent, original, Christian metaphysic. This metaphysical structure, this philosophical content, he tries to unravel, not by a purely analytic and deductive process, but more dynamically, by showing how, apropos of certain fundamental metaphysical problems (creation and anthropology), early Christianity became aware—not without groping and faltering, not without mistakes and polemics—of its own proper principles, its own specific metaphysical structure. It is Tresmontant's exciting thesis that God's gracious gift of himself through revelation and grace, far from vitiating philosophy, frees the human mind for the proper work of philosophizing.

[97] *Essai sur la pensée hébraïque*, Paris, Cerf, 1956²; *Etudes de métaphysique biblique*, Paris, Gabalda, 1955. The *Essai* has been translated by Michael Francis Gibson, *A Study of Hebrew Thought* (New York, Desclee, 1960).

[98] *La métaphysique du christianisme et la naissance de la philosophie chrétienne. Problèmes de la création et de l'anthropologie des origines à saint Augustin*, Paris, Seuil, 1961. Apparently a résumé of this larger work is Tresmontant's *Les origines de la philosophie chrétienne* (Paris, Fayard, 1962), which has been translated by Mark Pontifex, *The Origins of Christian Philosophy* (New York, Hawthorn, 1963).

SPIRITUALITY

An important facet of patristic thought that is remarkably relevant for our time is the spirituality latent therein. Patristic study, as John Courtney Murray observed some years ago,

admirably serves to bridge the gap that has been created, in the opinion of many, between theology and spirituality. The Fathers of the Church are not only teachers of Christian doctrine but masters of the spiritual life; not only do their works give guidance to the mind in its search for the truth of God, but they also afford inspiration to the whole soul in its search for God Himself. In this respect, patristic study offers a valuable completion of, and possibly a necessary corrective to, the more rigidly intellectualist mentality created by the student's immersion in Scholastic thought.[99]

One of their distinctive features is that the Fathers do not separate theology and spirituality. For them, Louis Bouyer has pointed out, "commentary on Scripture is steeped in tradition, especially in liturgical tradition, and leads directly to spirituality. Inversely, through the liturgical life of the Church spirituality finds its immediate source in the word of God." [100]

Here, too, the last decade has been good to us.[101] As general works I would recommend three. The first is the *Dictionnaire de spiritualité,* founded by Maurice Viller, Ferdinand Cavallera, and Joseph de Guibert, and now edited by André Rayez and Charles Baumgartner.[102] Four complete volumes are in print, and four fascicles of the fifth, reaching to "François." The DS consistently gives large space to the Fathers; it is an indispensable *instrument de travail* for anyone who would fathom the history of spirituality. The second general work is Bouyer's *The Spirituality of the New*

---

[99] *Theological Studies* 9, 1948, 250.

[100] "Le renouveau des études patristiques," *Vie intellectuelle* 15/1, 1947.

[101] See the rich (though selective), annotated bibliography by F. Refoulé, "La doctrine spirituelle des Pères de l'église. Bibliographie orgainsée," *Vie spirituelle* 102, 1960, 310-326.

[102] *Dictionnaire de spiritualité ascétique et mystique. Doctrine et histoire,* Paris, Beauchesne, 1937-. See also the volumes in *Sources chrétiennes;* many of the introductions are splendid analyses or syntheses of individual Fathers and their spiritual doctrine.

Testament and the Fathers.[103] His judgments are, for the most part, sound and penetrating; and monasticism plays a conspicuous part in his presentation. The third work is Irénée Hausherr's fine, savory study of spiritual direction in the East,[104] in which, among much else that is stimulating, the monastic idea of a spiritual father comes clear: not the extraordinary phenomena seen by Holl or Reitzenstein, but participation in the Spirit.

Specialized works, too, have come from "the decisive decade"; I shall simply point to some of the more significant. There is Henri Crouzel's distinguished study of Origen as a mystical theologian,[105] and Walther Völker's capital research on the spirituality of Gregory of Nyssa,[106] from which it transpires that Gregory's mysticism, despite borrowings from Greek thought, is thoroughly Christian and emphatically ecclesial. There is Olivier Rousseau's presentation of primitive monasticism not merely as a historical phenomenon, but also as an ideal for every vigorous religious life,[107] and there are a number of important studies on the spirituality of Antony the Hermit.[108] In the realm of the liturgy, Daniélou has communicated to us with consummate success the patristic vision of liturgical realities,[109] and Germain Hudon has shown how, for Leo

---

[103] Translated from the first French edition (1960), New York, Desclee, 1963. When writing this book, Bouyer was lecturing at the Institut Catholique in Paris, but now, owing to the quarrels occasioned by reviews of this and of another book published about the same time, he has removed to Strasbourg; see documentation of the affair in *Revue d'ascétique et de mystique* 37, 1961, 213-234, 528-531. As Joseph Crehan has pointed out (*Theological Studies* 25, 1964, 437), it is over Evagrius that his French critics found most fault with Bouyer and his book.

[104] *Direction spirituelle en Orient autrefois*, Rome, Istituto Orientale, 1955.

[105] *Origène et la "connaissance mystique,"* Bruges, Desclée de Brouwer, 1961. This splendid work will receive more attention later in this essay, in the section on Origen.

[106] *Gregor von Nyssa als Mystiker*, Wiesbaden, Steiner, 1955.

[107] Olivier Rousseau, *Monachisme et vie religieuse d'après l'ancienne tradition de l'église*, Chevetogne, Editions de Chevetogne, 1957.

[108] See, for example, the volume of fourteen essays edited by Basilius Steidle, *Antonius magnus eremita*, 356-1956. *Studia ad antiquum monachismum spectantia*, Rome, Herder, 1956. A helpful bibliographical essay in this volume (pp. 13-34) is Ludwig von Hertling's "Studi storici antoniani negli ultimi trent'anni."

[109] Jean Daniélou, *Bible et liturgie. La théologie biblique des sacrements et des fêtes d'après les Pères de l'église*, Paris, Cerf, 1951; ET *The Bible and the Liturgy*, Notre Dame, University of Notre Dame Press, 1956.

the Great in his sermons, man touches God by means of mystery (word and rite), through which the Word Incarnate, light and life of the Church, reveals and communicates himself.[110] In line with the effort to give the *lectio divina* its proper place in the life of each Christian, it is still worth recalling two books written in 1950: de Lubac's exposition of Origen's exegesis,[111] and Daniélou's research into the origins of biblical typology.[112] But surely one of the magisterial works of our time is de Lubac's gigantic attempt to recapture the exegesis of the Fathers and the Middle Ages under the rubric of "the four senses of Scripture." [113] It is neither a continuous history nor a scientific handbook; it is a synthesis, structured on a variety of essential themes which converge in the accumulated witness they bear to the four senses of Scripture, the profound concern of patristic and medieval exegetes.

THE IMAGE OF GOD IN MAN

One facet of patristic theology and spirituality that has engaged the attention of scholars this past decade and more is the image of God in man. Enthralling to the historian of ideas, the idea has not impressed the manualist, even though the image theme touches intimately the triune life of God and the sacramental life of the Christian, can command the history of salvation and the theology of redemption, illuminates the dark depths of sanctifying grace, and can add a different dimension to our understanding of sin as an offense against God. Perhaps this is due to a basic limitation within thesis theology: Themes like the image of God are not easily sche-

---

[110] Germain Hudon, *La perfection chrétienne d'après les sermons de saint Léon*, Paris, Cerf, 1959.

[111] Henri de Lubac, *Histoire et esprit. L'Intelligence de l'Ecriture d'après Origène*, Paris, Aubier, 1950. See the lengthy summary and critique of de Lubac's (a) exposition of Origen's exegesis and (b) plea for spiritual exegesis by John L. McKenzie, "A Chapter in the History of Spiritual Exegesis. De Lubac's *Histoire et esprit*," *Theological Studies* 12, 1951, 365-381.

[112] Jean Daniélou, *Sacramentum futuri. Etudes sur les origines de la typologie biblique*, Paris, Beauchesne, 1950; ET *From Shadows to Reality*, London, Burns & Oates, 1960.

[113] Henri de Lubac, *Exégèse médiévale. Les quatre sens de l'Ecriture*, 2 volumes, each with two parts, Paris, Aubier, 1959-1964. See the review article of volume 1 by Robert E. McNally, "Medieval Exegesis," *Theological Studies* 22, 1961, 445-454.

matized, do not fit into existing categories, overrun theses, and, more often than not, have no proof-number in Denzinger.

The image monographs of the fifties have centered on the Greek Fathers, particularly of the Alexandrian School: Origen,[114] Athanasius,[115] Gregory of Nyssa,[116] Cyril of Alexandria,[117] and John Damascene.[118] Out of these investigations has come a vast theological and spiritual world of ideas: creation and degradation and divinization, participation of the divine Logos by the human logos, ordination of the soul to God despite sin, conformity to Christ, the knowledge of God that is essentially union with God, reason perfected by faith and freedom perfected by grace, adoptive sonship through the Spirit of adoption, and so on.

What is needed at this point is a work at once of synthesis and of theology. The material is at hand for a theologian with roots in the past, who will gather together the patristic theologies of the image and reveal their thrust, the direction in which they point. Not simply the sheer facts: What did the Fathers say? Rather, the significance of the patristic vision for the development of doctrine. We need, on still broader lines, a corps of adventurous scholars and teachers, adventurous in this, that they will see whether the image of God can be made a central, unifying theme of a Christian anthropology, recapturing and deepening the patristic insight of

[114] Henri Crouzel, *Théologie de l'image de Dieu chez Origène*, Paris, Aubier, 1956.

[115] Régis Bernard, *L'Image de Dieu d'après saint Athanase*, Paris, Aubier, 1952.

[116] Roger Leys, *L'Image de Dieu chez saint Grégoire de Nysse. Esquisse d'une doctrine*, Brussels and Paris, Desclée de Brouwer, 1951. Also Hubert Merki, *Homoiōsis Theō. Von der platonischen Angleichung an Gott zur Gottähnlichkeit bei Gregor von Nyssa*, Fribourg, Paulusverlag, 1952.

[117] Walter J. Burghardt, *The Image of God in Man according to Cyril of Alexandria*, Washington, Catholic University of America Press; Woodstock, Woodstock College Press, 1957.

[118] James J. Meany, *The Image of God in Man according to the Doctrine of Saint John Damascene*, Manila, San José Seminary, 1954. Other authors and traditions besides the Alexandrian continue to be studied. John Edward Sullivan, *The Image of God. The Doctrine of St. Augustine and Its Influence* (Dubuque, Priory Press, 1963), emphasizes the image of the Trinity and unravels Augustine's relationship to the Fathers of the past and to Aquinas, with an epilogue on the Trinitarian image after St. Thomas. See also William R. Jenkinson, "The Image and the Likeness of God in Man in the Eighteen Lectures on the Credo of Cyril of Jerusalem (c. 315-387)," *Ephemerides Theologicae Lovanienses* 40, 1964, 48-71.

Christian life as a gradual transformation from an indestructible image that abides despite sin, to resurrectional likeness of the whole man to *the* Image, the risen Christ.

There is room, finally, for a different kind of book, on the pertinence of the image theme to ideas not *prima facie* relevant to the image—the kind of research that is revealed in Ladner's *The Idea of Reform*.[119] For, as Musurillo has pointed out, "Ladner's reform is neither Stoic moralism nor Lutheran illuminationism, but truly supernatural and Christian, founded on the restoration of the divine image and likeness in man through the atoning work of Jesus and the sacramental process of the Mystical Body."[120]

MARIOLOGY

Since 1954, the Mariology of the Fathers has been studied extensively and in depth. There are continuing efforts to survey the patristic field and the Marian privileges on a large scale: into this category one might fit M. Gordillo's comprehensive work on Eastern Mariology,[121] my own two chapters on patristic West and East in Juniper Carol's *Mariology*,[122] or even D. Montagna's volume on praise of and prayer to Mary in Greek texts from the fourth to the seventh centuries.[123] There are splendid works on individual authors: Henri Crouzel on Origen,[124] E. Beck on Ephraem,[125] S. Fe-

[119] Gerhart B. Ladner, *The Idea of Reform. Its Impact on Christian Thought and Action in the Age of the Fathers*, Cambridge (Mass.), Harvard University Press, 1959.

[120] *Theological Studies* 21, 1960, 473. On this theme of the image, see the fine summaries by Merki, "Ebenbildlichkeit," *Reallexikon für Antike und Christentum* 4, 1959, 459-479, and by Ladner, "Eikon," *ibid.*, 771-786, both with splendid select bibliographies.

[121] Mauricius Gordillo, *Mariologia orientalis*, Rome, Istituto Orientale, 1954.

[122] "Mary in Western Patristic Thought," in J. B. Carol, *Mariology* 1 (Milwaukee, Bruce, 1955), 109-155; "Mary in Eastern Patristic Thought," *ibid.*, 2 (Milwaukee, Bruce, 1957), 88-153.

[123] D. Montagna, *La lode alla Theotokos nei testi greci dei secoli IV-VII*, Rome, Marianum, 1963.

[124] *Origène. Homélies sur s. Luc*, text, Introduction, translation, and notes by Henri Crouzel, François Fournier, and Pierre Périchon, Paris, Cerf, 1962. Crouzel's Introduction, on Origen's Marian theology, covers pp. 11-64.

[125] E. Beck, "Die Mariologie der echten Schriften Ephräms," *Oriens christianus* 40, 1956, 22-39.

dyniak on the Cappadocians,[126] C. W. Neumann on Ambrose,[127] G. Jouassard on Epiphanius and Ambrose,[128] J. M. Cascante Dávila on Ildephonsus of Toledo,[129] P. Voulet on John Damascene.[130]

This sort of cataloguing, however, is unsatisfactory. More relevant to our purpose is the question: What are the important trends in the decade just past? In answer, we can say that significant investigation on patristic Mariology took place in at least four areas, stimulated respectively by a centenary, by dissatisfaction with a Marian theology in isolation, by the impact of biology on theology, and by a concern for doctrinal development.

The centenary in question commemorated the definition of the Immaculate Conception in 1854, and it occasioned an enormous amount of research and production on this prerogative: Scripture, tradition, and theology.[131] This research, even in its patristic dimensions, is far too vast to summarize here. Many a Mariological congress was dedicated to this subject; the efforts of individuals, too, have been remarkably prolific. I would suggest, by way of break-through, that the basic book, now and probably for a long time to come, is the volume edited by Edward O'Connor on the history and significance of the dogma.[132] It is the work of an inter-

---

[126] Sergius Stephanus Fedyniak, *Mariologia apud PP. Cappadoces*, Rome, Apud Curiam Ordinis Basiliani S. Josaphat, 1958.

[127] Charles W. Neumann, *The Virgin Mary in the Works of Saint Ambrose*, Fribourg, University Press, 1962.

[128] G. Jouassard, "Deux chefs de file en théologie mariale dans la seconde moitié du IVᵉ siècle: saint Epiphane et saint Ambroise," *Gregorianum* 42, 1961, 5-36.

[129] Juan M. Cascante Dávila, *Doctrina mariana de S. Ildefonso de Toledo*, Barcelona, Casulleras, 1958.

[130] *S. Jean Damascène. Homélies sur la nativité et la dormition*, text, Introduction, translation, and notes by Pierre Voulet, Paris, Cerf, 1961. Voulet's Introduction deals with the Marian homilies in Damascene's work (pp. 7-13) and with his Marian doctrine (pp. 14-40).

[131] See the bulletins consecrated to this theme by René Laurentin: "L'Immaculée conception. Les travaux du centenaire," *Vie spirituelle: Supplément* 8, 1955, 455-481; "L'Immaculée conception. Derniers travaux du centenaire de la définition dogmatique du Décembre 1854," *Vie spirituelle* 101, 1959, 538-563; and the several pages of follow-up in his Marian bulletin in *Revue des sciences philosophiques et théologiques* 46, 1962, 350-357.

[132] *The Dogma of the Immaculate Conception. History and Significance*, Notre Dame, University of Notre Dame Press, 1958. For Jouassard's article

national corps of scholars; it is learned and balanced; the bibliographies carry us into 1957; and, after the specialized monographs, it offers syntheses on important historical and theological aspects.

For this paper, the interest of the volume lies primarily in Jouassard's article on the Fathers and the Immaculate Conception. This article, and the centenary studies in general, reveal with impressive scholarship how far the Fathers were from an explicit awareness and understanding of the prerogative. The implications of Mary's holiness were only gradually uncovered. Though the problem was *posed* with sufficient clarity among the Latins in the fifth century, the Augustinian tradition on original sin and concupiscence blocked any satisfactory solution before the twelfth century; among the Greeks the terms of the problem were not adequately posed in patristic times. Jouassard's conclusion is persuasive: A dialogue between East and West would have hastened a solution. The conclusion has a broader significance for our age: For the progress of theology and for authentic ecumenism, East-West dialogue is imperative—now.

A second facet of Marian research stemmed from a smoldering dissatisfaction with a Marian theology that seemed to isolate the Mother of Christ from the physical Christ and from the mystical Christ. Theologians were increasingly aware of an indispensable condition for a dynamic, relevant, authentically theological Mariology: what Laurentin expressed so well in 1954 when he observed that Mariology must be kept in a fruitful tension between Christology and ecclesiology.

A close link between Mariology and Christology (including soteriology) was relatively easy to recover; it was, in large measure, a matter of reorientation, with renewed efforts to discover to what extent doctrines like Mary's role in redemption are germinal in such patristic themes as the Eve-Mary parallelism. Not so the relationship between Mariology and ecclesiology. Here a lost tradition was recaptured, with unsuspected possibilities for Mariological renewal. I mean the Mary-Church parallelism.

In this area, one of the most momentous works of the fifties was

on the Fathers, see pp. 51-86. See also M. Jugie, *L'Immaculée conception dans l'Ecriture sainte et dans la tradition orientale*, Rome, Officium libri catholici, 1952.

Alois Müller's detailed research in the patristic field, East and West, from the Apostolic Fathers to Cyril of Alexandria and Augustine.[133] Müller uncovers, with impressive documentation, three patristic insights. 1) In the mind of many Fathers, there is a striking *similarity* between the role of Mary and the role of the Church in God's redemptive plan. They are *alike* in that each, as virgin, as virgin bride, as virgin mother, brings Christ to birth by a voluntary yes which is man's response to God's invitation, the prelude to the union of human and divine in a single individual and in the whole Church. 2) A fair number of Fathers see in Mary a *type* of the Church, at least in the sense that in God's design she foreshadows in her own person, in her own activity, what the whole Church is to be and to do. 3) A few Fathers assert or imply that Mary *is* the Church, *identify* Mary and the Church. And one may argue with a certain suasiveness that they may well mean that our Lady not simply foreshadows the Church, but is the perfect realization of the Church's inner essence, of redeemed humanity.

This thesis, that Mary is type or figure of the Church, that in Mary redemption finds its consummate realization, that in her God achieves to perfection what he has designed for the whole Church, that what the Mother of God is, this the Church is destined to be—this thesis has breathed new life into Marian theology. For this vision of Mary preserves a gratifying balance between her humanness and her uniqueness; it clarifies and unifies her role in redemption; it makes for authentic Marian devotion.[134] And the role of the Fathers in producing this theological vision, if not indispensable, is surely not negligible.[135]

---

[133] *Ecclesia-Maria. Die Einheit Marias und der Kirche*, Fribourg, University Press, 1955[2].

[134] See, for fine indications of the theological issues, *Marian Studies* 9, 1958, 31-51, 107-128. For an effort at theological synthesis, see my "*Theotokos.* The Mother of God," in Edward D. O'Connor, *The Mystery of the Woman* (Notre Dame, University of Notre Dame Press, 1956), 3-33. Müller's own theological construction, at the close of his book, did not escape criticism, especially in the first edition; but I would have little fault to find with his reconstruction of the patristic evidence.

[135] H. Coathalem, *Le parallélisme entre la sainte Vierge et l'église dans la tradition latine jusqu'à la fin du XIIe siècle* (Rome, Università Gregoriana, 1954), has traced the Mary-Church parallelism in the Latin tradition down

In the fifties, a Marian prerogative that generated unexpected heat was Mary's virginity in parturition (*virginitas in partu*). For various reasons,[136] this doctrine, which had enjoyed a tranquil existence within the Church since the fourth century but had in latter years degenerated into a primarily physiological mystery, found itself under attack: It was regarded as dated, outmoded, anachronistic. Spurred by Albert Mitterer,[137] many a critic of the dogma saw a desirable solution to the problem: Retain the formula *virgo in partu*, but strip it of its traditional components, bodily integrity and painless childbearing. The arguments for this position were basically two. First, it was argued, these features do not belong to the concept of virginity and they run counter to the concept of maternity. Second, on the level of positive data, the highlights were the hesitations prior to the fourth century, the apparent influence of the apocrypha, and the physiological inadequacy of patristic terminology. Mitterer was attacked and defended; doctors and theologians entered the lists; the Holy Office issued a disciplinary decree (July 20th, 1960) forbidding publication of such articles on the subject as would offend against Christian delicacy and contradict traditional doctrine.[138]

On the patristic level, perhaps the most influential name in the controversy is René Laurentin. In a famous article,[139] long unpublished (save privately) for discretionary reasons, Laurentin took issue with the anatomical approach. The article is not uncommonly documented; the patristic evidence is adequate but not overwhelming. The significance of the article is rather that it is genuinely an essay in patristic theology—better, theology with deep roots in tra-

---

to the close of the twelfth century; but this fine work was finished in 1939 and had to be supplemented, even at the time of its appearance in 1954, by less dated research.

[136] See Laurentin's presentation of these reasons in his Marian bulletin, *Revue des sciences philosophiques et théologiques* 46, 1962, 357.

[137] Albert Mitterer, *Dogma und Biologie der Heiligen Familie nach dem Weltbild des hl. Thomas von Aquin und dem der Gegenwart* (Vienna, Herder, 1952), 82-132.

[138] For some of the literature in the controversy, see Laurentin, *Revue des sciences philosophiques et théologiques* 46, 1962, 357-358, n. 115.

[139] René Laurentin, "Le mystère de la naissance virginale. A propos d'un livre récent," *Ephemerides mariologicae* 10, 1960, 345-374.

dition. Laurentin insists that the problem is not primarily a biological issue; he refuses dialogue on this level. He finds it imperative to restore the meaning of the Fathers and Councils, that is, to restore the question to the theological level, to recapture the discretion and delicacy exemplified by the patristic approach. Not that the corporeal element of the mystery can or should be eliminated, but that we must renounce the possibility or advisability of a clinical description of Christ's birth; for here, as with the Assumption, we know almost nothing of the how, we have not the requisite theological criteria. And Laurentin thinks it needful to recall what partisans and adversaries of the traditional doctrine have frequently forgotten: the importance of rediscovering in patristic tradition the authentic meaning of the Incarnation and of Christian virginity, of which the mystery of *virginitas in partu* is no more than an element.[140]

It may well be that the most significant consequence of this sensitive controversy will be a more profound understanding of virginity and its place in God's redemptive design. Serious study has already been launched in this direction, with splendid contributions by, for example, Mariological societies such as the Spanish and the American.[141]

A fourth facet of Mariological research has grown out of the recognition, by Mariologists and patrologists in theological tune with the times, that the factual evolution of Marian doctrine and devotion cannot be disregarded. What are the stages that lead from Palestine to Rome, from the maid of Nazareth to the Queen of Heaven, from "Hail Mary, highly favored" to "Hail holy Queen, our life, our sweetness, and our hope"? In this area, many worthwhile contributions of limited scope have been made;[142] but I sug-

---

140 See *Revue des sciences philosophiques et théologiques* 46, 1962, 360. See also the theologically sensitive observations on this problem by G. Philips, *Marianum* 24, 1962, 26-35.

141 *Estudios Marianos* 21, Madrid, Sociedad Mariológica Española, 1960. Also *Marian Studies* 13, Paterson, N. J., Mariological Society of America, 1962.

142 By "contributions of limited scope" I mean studies such as my own *The Testimony of the Patristic Age concerning Mary's Death* (Westminster, Newman, 1957), with its summary conclusion (p. 41): "From the evidence of the patristic age there emerges a widespread conviction of the early Church that our Lady died a natural death. This conviction, especially between the fifth and eighth centuries, was shared by hierarchy and faithful, preached by

gest that work of broader compass is imperative, along the lines sketched so impressively by C. Dillenschneider[143] and Laurentin,[144] so as to reveal not only in its labyrinthine detail, but especially in its extraordinary sweep the Church's growth in her understanding of Mary.

CHRISTOLOGY

One of the finer ongoing efforts in patristic research has to do with the Christology of the latter half of the fourth century and the first half of the fifth. Here the specific areas of greatest concern have been Chalcedon and the Antioch-Alexandria conflict. For Chalcedon, as indeed for its antecedents and consequences, we have the magisterial three volumes edited by Alois Grillmeier and Heinrich Bacht on the occasion of the Council's fifteenth centenary,[145] and R. V. Sellers' much smaller but dense and important study.[146] On several root questions of historical Christology the debate intensifies. How are we to understand and/or justify the *assumptus homo* formulas of patristic theology? Was Nestorius a Nestorian in the

theologians, publicly affirmed in the liturgy. There is no comparable conviction to offset it; for in dissent we find only individuals, not a tradition. However, the nature of much of the evidence—sporadic comments before Ephesus, apocrypha obscure in origin and impalpable in weight, a feast still hidden in history—is too fragile to sustain an apodictic conclusion on the theological significance of this convicton. But the conviction is there. More than that, the consistency of its liturgical expression and the uniformity of its homiletic articulation warrant the conclusion that it was conscious, abiding, and informed."

[143] Clément Dillenschneider, *Le sens de la foi et le progrès dogmatique du mystère marial*, Rome, Academia Mariana Internationalis, 1954. Dillenschneider has some excellent observations on the value of the dormition apocrypha and on the development of belief in the Assumption in the early homilies.

[144] René Laurentin, *Court traité du théologie mariale*, Paris, Lethielleux, 1954. See the fourth edition, 1959. The English translation by Gordon Smith, *Queen of Heaven. A Short Treatise on Marian Theology* (Dublin, Clonmore & Reynolds, 1956), unfortunately omits the highly helpful Table of Corrections on spurious or disputed Marian texts in Migne (*Court traité*, first edition, 118-173). See also Charles Journet, *Esquisse du développement du dogme marial*, Paris, Alsatia, 1954.

[145] Alois Grillmeier and Heinrich Bacht (eds.), *Das Konzil von Chalkedon. Geschichte und Gegenwart*, 3 volumes, Würzburg, Echter, 1951, 1953, 1954.

[146] R. V. Sellers, *The Council of Chalcedon. A Historical and Doctrinal Survey*, London, S.P.C.K., 1953.

classical sense? Was Theodore of Mopsuestia theologically the father of Nestorianism, and was his condemnation justified on the evidence? The student who would come abreast of the issues involved and the solutions proposed should read H. M. Diepen's articles on the *assumptus homo* problem in the patristic age,[147] L. Scipioni's work on Nestorius and the *Book of Heraclides*,[148] Grillmeier's insightful article on the theological importance of Nestorius,[149] the significant studies of Theodore by F. A. Sullivan, P. Galtier, John L. McKenzie, R. A. Greer, and R. A. Norris,[150] and P. Smulders' effort to trace the development of Christology in the patristic age and to make it more understandable from patristic soteriology.[151]

ORIGEN

"No comparable period in the history of the Church," Herbert Musurillo remarks, "has seen such a renascence of Origen studies." [152] The revival has been stimulated, in great part, by critical editions of Origen's works and by new discoveries such as the

---

[147] H. M. Diepen, " 'L'*Assumptus homo*' patristique," *Revue thomiste* 63, 1963, 225-245, 363-388; 64, 1964, 32-52.

[148] Luigi I. Scipioni, *Ricerche sulla cristologia del "Libro di Eraclide" di Nestorio. La formulazione teologica e il suo contesto filosofico*, Fribourg, University Press, 1956.

[149] Alois Grillmeier, "Das Scandalum oecumenicum des Nestorius in kirchlich-dogmatischer und theologiegeschichtlicher Sicht," *Scholastik* 36, 1961, 321-356.

[150] Francis A. Sullivan, *The Christology of Theodore of Mopsuestia*, Rome, Università Gregoriana, 1956; P. Galtier, "Théodore de Mopsueste. Sa vraie pensée sur l'Incarnation," *Recherches de science religieuse* 45, 1957, 161-186, 338-360; John L. McKenzie, "Annotations on the Christology of Theodore of Mopsuestia," *Theological Studies* 19, 1958, 345-373; Francis A. Sullivan, "Further Notes on Theodore of Mopsuestia. A Reply to Fr. McKenzie," *ibid.*, 20, 1959, 264-279; Rowan A. Greer, *Theodore of Mopsuestia, Exegete and Theologian*, London, Faith Press, 1961; R. A. Norris, Jr., *Manhood and Christ. A Study in the Christology of Theodore of Mopsuestia*, Oxford, Clarendon, 1963.

[151] P. Smulders, "De ontwikkeling van het christologisch dogma," *Bijdragen* 22, 1961, 357-424.

[152] "The Recent Revival of Origen Studies," *Theological Studies* 24, 1963, 250. I am indebted to this article (pp. 250-263) for useful information and deep insights.

1941 find of a cache of Origen and Didymus papyri in some ruins near Tourah, some twelve or thirteen miles south of Cairo.

While the revival broadens the cleavage between two schools on the question of the essential Origen, it deepens our detailed understanding of his work and its meaning. Christian theologian or Neoplatonist philosopher? Hans Jonas,[153] in the wake of de Faye, Koch, and Ivanka, sees Origen's system as essentially philosophical, with Christian elements inserted in sheerly material fashion. For this school, Origen was hardly a Christian theologian; he had little grasp of Christianity's authentic message; his use of the Bible is but a façade. Diametrically opposed are scholars of the stamp of Molland, Bardy, Völker, de Lubac, and Daniélou, who see in Origen a biblical theologian, with personal asceticism and authentic mysticism as the focal point of his entire system—a Christian theologian in a philosophical and cultural climate that is specifically Alexandrian.[154] For many in this school, Origen's system is a *Logosmystik*, "a personal Christianity based on a mystical union with the Logos; this is the pinnacle of all ascetical as well as theological effort, the culmination of God's creative and redemptive gesture, and the goal to which all prayer and study lead. Towards this are ordered the various levels of knowledge (shadow-image-reality), the three levels of scriptural interpretation, indeed all the studies of the secular schools." [155]

[153] *Gnosis und spätantiker Geist* 2/1. *Von der Mythologie zur mystischen Philosophie*, Göttingen, Vandenhoeck & Ruprecht, 1954 (see n. 91 above). Jonas tries to show that Origen's thought is linked to that of Valentinus and Plotinus by a special characteristic, the vital principle of system: the truth of a philosophy is judged not by its relation to objective reality but according to its inner consistency. It is deduced totally *a priori*, from an essential schema which is the unfolding of the genesis of the many from the one. Daniélou (*Recherches de science religieuse* 43, 1955, 579-580) agrees that this is one of the characteristic features of the *spätantiker Geist*, and notes that this type of thinking is to be found in the fourth century in the masterful construction of Eunomius, that it characterizes Gregory of Nyssa's *theōria*, that it will find its final form in Proclus; we have here a single intellectual family.

[154] A fine little work by K. O. Weber, *Origenes der Neuplatoniker* (Munich, Beck, 1962), decides the question, Christian theologian or Neoplatonist philosopher, in favor of a duality, and tries to reconstruct the principal features of Origen's Neoplatonism on (mainly) the basis of Proclus' statements.

[155] Musurillo, *art. cit.* (n. 152 above), 254.

Of this latter group, three scholars who have marked and sparked the Origen revival in the past decade merit special mention: Harl, Gruber, and Crouzel. Marguerite Harl's monograph on the revelatory role of the Incarnate Word [156] is fashioned on the terminology Origen employs to construct a Christocentric theology. She finds the focal point of his thought in the crucial, decisive concept of *logos* as it exists on three levels: in God, in Christ the Savior, and in the redeemed. She concludes that "Origen has the ability to borrow very precise terms from a vocabulary other than that of the Christians, without modifying in any way his profound inspiration, which is Christian. He borrows words, formulas, images, but the totality of his thought forms, in most instances, a radically different whole from the source from which he takes part of his language." [157]

Gerhard Gruber's monograph analyzes Origen's concept of life; [158] he finds in *zōē* a transcendental notion parallel with *sophia*, *logos*, and *phōs*; he sees it not only in its application to the Godhead and to Jesus, but as an activating, actuating force whereby the redeemed are raised to participation in Trinitarian life. And though Gruber tends to see Origen's thought as somehow derivative from the Valentinian *gnōsis*, he insists that "Origen in his distinction of the various levels of participation [of human nature in the divine life] has far surpassed the system of the Gnostics— even though Origen himself was not always aware of the consequences of his own thought." [159]

The most knowledgeable and prolific Origen scholar of our time is Henri Crouzel. Apart from a number of articles, Crouzel has produced four full-length books on Origen in eight years. His earliest study, on the image of God, [160] reveals, against the inclinations of some earlier scholars, the high significance of the image theme in Origen's total theological vision. His second work, on mystical

[156] *Origène et la fonction révélatrice du Verbe incarné*, Paris, Seuil, 1958.

[157] Harl, *op. cit.*, 347; translated by Musurillo, *art. cit.* (n. 152 above), 254.

[158] Gruber, *ZŌĒ. Wesen, Stufen und Mitteilung des wahren Lebens bei Origenes*, Munich, Hueber, 1962. This is a revised text, on the basis of more intensive study, of what was originally undertaken as a dissertation for the Gregorian University, Rome, in 1956.

[159] Gruber, *op. cit.*, 330; translated by Musurillo, *art. cit.* (n. 152 above), 258.

[160] *Théologie de l'image de Dieu chez Origène*, Paris, Aubier, 1956.

158

knowledge,[161] complements Völker's research: It establishes Origen's authentically Christian mysticism against Koch and others, and sees its basis in the shadow-truth-reality triplet implicit in his allegorical interpretation of Scripture and in the typological response between the two Testaments.[162] The third study, on philosophy,[163] is a documented reply to the charge that Origen's contribution was but a brilliant Hellenization of Christianity, a clever structuring of certain aspects of Christianity in line with the eclectic philosophy of the Alexandrian schools, neo-Stoic, Gnostic, and Platonic. Not a system, not free of contradictions, Origen's theology is shown to be soundly Christian in inspiration, with his whole thought ultimately unified by the final restoration of the divine image-likeness in man: the mystical vision of God in this life, to be consummated hereafter, when God is all in all. Crouzel's most recent book, on Origen's theology of virginity and marriage,[164] provides, among much else, a corrective for the imbalance of Nygren's treatment of *agapē* and *erōs*; it illustrates Origen's increasingly pastoral concerns with the mystery and the sacramental character of marriage modeled on the relationship between Christ and the Church; significantly, it begins with a splendid treatment of Origen's ideas on the mystery of the Church in her pre-creational existence, thus laying the spiritual and metaphysical foundations for the essentially mystical pattern of his thought.

Crouzel's four books should be read as a unity. They give added weight to the conviction of many that the real Origen is not the philosopher, but the theologian and mystic who has transcended the limited categories of eclectic Neoplatonism, and who is in large

[161] *Origène et la "connaissance mystique,"* Bruges, Desclée de Brouwer, 1961.

[162] On this aspect of Origen, see the fine introduction by Olivier Rousseau to his translation of the *Homélies sur le Cantique des cantiques* ("Sources chrétiennes" 37, Paris, Cerf, 1954). Origen's mysticism is at once liturgical and biblical. Here the mystical experience is *gnōsis*, contemplative wonderment at the mysteries hidden in Scripture and to which the Spirit introduces pure hearts. Though experiential and personal, this mysticism is even more ecclesial. Frédéric Bertrand, *Mystique de Jésus chez Origène* (Paris, Aubier, 1951), had already shown that devotion to the person of Jesus is an essential trait of Origen's spirituality; he is not an intellectualist preoccupied exclusively with the Logos; he heralds Bernard.

[163] *Origène et la philosophie*, Paris, Aubier, 1962.

[164] *Virginité et mariage selon Origène*, Bruges, Desclée de Brouwer, 1963.

measure responsible for the flowering of mystical theology and asceticism under the Cappadocians in the East and under Augustine and his successors in the West.

It is worth noting that, for some years now, Crouzel has been engaged on a critical bibliography of Origen. It will include, as far as this is possible, the editions, translations, and studies (books, parts of books, articles in journals and in dictionaries or encyclopedias) that have been published since the invention of printing. The subject matter comprised therein embraces 1) Origen and his works, including the *Hexapla*; 2) Ammonius Saccas and the problem of "Origen the pagan"; 3) Heracleon and Celsus; 4) Gregory Thaumaturgus' panegyric on Origen; 5) the history of Origenism and the struggles it occasioned; 6) pseudo-Origeniana, to the moment when the attribution to another author has been commonly accepted. Unpublished dissertations will enter the bibliography to the extent that Crouzel can consult them. In all probability, the bibliography will be organized along chronological lines, with a systematic *index rerum* and an *index auctorum* to facilitate its use. It will indicate the content of the articles, unless the titles are indication enough, and the content of the books, restricted of course to pertinent Origen material. Frequently, a critical judgment will be offered, as well as references to the more significant reviews, when there is question of modern books devoted, in whole or in part, to Origen and related topics.

Other important works of the decade present Origen as a teacher,[165] his doctrine on sin,[166] his philosophy of matter,[167] his understanding of tradition,[168] his exegesis,[169] his Mariology,[170] his

[165] G. I. Mantzaridēs, *To didaskalikon ergon tou Ōrigenous*, Thessalonica, 1960.

[166] Georg Teichtweier, *Die Sündenlehre des Origenes*, Regensburg, Pustet, 1958.

[167] H. Cornélis, *Les fondements cosmologiques de l'eschatologie d'Origène*, Paris, Vrin, 1959.

[168] R. P. C. Hanson, *Origen's Doctrine of Tradition*, London, S.P.C.K., 1954.

[169] R. P. C. Hanson, *Allegory and Event. A Study of the Sources and Significance of Origen's Interpretation of Scripture*, London, SCM, 1959. For the tools at Origen's disposal in his approach to the New Testament, see Robert M. Grant, *The Earliest Lives of Jesus*, New York, Harper, 1961. See also the introductions to the *Sources chrétiennes* volumes on Origen: 7 (Homi-

conception of holiness,[171] his theology of light,[172] and his vision of God as father.[173]

The significance of the Origen revival transcends the commendable endeavor to understand, or even to rehabilitate, a fascinating Christian thinker. Incarnate in Origen, basic to Origen studies, are several questions of contemporary concern: What is the role of the Christian theologian? To what extent, if any, is philosophy legitimate in the effort to fathom the faith? Is any given philosophy perennially adequate to this task? What is biblical theology, and how is it carried on? How is the Christian to interpret Scripture, especially the Old Testament? What is tradition, and what is its relationship to Scripture?

DOCTRINAL DEVELOPMENT

Perhaps the most crucial theological problem of our time, in itself and for the ecumenical dialogue, is doctrinal development: "the nature of development, its validity, the permanent or ephemeral value of developed forms, the relative character of conception that is the presupposition of all development in doctrine." [174] In a sense, every book or article on patristic theology is relevant to the problem of development; for in this way the actual process of evolution gradually transpires and the facts come to light without which any theory of development must remain irritatingly broad and nebulous.

In the realm of developmental theory, the classical authors of

---

lies on Genesis), 16 (Exodus), 29 (Numbers), 37 (Song of Songs, 71 (Joshua), 87 (Luke).

[170] See n. 124 above. Crouzel here recaptures Origen's ideas on Mary's maternity, virginity, holiness, and role in redemption, with the care and insight we have come to expect of him wherever he deals with Origen.

[171] Franz Faessler, *Der Hagiosbegriff bei Origenes. Ein Beitrag zum Hagios-Problem*, Fribourg, University Press, 1958.

[172] Marcelo Martínez Pastor, *Teología de la luz en Orígenes* (*De princ. et In Ioh.*), Comillas-Santander, Universidad Pontificia, 1963.

[173] Peter Nemeshegyi, *La paternité de Dieu chez Origène*, Tournai, Desclée et Cie, 1960.

[174] Frederick E. Crowe, "Development of Doctrine and the Ecumenical Problem," *Theological Studies* 23, 1962, 45.

the distant past have been Cardinal Newman, R. M. Schultes, and F. Marin-Sola.[175] From 1937 on, for more than a decade, we had the books and especially the articles touching immutability and development which led to and surrounded the distressing accusations of a "new theology." Here perhaps the most significant names immediately pertinent to development were Draguet and Simonin, Taymans and Mersch, de Lubac and Bouillard, Boyer and Garrigou-Lagrange.[176] In the past decade, I find three authors uncommonly significant on the level of theory, each with deep roots in and important implications for patristic theology: Owen Chadwick, Karl Rahner, and Bernard Lonergan. Chadwick's *From Bossuet to Newman*[177] tries to establish a contrast, even a contradiction, between Bossuet's insistence on unchanging tradition and Newman's theory of doctrinal growth, with the Roman Church clutching gratefully at Newman's *Essay* for the theoretical justification of her variations in doctrine, her additions to the original revelation. "Learned and in intention fair," delightful and often exhilarating, the distinguished Cambridge scholar has been criticized for assuming that immutability and development are simply contrasts, and because he "has been badly briefed on the facts" of the history of dogmas.[178]

---

[175] See John Henry Newman's last work as an Anglican, *An Essay on the Development of Christian Doctrine* (London, 1845, 1878[2]; Image Book edition, with Foreword by Gustave Weigel, S.J., Garden City, Doubleday, 1960), with its seven qualities of true development: chronic vigor, preservation of type, power of assimilation, continuity of principle, logical sequence, conservation of action, and anticipation of the future. The much-debated *Introductio in historiam dogmatum* by Reginald-M. Schultes (Paris, 1922) deals with the notion of dogma, the evolution of dogmas, and the history of dogmas. Francisco Marin-Sola's *La evolución homogénea del dogma católico* (Madrid, 1923) centers on the virtually revealed.

[176] For some detailed discussion of the theories involved, see John J. Galvin, "A Critical Survey of Modern Conceptions of Doctrinal Development," *Proceedings of the Fifth Annual Meeting, The Catholic Theological Society of America*, 1950 (New York, 1951), 45-63; also Philip J. Donnelly, "On the Development of Dogma and the Supernatural," *Theological Studies* 8, 1947, 471-491; and Donnelly's follow-up, "Theological Opinion on the Development of Dogma," *ibid.*, 668-699.

[177] *From Bossuet to Newman. The Idea of Doctrinal Development*, Cambridge, Cambridge University Press, 1957.

[178] So Anthony A. Stephenson, "The Development and Immutability of Christian Doctrine," *Theological Studies* 19, 1958, 481, 483. Stephenson's own understanding of doctrinal development in this article (pp. 481-532) is

Even more significant are Rahner and Lonergan. Karl Rahner discovers the correct understanding of development in the correct understanding of revelation itself as part of salvation history. And in its deepest dimension doctrinal explication is not a movement from proposition to proposition, but a movement from prereflective possession of an entire truth to its more reflective, though necessarily only partial, appropriation in and through propositional formulation.[179] Bernard Lonergan, without ever having published a specific work on the problem of development, has shown impressively,[180] with emphasis on Nicaea and Chalcedon among others, how doctrinal evolution is a complex historical process involving three movements or dimensions of movement: the transcultural, the theological, and the strictly dogmatic. The transcultural involves transposition not merely from one use of words to another, but from one underlying mentality to another. As theological, the movement takes a precise direction—towards theological *understanding* in a highly particularized sense: analytical reduction from what is first, or immediate, in the order of human experience, to what is first, or immediate, in the order of things as they are in themselves objectively.

I would note, finally, that John Courtney Murray, in his small

---

open to serious criticism: In his effort to preserve immutability, he seems to make development (e.g., *homoousios*, seven sacraments) a sheerly verbal thing.

[179] See "Zur Frage der Dogmenentwicklung," *Schriften zur Theologie* 1 (Einsiedeln, Benziger, 1954), 49-90; ET *Theological Investigations* 1 (Baltimore, Helicon, 1961), 39-97. See also Rahner's "Dogmenentwicklung," *Lexikon für Theologie und Kirche* 3, 1959², 457-463. For a penetrating analysis of the former article and a comparison with Lonergan, see Robert L. Richard, "Rahner's Theory of Doctrinal Development," *Proceedings of the Eighteenth Annual Convention, The Catholic Theological Society of America*, 1963 (New York, 1964), 157-189.

[180] Lonergan's longest and most complete discussion is discoverable in sections 6 and 7 (pp. 28-41) towards the end of the introductory Chapter 1 of the Trinitarian treatise *Divinarum personarum conceptio analogica* (Rome, Università Gregoriana, 1957); this should be complemented by the historical analyses in *De Verbo incarnato* (Rome, Università Gregoriana, 1961²) and *De Deo trino* (2 volumes, second edition of volume 1, and third edition of volume 2; Rome, Università Gregoriana, 1964). An English translation of *De Deo trino* is now being prepared in cooperation with the author, and will be published in 1966 by Herder and Herder, New York.

but distinguished book, *The Problem of God*,[181] has indicated with rich suggestiveness the balance of immutability and development in the *homoousios* of Nicaea. It has been observed that Murray's explication calls for Lonergan's epistemology, but I do not find this at all repellent or undesirable.[182]

This type of ten-year survey demands not a final summary, but a renewed warning. The survey is selective, not complete; it is suggestive rather than profound. For any student of patristic thought, it should mark not an end, but a beginning. Only from such a viewpoint, as realistic as it is gracious, will he find the survey serviceable.

Bibliography

1. GENERAL WORKS

MANUALS OF PATROLOGY AND HISTORIES OF CHRISTIAN LITERATURE

ALTANER, BERTHOLD. *Patrologie. Leben, Schriften und Lehre der Kirchenväter*, Freiburg, Herder, 1958⁵; ET *Patrology*, New York, Herder and Herder, 1960. See the sixth German edition, corrected and supplemented by Alfred Stuiber, Freiburg, Herder, 1960.

BECK, HANS-GEORG. *Kirche und theologische Literatur im byzantinischen Reich*, Munich, Beck, 1959.

CAMPENHAUSEN, HANS VON. *Die griechischen Kirchenväter*, Stuttgart,

[181] New Haven, Yale University Press, 1964.

[182] See also the collaborative work, *Lo sviluppo del dogma secondo la dottrina cattolica. Relazioni lette nella Seconda Settimana Teologica, 24-28 Settembre, 1951* (Rome, Università Gregoriana, 1953), with studies by Flick, Spiazza, Rambaldi, Bea, Balič, Filograssi, Dhanis, and Boyer. These studies cover the important points of dogmatic development: the close of revelation with the Apostles, the immutability of dogma and its formulas, tradition, the Christian sense, interpretation of Scripture, the role of theologian and philosopher in dogmatic progress, and the manner in which new dogmas are related to the deposit. An initial essay outlines the various theories on development and the state of theological thinking on the matter at the time.

Kohlhammer, 1956[2]; ET *The Fathers of the Greek Church,* New York, Pantheon, 1959.

CAMPENHAUSEN, HANS VON. *Lateinische Kirchenväter,* Stuttgart, Kohlhammer, 1960; ET *The Fathers of the Latin Church,* London, A. & C. Black, 1964.

CROSS, F. L. *The Early Christian Fathers,* London, Duckworth, 1960.

DEKKERS, ELIGIUS. *Clavis patrum latinorum,* Bruges, Beyaert, 1961[2].

GRAF, GEORG. *Geschichte der christlichen arabischen Literatur,* 5 volumes, Vatican City, Bibliotheca Apostolica Vaticana, 1944-1953.

ORTIZ DE URBINA, IGNATIUS. *Patrologia syriaca,* Rome, Istituto Orientale, 1958.

QUASTEN, JOHANNES. *Patrology* 1. *The Beginnings of Patristic Literature;* 2. *The Ante-Nicene Literature after Irenaeus;* 3. *The Golden Age of Greek Patristic Literature. From the Council of Nicaea to the Council of Chalcedon,* Westminster, Newman, 1950, 1953, 1960; FT *Initiation aux Pères de l'église,* 3 volumes, Paris, Cerf, 1955, 1957, 1963; ST *Patrología,* 2 volumes, Madrid, La Editorial Católica, 1961, 1962.

HISTORIES OF DOGMA AND DOCTRINE

KELLY, J. N. D. *Early Christian Doctrines,* London, A. & C. Black, 1960[2].

SCHMAUS, MICHAEL, AND GRILLMEIER, ALOIS (editors), *Handbuch der Dogmengeschichte:*

1/4. BEUMER, JOHANNES. *Die mündliche Ueberlieferung als Glaubensquelle,* Freiburg, Herder, 1962.

2/2a. SCHEFFCZYK, LEO. *Schöpfung und Vorsehung,* Freiburg, Herder, 1963.

4/2. NEUNHEUSER, BURKHARD. *Taufe und Firmung,* Freiburg, Herder, 1956 (see below).

4/3. POSCHMANN, BERNHARD. *Busse und Letzte Oelung,* Freiburg, Herder, 1951 (see below).

4/4b. NEUNHEUSER, BURKHARD. *Eucharistie in Mittelalter und Neuzeit,* Freiburg, Herder, 1963.

The *Handbuch der Dogmengeschichte* is being presented in English under the series title, "The Herder History of Dogma," published by Herder and Herder, New York. Titles published thus far are:

NEUNHEUSER, BURKHARD. *Baptism and Confirmation,* New York, Herder and Herder, 1964.

Poschmann, Bernhard. *Penance and the Anointing of the Sick,* New York, Herder and Herder, 1964.

Histories of Philosophy

Copleston, Frederick. *Medieval Philosophy. Augustine to Scotus,* Westminster, Newman, 1950.

Fraile, Guillermo. *El judaísmo y la filosofía. El cristianismo y la filosofía: El islamismo y la filosofía,* Madrid, La Editorial Católica, 1959.

Geyer, Bernhard. *Die patristische und scholastische Philosophie,* Basel, Schwabe, 1951[12].

Gilson, Etienne. *History of Christian Philosophy in the Middle Ages,* New York, Random House, 1955.

Wolfson, Harry Austryn. *The Philosophy of the Church Fathers* 1. *Faith, Trinity, Incarnation,* Cambridge (Mass.), Harvard University Press, 1956.

Editions

Corpus christianorum, Series latina, Turnhout, Brepols, 1953-.

Corpus scriptorum christianorum orientalium, under the secretary-generalship of René Draguet, Louvain, Secrétariat du Corpus-SCO, 1903-.

Patrologiae cursus completus, Series latina, Supplementum 1, 2, and 3/1, edited by Adalbert Hamman, Paris, Garnier, 1958-.

Sources chrétiennes, under the direction of Henri de Lubac, Jean Daniélou, and Claude Mondésert, Paris, Cerf, 1942-.

Translations

Ancient Christian Writers, edited by Johannes Quasten and Walter J. Burghardt, Westminster, Newman, 1946-.

The Fathers of the Church, under the editorial direction of Roy J. Deferrari, Washington, Catholic University of America Press, 1947-.

Sources chrétiennes, under the direction of Henri de Lubac, Jean Daniélou, and Claude Mondésert, Paris, Cerf, 1942-.

Encyclopedias and Dictionaries

Lexikon für Theologie und Kirche, edited by Josef Höfer and Karl Rahner, Freiburg, Herder, 1957-[2].

The Oxford Dictionary of the Christian Church, edited by F. L. Cross, New York, Oxford University Press, 1957.

Reallexikon für Antike und Christentum, edited by THEODOR KLAUSER, Stuttgart, Hiersemann, 1950-.
Die Religion in Geschichte und Gegenwart, edited by KURT GALLING. 6 volumes; index volume to follow; Tübingen, Mohr, 1957-1962³.
Twentieth Century Encyclopedia of Religious Knowledge, edited by LEFFERTS A. LOETSCHER, 2 volumes, Grand Rapids, Baker, 1955.

LEXICONS

BAUER, WALTER. *Griechisch-deutsches Wörterbuch zu den Schriften des Neuen Testaments und der übrigen urchristlichen Literatur,* Berlin, Töpelmann, 1958⁵. ET and adaptation of the fourth edition (1952): *A Greek-English Lexicon of the New Testament and Other Early Christian Literature,* Chicago, University of Chicago Press, 1957.
BLAISE, ALBERT. *Dictionnaire latin-français des auteurs chrétiens,* Strasbourg, "Le Latin Chrétien," 1954.
NIERMEYER, J. F. *Mediae latinitatis lexicon minus,* Leiden, Brill, 1954-.
A Patristic Greek Lexicon, edited by G. W. H. LAMPE, Oxford, Clarendon, 1961-.
Thesaurus linguae latinae, Leipzig, Teubner, 1904-.

PERIODICALS AND BIBLIOGRAPHICAL AIDS

Augustinus, Madrid, 1956-.
Bibliographia patristica, edited by WILHELM SCHNEEMELCHER, Berlin, de Gruyter, 1950-.
Jahrbuch für Antike und Christentum, Münster, Aschendorff, 1958-.
Oriens christianus, Wiesbaden, 1953-.
L'Orient syrien, Paris, 1956-.
Revue des études augustiniennes, Paris, 1955-.

2. THEOLOGICAL THEMES

JUDAISM, GNOSTICISM, HELLENISM

ANDRESEN, CARL. *Logos und Nomos. Die Polemik des Kelsos wider das Christentum,* Berlin, de Gruyter, 1955.
DANIÉLOU, JEAN. *Histoire des doctrines chrétiennes avant Nicée 1. Théologie du judéo-christianisme; 2. Message évangélique et culture hellénistique aux IIe et IIIe siècles,* Tournai, Desclée et Cie., 1958, 1961.

GOODENOUGH, ERWIN R. *Jewish Symbols in the Greco-Roman Period* 1-11, New York, Pantheon, 1953-64. Volume 12 is scheduled for publication in 1965.

GOPPELT, LEONHARD. *Christentum und Judentum im ersten und zweiten Jahrhundert. Ein Aufriss der Urgeschichte der Kirche*, Gütersloh, Bertelsmann, 1954.

GRANT, ROBERT M. *Gnosticism and Early Christianity*, New York, Columbia University Press, 1959.

HOUSSIAU, ALBERT. *La christologie de saint Irénée*, Louvain, Publications Universitaires, 1955.

JONAS, HANS. *Gnosis und spätantiker Geist* 2/1. *Von der Mythologie zur mystischen Philosophie*, Göttingen, Vandenhoeck & Ruprecht, 1954.

———. *The Gnostic Religion. The Message of the Alien God and the Beginnings of Christianity*, Boston, Beacon, 1958.

ORBE, ANTONIO. *Estudios Valentinianos:*

1/1 and 1/2. *Hacia la primera teología de la procesión del Verbo*, Rome, Università Gregoriana, 1958.

2. *En los albores de la exegesis Iohannea (Ioh. I, 3)*, Rome, Università Gregoriana, 1955.

3. *La unción del Verbo*, Rome, Università Gregoriana, 1961.

5. *Los primeros herejes ante la persecución*, Rome, Università Gregoriana, 1956.

PETERSON, ERIK. *Frühkirche, Judentum und Gnosis. Studien und Untersuchungen*, Rome, Herder, 1959.

TESTA, P. E. *Il simbolismo dei Giudeo-Cristiani*, Jerusalem, Tipografia dei PP. Francescani, 1962.

TRESMONTANT, CLAUDE. *La métaphysique du christianisme et la naissance de la philosophie chrétienne. Problèmes de la création et de l'anthropologie des origines à saint Augustin*, Paris, Seuil, 1961.

———. *Les origines de la philosophie chrétienne*, Paris, Fayard, 1962; ET *The Origins of Christian Philosophy*, New York, Hawthorn, 1963.

SPIRITUALITY

BOUYER, LOUIS. *La spiritualité du Nouveau Testament et des Pères*, Paris, Aubier, 1960; ET *The Spirituality of the New Testament and the Fathers*, New York, Desclée, 1963.

CROUZEL, HENRI. *Origène et la "connaissance mystique,"* Bruges, Desclée de Brouwer, 1961.

DANIÉLOU, JEAN. *Sacramentum futuri. Etudes sur les origines de la typologie biblique*, Paris, Beauchesne, 1950; ET *From Shadows to Reality*, London, Burns & Oates, 1960.

————. *Bible et liturgie. La théologie biblique des sacrements et des fêtes d'après les Pères de l'église*, Paris, Cerf, 1951; ET *The Bible and the Liturgy*, Notre Dame, University of Notre Dame Press, 1956.

Dictionnaire de spiritualité ascétique et mystique. Doctrine et histoire, edited by ANDRÉ RAYEZ AND CHARLES BAUMGARTNER, Paris, Beauchesne, 1937-.

HAUSHERR, IRÉNÉE. *Direction spirituelle en Orient autrefois*, Rome, Istituto Orientale, 1955.

HUDON, GERMAIN. *La perfection chrétienne d'après les sermons de saint Léon*, Paris, Cerf, 1959.

LUBAC, HENRI DE. *Histoire et esprit. L'Intelligence de l'Ecriture d'après Origène*, Paris, Aubier, 1950.

————. *Exégèse médiévale. Les quatre sens de l'Ecriture*, 2 volumes, each with two parts; Paris, Aubier, 1959-1964.

ROUSSEAU, OLIVIER. *Monachisme et vie religieuse d'après l'ancienne tradition de l'église*, Chevetogne, Editions de Chevetogne, 1957.

STEIDLE, BASILIUS (editor). *Antonius magnus eremita, 356-1956. Studia ad antiquum monachismum spectantia*, Rome, Herder, 1956.

VÖLKER, WALTHER. *Gregor von Nyssa als Mystiker*, Wiesbaden, Steiner, 1955.

THE IMAGE OF GOD IN MAN

BERNARD, RÉGIS. *L'Image de Dieu d'après saint Athanase*, Paris, Aubier, 1952.

BURGHARDT, WALTER J. *The Image of God in Man according to Cyril of Alexandria*, Washington, Catholic University of America Press; Woodstock, Woodstock College Press, 1957.

CROUZEL, HENRI. *Théologie de l'image de Dieu chez Origène*, Paris, Aubier, 1956.

JENKINSON, WILLIAM R. "The Image and the Likeness of God in Man in the Eighteen Lectures on the Credo of Cyril of Jerusalem (c. 315-387)," *Ephemerides Theologicae Lovanienses* 40, 1964, 48-71.

LADNER, GERHART B. "Eikon," *Reallexikon für Antike und Christentum* 4, 1959, 771-786.

————. *The Idea of Reform. Its Impact on Christian Thought and Action in the Age of the Fathers*, Cambridge (Mass.), Harvard University Press, 1959.

LEYS, ROGER. *L'Image de Dieu chez saint Grégoire de Nysse. Esquisse d'une doctrine*, Brussels and Paris, Desclée de Brouwer, 1951.

MEANY, JAMES J. *The Image of God in Man according to the Doctrine of Saint John Damascene*, Manila, San José Seminary, 1954.

MERKI, HUBERT. *Homoiōsis Theō. Von der platonischen Angleichung an Gott zur Gottähnlichkeit bei Gregor von Nyssa*, Fribourg, Paulusverlag, 1952.

————. "Ebenbildlichkeit," *Reallexikon für Antike und Christentum* 4, 1959, 459-479.

SULLIVAN, JOHN EDWARD. *The Image of God. The Doctrine of St. Augustine and Its Influence*, Dubuque, Priory Press, 1963.

MARIOLOGY

BECK, E. "Die Mariologie der echten Schriften Ephräms," *Oriens christianus* 40, 1956, 22-39.

BURGHARDT, WALTER J. "Mary in Western Patristic Thought," in J. B. Carol, *Mariology* 1, Milwaukee, Bruce, 1955, 109-155.

————. "Theotokos: The Mother of God," in Edward D. O'Connor, *The Mystery of the Woman*, Notre Dame, University of Notre Dame Press, 1956, 3-33.

————. "Mary in Eastern Patristic Thought," in J. B. Carol, *Mariology* 2, Milwaukee, Bruce, 1957, 88-153.

————. *The Testimony of the Patristic Age concerning Mary's Death*, Westminster, Newman, 1957.

CASCANTE DÁVILA, JUAN M. *Doctrina mariana de S. Ildefonso de Toledo*, Barcelona, Casulleras, 1958.

COATHALEM, H. *Le parallélisme entre la sainte Vierge et l'église dans la tradition latine jusqu'à la fin du XIIe siècle*, Rome, Università Gregoriana, 1954.

DILLENSCHNEIDER, CLÉMENT. *Le sens de la foi et le progrès dogmatique du mystère marial*, Rome, Academia Mariana Internationalis, 1954.

FEDYNIAK, SERGIUS STEPHANUS. *Mariologia apud PP. Cappadoces*, Rome, Apud Curiam Ordinis Basiliani S. Josaphat, 1958.

GORDILLO, MAURICIUS. *Mariologia orientalis*, Rome, Istituto Orientale, 1954.

S. *Jean Damascène. Homélies sur la nativité et la dormition*, text, introduction, translation, and notes by Pierre Voulet, Paris, Cerf, 1961.

JOUASSARD, G. "Deux chefs de file en théologie mariale dans la seconde moitié du IVe siècle: saint Epiphane et saint Ambroise," *Gregorianum* 42, 1961, 5-36.

JOURNET, CHARLES. *Esquisse du développement du dogme marial,* Paris, Alsatia, 1954.

JUGIE, M. *L'Immaculée conception dans l'Ecriture sainte et dans la tradition orientale,* Rome, Officium libri catholici, 1952.

LAURENTIN, RENÉ. *Court traité du théologie mariale,* Paris, Lethielleux, 1954, 1959[4]; ET *Queen of Heaven. A Short Treatise on Marian Theology,* Dublin, Clonmore & Reynolds, 1956.

————. "Le mystère de la naissance virginale. A propos d'un livre récent," *Ephemerides mariologicae* 10, 1960, 345-374.

MITTERER, ALBERT. *Dogma und Biologie der Heiligen Familie nach dem Weltbild des hl. Thomas von Aquin und dem der Gegenwart,* Vienna, Herder, 1952.

MONTAGNA, D. *La lode alla Theotokos nei testi greci dei secoli IV-VII,* Rome, Marianum, 1963.

MÜLLER, ALOIS. *Ecclesia-Maria. Die Einheit Marias und der Kirche,* Fribourg, University Press, 1955[2].

NEUMANN, CHARLES W. *The Virgin Mary in the Works of Saint Ambrose,* Fribourg, University Press, 1962.

O'CONNOR, EDWARD D. (editor). *The Dogma of the Immaculate Conception. History and Significance.* Notre Dame, University of Notre Dame Press, 1958.

Origène. Homélies sur s. Luc, text, introduction, translation, and notes by HENRI CROUZEL, FRANÇOIS FOURNIER, AND PIERRE PÉRICHON, Paris, Cerf, 1962.

CHRISTOLOGY

DIEPEN, H. M. " 'L'*Assumptus homo*' patristique," *Revue thomiste* 63, 1963, 225-245, 363-388; 64, 1964, 32-52.

GALTIER, P. "Théodore de Mopsueste. Sa vraie pensée sur l'Incarnation," *Recherches de science religieuse* 45, 1957, 161-186, 338-360.

GREER, ROWAN A. *Theodore of Mopsuestia, Exegete and Theologian,* London, Faith Press, 1961.

GRILLMEIER, ALOIS. "Das Scandalum oecumenicum des Nestorius in kirchlich-dogmatischer und theologiegeschichtlicher Sicht," *Scholastik* 36, 1961, 321-356.

GRILLMEIER, ALOIS, AND BACHT, HEINRICH (editors). *Das Konzil von Chalkedon. Geschichte und Gegenwart*, 3 volumes, Würzburg, Echter, 1951, 1953, 1954.

McKENZIE, JOHN L. "Annotations on the Christology of Theodore of Mopsuestia," *Theological Studies* 19, 1958, 345-373.

NORRIS, R. A., JR. *Manhood and Christ. A Study in the Christology of Theodore of Mopsuestia*, Oxford, Clarendon, 1963.

SCIPIONI, LUIGI I. *Ricerche sulla cristologia del "Libro di Eraclide" di Nestorio. La formulazione teologica e il suo contesto filosofico*, Fribourg, University Press, 1956.

SELLERS, R. V. *The Council of Chalcedon. A Historical and Doctrinal Survey*, London, S.P.C.K., 1953.

SMULDERS, P. "De ontwikkeling van het christologisch dogma," *Bijdragen* 22, 1961, 357-424.

SULLIVAN, FRANCIS A. *The Christology of Theodore of Mopsuestia.* Rome, Università Gregoriana, 1956.

———. "Further Notes on Theodore of Mopsuestia. A Reply to Fr. McKenzie," *Theological Studies* 20, 1959, 264-279.

ORIGEN

CORNÉLIS, H. *Les fondements cosmologiques de l'eschatologie d'Origène*, Paris, Vrin, 1959.

CROUZEL, HENRI. *Théologie de l'image de Dieu chez Origène*, Paris, Aubier, 1956.

———. *Origène et la "connaissance mystique,"* Bruges, Desclée de Brouwer, 1961.

———. *Origène et la philosophie*, Paris, Aubier, 1962.

———. *Virginité et mariage selon Origène*, Bruges, Desclée de Brouwer, 1963.

FAESSLER, FRANZ. *Der Hagiosbegriff bei Origenes. Ein Beitrag zum Hagios-Problem*, Fribourg, University Press, 1958.

GRUBER, GERHARD. *ZŌĒ. Wesen, Stufen und Mitteilung des wahren Lebens bei Origenes*, Munich, Hueber, 1962.

HANSON, R. P. C. *Origen's Doctrine of Tradition*, London, S.P.C.K., 1954.

———. *Allegory and Event. A Study of the Sources and Significance of Origen's Interpretation of Scripture*, London, SCM, 1959.

HARL, MARGUERITE. *Origène et la fonction révélatrice du Verbe incarné*, Paris, Seuil, 1958.

MANTZARIDĒS, G. I. *To didaskalikon ergon tou Ōrigenous*, Thessalonica, 1960.

MARTÍNEZ PASTOR, MARCELO. *Teología de la luz en Orígenes* (*De princ. et In Ioh.*), Comillas-Santander, Universidad Pontificia, 1963.

NEMESHEGYI, PETER. *La paternité de Dieu chez Origène*, Tournai, Desclée et Cie., 1960.

TEICHTWEIER, GEORG. *Die Sündenlehre des Origenes*, Regensburg, Pustet, 1958.

WEBER, K. O. *Origenes der Neuplatoniker*, Munich, Beck, 1962.

DOCTRINAL DEVELOPMENT

CHADWICK, OWEN. *From Bossuet to Newman. The Idea of Doctrinal Development*, Cambridge, Cambridge University Press, 1957.

LONERGAN, BERNARD. *Divinarum personarum conceptio analogica.* Rome, Università Gregoriana, 1957.

MURRAY, JOHN COURTNEY. *The Problem of God*, New Haven, Yale University Press, 1964.

RAHNER, KARL. "Zur Frage der Dogmenentwicklung," in *Schriften zur Theologie* 1, Einsiedeln, Benziger, 1954; ET "The Development of Dogma," in *Theological Investigations* 1, Baltimore, Helicon, 1961.

Lo sviluppo del dogma secondo la dottrina cattolica. Relazioni lette nella Seconda Settimana Teologica, 24-28 Settembre, 1951, Rome, Università Gregoriana, 1953.

Liturgical Studies

John H. Miller, C.S.C.

Preparing this report has been nothing short of a traumatic experience. If a far from adequate coverage of one year's liturgical publications extends to one thousand and seventy-eight entries in the fourth volume of the *Yearbook of Liturgical Studies*, what should a thorough examination of such work amount to for a period of ten years? If for nothing else, these ten years have been decisive for the sheer quantity of studies produced in the field of liturgy.

By force of circumstances, I have had to limit myself to those contributions that I considered to be outstanding, if not for new and daring insights, at least for the excellence of their synthetic attempt and their bibliographical value. To make this report a little less wearisome and a little more helpful in gaining a general impression of the period, I shall divide it according to the following areas: liturgical doctrine, general studies, liturgical history, language, liturgical year, the Mass, the Office, Oriental studies, preaching, questions of reform, and questions concerning the ritual of sacraments and sacramentals. Within these categories, I shall assemble the material, in so far as possible, around certain topical ideas.

DOCTRINE

The points of liturgical doctrine that seem to have attracted most attention were the nature and definition of the liturgy, liturgy and spirituality, the *Mysterium* theology of Odo Casel, O.S.B., the sacramental character, the ecclesial and sacramental dimensions of the liturgy, and the relationship of liturgy to the Word of God. Each study in this category has contributed more or less consciously towards a genuine theology about the liturgy; there has been a definite upsurge of interest in the theological foundations, implications, and meaning of the liturgy as opposed to its merely historical development.

Before I go on to discuss these individual topics, I should first call attention to two very important collections. While they are not contributions precisely of this period, the compilations as such are —I refer to Bernard Capelle's *Travaux liturgiques* 1. *Doctrine*,[1] and Lambert Beauduin's *Mélanges liturgiques*.[2] Besides Odo Casel, it would be difficult to find any scholar who has made a greater contribution towards the construction of a theology of the liturgy than these two Benedictine theologians.

Though liturgists have been discussing the definition and nature of the liturgy for decades now, the question has not been settled. My article, "The Nature and Definition of the Liturgy," [3] drew a few negative comments from Josef A. Jungmann, S.J., and Karl Rahner, S.J. After attending to the various definitions and explanations of the nature of the liturgy, I tried to determine what the inner nature of the liturgy is, namely, a priestly-sacramental act of Jesus Christ in and through his Mystical Body. This caused no particular difficulty. What did was the reaction to my answer to the question: How does an act of the virtue of religion receive this liturgical quality, that is to say, by means of a juridical act or decision on the part of the Holy See? While in earlier writings Jungmann would not admit that only what the Holy See approved as liturgy was truly such, in his article, "Pia Exercitia and Liturgy," [4] he agreed that the *Instruction on Sacred Music and Liturgy* of 1958 made it clear that this is the case. Having said so much, he then went on to deny that there is any intrinsic difference between the liturgical and nonliturgical prayer, claiming that the higher rank accorded liturgical worship is merely juridical and indicates no necessary objectively higher religious value in liturgical worship.

Karl Rahner concurs in this opinion. In his study, "Thesen über

[1] Louvain, Mont-César, 1955.
[2] Louvain, Mont-César, 1954.
[3] *Theological Studies* 18, 1957, 325-356.
[4] *Worship* 33, 1959, 616-622.

das Gebet im Namen der Kirche," [5] he holds that the value of prayer stems from the devotion with which one prays under the impulse of grace. Prayer, no matter what kind, when performed by one in sin has no value before God. All good actions of Christians in the state of grace can and must be called acts of the Church, for all such come from members influenced by Christ the Head and benefit other members. Hence liturgical prayer possesses no greater value before God than other prayer inspired by the Holy Spirit. It would seem that both Jungmann and Rahner understand the deputation to act as a liturgical minister as giving a purely juridical legitimacy, but not as activating the sacramental character which gives rise to an objectively greater value in liturgical prayer as done *ex opere operantis Christi et ecclesiae.*

In a brief but pointed article,[6] J. Pascher follows Rahner thesis by thesis and usually singles out factors that the latter failed to consider, among others the sacramental characters.

Jacques and Raïssa Maritain unleashed quite a controversy when they published their article, "Liturgy and Contemplation." [7] While they professed to defend the rights of both liturgy and contemplation, in the opinion of numerous theologians the Maritains would seem to have undervalued the sacramental nature of the liturgy when they contended that contemplation is superior to liturgical worship. In an issue of *Worship* (34, October, 1960) entirely devoted to this question, Bernard Häring's contribution, "Liturgical Piety and Christian Perfection" (523-535), refutes the Maritains' article as smacking of disincarnated spiritualism contrary to the whole meaning of redemptive Incarnation, opposed therefore to the essentially sacramental and communal nature of Christianity.

In a well-reasoned article,[8] Gregory Stevens, O.S.B., also takes issue with the Maritains. He insists on the unique superior value of

---

[5] *Zeitschrift für katholische Theologie* 83, 1961, 307-324.

[6] "Thesen über das Gebet im Namen der Kirche. Ergänzungen zu den gleichnamigen Aufsatz von Karl Rahner," *Liturgisches Jahrbuch* 12, 1962, 58-62.

[7] *The Spiritual Life* 5, 1959, 94-131; later published in book form under the same title (New York, Kenedy, 1960).

[8] "Liturgy and Contemplation," *American Ecclesiastical Review* 142, 1960, 108-115.

liturgical prayer because the acts of the virtues elicited in liturgical action are done by the power of the sacramental character and thus participate in the action of Christ.[9]

Of fundamental importance to questions such as the definition and juridical aspects of the liturgy and its relationship to spirituality is the more basic issue of the sacramental nature of the liturgy itself. Though the *Mysterium* theology of Odo Casel, O.S.B., has met with varying response on the part of theologians, all will agree that his insights have served to draw minds once again to the core of the liturgical question, the priestly-sacramental content of liturgical worship and all that that content implies. Unfortunately, his chief work appeared in English translation rather late in the controversy,[10] fifteen years after he died. The English-speaking world had to be content with knowing this scholar's thought and the ensuing controversy through secondhand reports not always so objective. T. Filthaut has provided an excellent résumé of all contributions to the question up to 1947 in his doctoral dissertation, *Die Kontroverse über die Mysterienlehre*.[11] From 1947 to the present time, good reviews of the various positions taken by theologians are given by B. Neunheuser, O.S.B.,[12] and J. Gaillard, O.S.B.[13] Nor should we overlook the magnificent expression given to Caselian

[9] Among the many studies given rise to by the Maritains' article, the following should be singled out: B. Bernard, O.P., "Peut-on passer de la liturgie?" *La Vie spirituelle* 102, 1960, 5-32; L. Bouyer, "Liturgie et contemplation," *ibid.*, 102, 1960, 406-409; M. M. Labourdette, O.P., "Principes pour la prière liturgique," *ibid.*, 102, 1960, 493-505; G. Lefèbvre, O.S.B., "Oraison et liturgie," *ibid.*, 102, 1960, 428-439; P. Régamey, O.P., "L'orientation contemplative de la prière liturgique," *ibid.*, 102, 1960, 469-492; H. A. Reinhold, "Liturgy and Contemplation," *The Spiritual Life* 6, 1960, 207-217; A. M. Roguet, O.P., "Liturgie et prière personnelle," *La Maison-Dieu* 72, 1962, 99-119; C. Vagaggini, O.S.B., "Contemplazione durante l'atto liturgico et contemplazione extraliturgica," *Rivista di ascetica e mistica* 7, 1962, 8-34; I. van Houtryve, O.S.B., "Liturgie et contemplation," *Questions liturgiques et paroissiales* 41, 1960, 105-110; F. Vandenbroucke, O.S.B., "Prière individuelle et prière communautaire," *La Maison-Dieu* 64, 1960, 143-158.

[10] *The Mystery of Christian Worship*, Westminster, Newman, 1962.

[11] Warendorf, Schnell, 1947. For the benefit of those who do not read German with ease, a French translation appeared in 1954: *La théologie des mystères. Exposé de la controverse* (Tournai, Desclée et Cie.).

[12] "Ende des Gesprächs um die Mysteriengegenwart?" *Archiv für Liturgiewissenschaft* 4, 1956, 316-324; "Neue Aeusserungen zur Frage der Mysteriengegenwart," *ibid.*, 5, 1958, 333-353.

[13] "La théologie des mystères," *Revue thomiste* 57, 1957, 510-551.

doctrine by I. H. Dalmais, O.P., "Liturgie et mystère du salut," [14] and his *Introduction to the Liturgy*.[15]

Since 1954, there have been several good monographs on Caselian thought. The first was L. Bouyer's monumental work, *Liturgical Piety*,[16] at the center of which stands an exposé of the *Mysterium*. Chapter 5 of the popular and highly informative book of Charles Davis, *Liturgy and Doctrine*,[17] succeeds admirably in giving a clear, succinct explanation of "Liturgy and Mystery."

Viktor Warnach, O.S.B., has made an exegetical study of the Epistle to the Romans and supports Casel's claim that in the liturgy we have, according to St. Paul, a making present of salvation history under cultic symbols.[18] A similar scriptural investigation was made by H. Schürmann;[19] he maintains that John 6 portrays the Eucharist as representing, applying, and making present Christ's salvific event.

Although M. B. de Soos, O.S.B., does not unreservedly endorse Casel's position, his critical and systematic interpretation of Leo the Great's writings in *Le mystère liturgique d'après saint Léon le Grand*[20] shows unquestionably how correct was Casel's basic contention that the mysteries of Christ are celebrated in the liturgy, not only as events belonging to the past, but as present. Aquinas's teaching that the sacrifice of the Mass is *idem actus numero* as the sacrifice on the cross, according to M. Matthijs, O.P.,[21] also lends strong support to Casel. And in the first systematic attempt at a speculative foundation for Caselian thought ever made, P. Wegenaer, O.S.B., proceeds from the principles of St. Thomas and shows

[14] In A. G. Martimort, *L'Eglise en prière*, Tournai, Desclée et Cie., 1961, 198-219.

[15] Baltimore, Helicon, 1961, 56-95.

[16] Notre Dame, University of Notre Dame Press, 1955.

[17] New York, Sheed & Ward, 1960, 75-92.

[18] "Taufe und Christusgeschehen nach Römer 6," *Archiv für Liturgiewissenschaft* 3, 1954, 284-366; and "Die Tauflehre des Römerbriefes in der neueren theologischen Diskussion," *ibid.*, 5, 1958, 274-332.

[19] "Die Eucharistie als Repräsentation und Applikation des Heilsgeschehens nach Joh. 6.53-58," *Trierer theologische Zeitschrift* 68, 1959, 30-45, 108-118.

[20] Münster, Aschendorff, 1958. De Soos also published a résumé of his conclusions in "Présence du mystère du salut dans la liturgie d'après saint Léon," *Ephemerides Liturgicae* 73, 1959, 116-135.

[21] "Mysteriengegenwart secundum sanctum Thomam," *Angelicum* 34, 1957, 393-399.

the speculative possibilities and limits of a presence of Christ's salvific work in the liturgy.[22]

There is no doubt that the greatest contributions to the theology of the liturgy within the last decade were made by F. X. Durrwell, C.SS.R., and E. H. Schillebeeckx, O.P. While Durrwell's book[23] was manifestly a work of biblical theology, it marvelously coincided with the thesis of E. H. Schillebeeckx's *Christ the Sacrament of the Encounter with God*[24] that Christ is the chief sacrament, the primordial sacrament from whom flow his sacramental prolongations, the Church and the sacraments. Both works clearly support Casel's basic ideas. Christ as sacrament and the Resurrection as the epitome of his sacramental role in the economy of salvation are central to the sacramental principle that is of the essence of liturgy. Through sacramental or sign language the work of redemption is made really present in the liturgical celebration, that is, the eternal act of Christ's glorification, his sacrifice eternally fixed at its climactic point, his Resurrection.[25]

While C. Vagaggini, O.S.B., does not give a very sympathetic hearing to Casel, or relate Casel's position to that of Durrwell, or even offer any appraisal of the evolution of the Maria Laach school in the writings of B. Neunheuser, J. Hild, I. H. Dalmais and others, his work, *Il senso teologico della liturgia*,[26] was nonetheless one of the first attempts to treat the liturgy from a strictly theological viewpoint, to arrive at a theology about the liturgy. In general, it is greatly successful. He rightly situates the liturgy in the perspective of salvation history, thus showing the liturgy to be the mystery of Christ, the climax of salvation history, still operative in his Church. His treatment of the sacramental principle (that is, a complexus of signs) behind the liturgy is exceptionally well done. However, his explanation of the *ex opere operantis Ecclesiae*

[22] *Heilsgegenwart*, Münster, Aschendorff, 1958.
[23] *The Resurrection*, New York, Sheed & Ward, 1960.
[24] New York, Sheed & Ward, 1963.
[25] Both Balthasar Fischer in "Liturgy and the Risen Christ," *Theology Digest* 8, 1960, 123-126 (the original: "Der verherrlichte Mensch Christus und die Liturgie," *Liturgisches Jahrbuch* 8, 1958, 205-217), and Charles Davis in Chapter 2 of his book, *Liturgy and Doctrine*, 25-43, ably summarize this solution.
[26] Rome, Paoline, 1957; partially translated, partially abridged in *Theological Dimensions of the Liturgy*, Collegeville, Liturgical Press, 1959.

179

doctrine in relation to the liturgy is not very satisfying. He states that the *opus operantis* of the Church is not always a liturgical act; public nonliturgical parochical devotions enjoy this efficacy and nature. Thus his distinction between *a* prayer of the Church and *the* prayer of the Church is extremely weak. Since, according to him, both liturgical and nonliturgical public prayer enjoy the nature of *opus operantis Ecclesiae*, the only really distinctive difference between them is that the first is official, the second is not. If, as Vagaggini rightly declares, the power behind liturigcal prayer is the holiness of the Church and her Head because it is an action of her and her Spouse, would this not also be true of nonliturgical prayer, since, according to him, it is an *opus operantis Ecclesiae?*

The fact that priestliness is one of the essential elements of liturgical prayer is not emphasized sharply enough. Although Vagaggini insists that the peculiar value of Christian worship comes from its being a prolongation of and participation in Christ's worship, and that through the sacramental characters Christ exercises his own priesthood, his worship of his Father, in his members as in instruments, he does not say how important this fact is for the distinction between liturgical and nonliturgical prayer.

Nor has this question of the function of the priestly characters of Baptism, Confirmation, and Holy Orders in the liturgy been neglected in the work of the last decade. In his encyclopedia work,[27] J. Lécuyer, C.S.Sp., delves deeply into scriptural and patristic sources to elaborate a doctrine on the sacramental characters, but he barely touches on the speculative analysis of the question which has great relevance for the nature and practice of the liturgy.

What Lécuyer fails to do, four other theologians tackle straight on: Yves Congar, O.P., Kevin McNamara, C. O'Neill, O.P., and C. A. Schleck, C.S.C.

While Congar in his *Lay People in the Church*[28] lays a solid foundation for the lay priesthood in his inquiry into scriptural and patristic sources, he goes beyond and shows the relevance of St. Thomas's thought on the matter. He points out that for Aquinas the sacramental character empowers one to engage in divine worship, or ritual, social, official worship. The character enables the

[27] *What is a Priest?*, New York, Hawthorn, 1959.
[28] Westminster, Newman, 1957.

possessor to participate in Christ's own worship of his Father in and through his Church, a worship of God which rightly and ultimately has Christ as the responsible person and effective power behind it.

Carefully analyzing St. Thomas's teaching on the character as an instrumental power, C. O'Neill in two profound studies[29] places the whole discussion about the character on the level of sacramental signification. The precise function of sacramental characters is to produce supernatural, life-giving *signs*. The character enables the one who bears it to make natural actions signs of a supernatural transaction; it raises what may seem to be ordinary activities of men to the level of sacramental sign language, making them valid sacramental signs which God uses to produce grace instrumentally. The character secures validity for the acts of the Church's members in her ritual, making them signs serving Christ as his instruments of worship and salvation.

While Kevin McNamara[30] substantially echoes Congar and emphasizes the fact that the characters of the layman are exercised in the liturgical order but lays the basis for the possibility of his exercise of the priesthood of a good life, C. A. Schleck, C.S.C.,[31] directs O'Neill's thought towards the Mass and says that the character enables the bearer to designate Christ's sacrifice as the sign of his own charity. Schleck claims further that each of the characters in its own order can be said to be a real and true priesthood; only one of them, that of Holy Orders, can be said to be a real and true priesthood, if we limit these words to the sacrificial office. In the latter case, the lay priesthood would not be a priesthood properly speaking, but only improperly and probably equivocally, since it is of another order than that of the ministerial priesthood.

The role of the Church as the mystery of Christ, his sacramental continuation, in the earthly expression of his worship of his Father has also received attention at the hands of liturgists during this

---

[29] "The Instrumentality of the Sacramental Character," *Irish Theological Quarterly* 25, 1958, 262-268; and "The Role of the Recipient and Sacramental Signification," *The Thomist* 21, 1958, 257-301, 508-540.

[30] "Aspects of the Layman's Role in the Mystical Body," *Irish Theological Quarterly* 25, 1958, 124-143.

[31] "The Lay Priesthood and the Mass," *Sciences ecclésiastiques* 12, 1960, 83-103.

period. Besides Durrwell and Schillebeeckx, A. G. Martimort explained the concrete worshipping community as the extension and sacramental organ of Christ.[32] In his exciting article, "Théologie de l'initiation chrétienne chez les Pères," [33] J. Lécuyer brings out three salient points from his study of the Father's teaching on the sacraments of initiation: the continuity of salvation history, the Church as the community of redeemed worshippers, and Confirmation as the "perfecting" of Baptism.

Otto Semmelroth, S.J., offers a very thought-provoking insight into the nature of the Church and her worship in "Towards a Unified Concept of the Church." [34] He sees the sacramental nature of the Church as the basis for unity among the different scriptural images of the Church. As the life-giving soil from which the seven sacraments receive their sacramental efficacy, the Church must hold a sacramental nature in common with them; she is the prime or root sacrament. The concept of the People of God as organized and institutional places emphasis on the sacramental signification of the Church; that of the Lord's Mystical Body, on the sacramental efficacy of the sign; that of the Bride of Christ, on the personal disposition with which the Church encounters her Bridegroom.

We must not overlook the immense value—for our understanding of the salvation-history perspective against which the whole of the liturgical question is situated—of such works as *The Liturgy and the Word of God*,[35] and the anthology recently edited by C. Luke Salm, F.S.C., *Studies in Salvation History*.[36]

I have tried to summarize all these developments in the theology of the liturgy in my recent work, *Signs of Transformation in Christ*.[37] Godfrey Diekmann, O.S.B., has been speaking and writ-

[32] "L'assemblée liturgique, mystère du Christ," *La Maison-Dieu* 40, 1954, 5-29. In a similar vein, Michael Schmaus wrote of the liturgy as the expression of the life of the Church in "Die Liturgie als Lebensausdruck der Kirche," *Liturgisches Jahrbuch* 5, 1955, 80-95, and F. Mussner discussed the Church as a worshipping community in "Kirche als Kultgemeinde," *Liturgisches Jahrbuch* 6, 1956, 50-67.

[33] *La Maison-Dieu* 58, 1959, 5-26.

[34] *Yearbook of Liturgical Studies* 2, 1961, 85-102.

[35] Edited by A. G. Martimort, Collegeville, Liturgical Press, 1959.

[36] Englewood Cliffs, Prentice-Hall, 1964.

[37] Englewood Cliffs, Prentice-Hall, 1963. A similar attempt is the book of A. G. Martimort, *The Signs of the New Covenant*, Collegeville, Liturgical Press, 1963.

ing on these themes for more than a decade now, and his major contributions to these questions have been gathered together in *Come, Let us Worship*.[38] Another very useful anthology has been edited by C. Stephen Sullivan, F.S.C., *Readings in Sacramental Theology*.[39] And at the risk of repeating myself, I must again call attention to the superb introduction to these matters of Charles Davis.[40]

GENERAL

In the area of general works, I will mainly speak of text books, introductory works, and symposia which treat of a variety of liturgical matters. In the first place, there are the historical and pastoral-theological studies that have been made available through the publication of talks given at liturgical conferences and study days: *The Assisi Papers*,[41] *Studies in Pastoral Liturgy*,[42] the *Proceedings of the North American Liturgical Weeks*,[43] of which eleven volumes have appeared since 1954; *Liturgy and the Missions*, edited by J. Hofinger, S.J.,[44] containing the papers delivered at the International Study Week on Missions and Liturgy held at Nijmegen in September, 1959.

This decade, it seems to me, will go down in history for the number of handbooks, textbooks, and symposia.[45]

Of particular interest to seminary professors is the penetrating

[38] Baltimore, Helicon, 1961.
[39] Englewood Cliffs, Prentice-Hall, 1964.
[40] *Liturgy and Doctrine* (see n. 17).
[41] Collegeville, Liturgical Press, 1957.
[42] Maynooth, Furrow Trust, 2 volumes, 1961, 1963.
[43] Washington, Liturgical Conference.
[44] New York, Kenedy, 1960.
[45] Let a simple mention of them suffice here: L. Eisenhofer and J. Lechner, *The Liturgy of the Roman Rite*, New York, Herder and Herder, 1961; J. A. Jungmann, S.J., *Public Worship. A Survey*, Collegeville, Liturgical Press, 1957; J. W. King, S.J., *The Liturgy and the Laity*, Westminster, Newman, 1963; C. M. Magsam, M.M., *The Inner Life of the Liturgy*, St. Meinrad, Grail, 1958; A. G. Martimort (editor), *L'Eglise en prière*, Tournai, Desclée et Cie., 1961; J. H. Miller, C.S.C., *Fundamentals of the Liturgy*, Notre Dame, Fides, 1960; W. J. O'Shea, S.S., *The Worship of the Church*, Westminster, Newman, 1957; R. Peil, *A Handbook of the Liturgy*, New York, Herder and Herder, 1960; H. Schmidt, S.J., *Introductio in liturgiam occidentalem*, Rome, Herder, 1960.

and forward-looking contribution to the liturgical formation of seminarians by J. R. Quinn, "The Necessity of an Ecclesial Formation of Seminarians." [46] The emphasis throughout his article is on the place in the Church of the priest as her agent, her leader, as sacramental embodiment of her reality.

Although G. Braso, O.S.B., entitled his work *Liturgy and Spirituality*[47] the book amounts to a general introduction to the liturgy. As such, it is both solid and valuable. He does go into a discussion of what spirituality means, how the Church's liturgy constitutes her spirituality, and the relationship between her own and other spiritualities. However, he does not dig very deeply into the theoretical problems involved in all of this. His stand against adaptation or reform of the liturgy is somewhat utopian and unpastoral. He says: "it is not a question of adapting the liturgy to those who assist at it (this would be to destroy it), but of adapting the people to the liturgy." Such a statement appears in a chapter entitled "Liturgy and Pastoral Action." It would seem that he thinks liturgical education is all that is necessary for renewal, the fossilized and time-bound condition of much of the liturgy is no problem to him.

Liturgy for the People[48] is a *Festschrift* honoring the late Gerald Ellard, S.J. Not attempting any systematic or cohesive development of subject matter, this book is a collection of excellent contributions probing a variety of aspects of liturgical doctrine, history, and practice. Liturgical music is particularly well-covered—and from conflicting viewpoints. The last ten pages offer a complete bibliography of Ellard.

Another symposium, a highly successful one, is that edited by Frederick R. McManus.[49] It is a collection of essays offered to Godfrey Diekmann, O.S.B., on the occasion of his completion of twenty-five years as editor of *Worship*, and it makes for extraordinarily good reading. McManus's own essay, "The Future: Its Hopes and Difficulties," offers much sage advice. Also genuine contributions to the liturgical revival are Gerald Sloyan's "Liturgy and Catechetics," W. J. O'Shea's "Liturgical Formation of Candidates

---

[46] *Yearbook of Liturgical Studies* 3, 1962, 63-89.
[47] Collegeville, Liturgical Press, 1960.
[48] Edited by W. J. Leonard, S.J., Milwaukee, Bruce, 1963.
[49] *The Revival of the Liturgy*, New York, Herder and Herder, 1963.

for the Priesthood," and C. McNaspy's "The Sacral in Liturgical Music."

Of great interest is the symposium edited by L. C. Sheppard.[50] It is a collection of papers delivered at a meeting held in the Abbey of Bec. The subject matter varies widely, but the papers are the fruit of long study and offer valuable insights.

HISTORY

Of prime importance to the history of the liturgy are the various modern editions of liturgical sources: the fifth volume of *Andrieu's Les Ordines Romani du haut moyen-âge*[51] and the collection edited by K. Mohlberg, O.S.B., and P. Siffrin, O.S.B.[52]

A newly reconstructed text of the *Apostolic Tradition* of Hippolytus has been published by B. Botte, O.S.B.[53] Besides furnishing a completely reconstructed text with variant readings in Latin and French, Botte relates the discovery of the original document, discusses the identity of Hippolytus and the character of the *Apostolic Tradition*, and describes the sources of his text. Regarding the person of Hippolytus, Botte accepts the common opinion that he was indeed the author of the *Tradition*, lived in Rome as the head of a dissident community and died as a martyr (his feast: August 13th). While claiming the document to be Roman, Botte warns against believing that it represents *exactly* the Roman discipline of the third century, for the simple reason that improvisation of liturgical prayers was still the rule. The *Tradition*, on the whole, is a good indication of Roman practice, however. Thus Botte emphatically rejects the thesis that its liturgy is an import from Alexandria, a thesis proposed by J. M. Hanssens, S.J.[54]

Many problems concerning the origin and character of the Gelasian Sacramentary receive light from the study of A. Chavasse, *Le*

[50] *True Worship*, Baltimore, Helicon, 1963.

[51] Louvain, Spicilegium Sacrum Lovaniense, 1961.

[52] *Sacramentarium Veronense* (1956); *Missale Francorum* (1957); *Missale Gallicanum Vetus* (1958); and *Missale Gothicum* (1961), all published by Herder, Rome.

[53] *La Tradition Apostolique de saint Hippolyte. Essai de reconstitution*, Münster, Aschendorff, 1963.

[54] In *La liturgie d'Hippolyte*, Rome, Istituto Orientale, 1959.

sacramentaire Gélasien (Tournai, Desclée et Cie., 1958). His major thesis is that the book substantially served as a sacramentary in the Roman titular churches of the seventh century, particularly St. Peter in Chains. Most reviewers have written laudatory and long résumés of this work. Few have insisted on the considerably hypothetical quality of the book; even fewer have taken issue with Chavasse. To my knowledge, there were only two serious critics of this work: J. A. Jungmann, S.J.,[55] and C. Coebergh, O.S.B.[56] According to Coebergh, the ancient Gelasian was the work of non-Roman romanizing clerics who used Roman sources to produce a book for their own use.

In *Leo der Grosse und die Texte des Altgelasianums,*[57] A. P. Lang, S.V.D., has tried to discover precisely which formulas of the old Gelasian Sacramentary are the work of Leo the Great. By using good historical, literary, and theological criteria, he has been able to establish seventy-eight formulas as having been composed by Leo.

The origin and Gregorian authorship of the so-called Gregorian Sacramentary has been challenged in recent times by H. Ashworth, O.S.B.[58] He attempts to prove that Gregory did compose a certain number of prayers, but not a sacramentary; at some later date (perhaps under Boniface IV in the seventh century), Gregory's prayers were incorporated into an official book for papal stational use. Despite Ashworth's arguments, K. Gamber denies his claim and reasserts the traditional opinion of scholars that Gregory did indeed compose a sacramentary.[59]

Of outstanding value for the understanding of symbolism, the patristic typologies, and their use in liturgy are the three works of Jean Daniélou, S.J.: *The Bible and the Liturgy,*[60] *From Shadows to Reality,*[61] and *Primitive Christian Symbols.*[62]

---

[55] In *Zeitschrift für katholische Theologie* 81, 1959, 236-239.

[56] "Le sacramentaire Gélasien ancien," *Archiv für Liturgiewissenschaft* 7, 1961, 45-88.

[57] Steyl, Steyler Verlagsbuchhandlung, 1957.

[58] "St. Gregory the Great and the Gregorian Sacramentary," *Liturgy* 31, 1962, 12-15.

[59] "Hat Gregor der Grosse ein Sakramentar verfasst?", *Ephemerides Liturgicae* 73, 1959, 139-140.

[60] Notre Dame, University of Notre Dame Press, 1956.

[61] Westminster, Newman, 1960.

[62] Baltimore, Helicon, 1963.

J. A. Jungmann's *Pastoral Liturgy*[63] brings together many of his previously published articles. The opening essay is his classic contribution to the history of ideas, the influence of the Church's anti-Arian struggle on the reshaping of religious thought in the Middle Ages. His valuable essays on the historical development of the Divine Office come next, and these are followed by other historical and pastoral treatises of great value. The publication of his 1949 Notre Dame lectures, *The Early Liturgy*,[64] with minor reservations, can be said to bring a welcome and well-balanced introduction to the general historical and conceptual development of the liturgy up to the time of Gregory the Great.

No one can gainsay the immense contribution made by A. A. King's many volumes on the various liturgies of the Church. In the last decade, he has published three more treating the rites of the West: *Liturgies of the Religious Orders* (1956), *Liturgies of the Primatial Sees* (1957), and *Liturgies of the Past* (1959).[65] The last discusses the rites of the West that have fallen into disuse, such as Gallican rites, and those of Aquileia and Benevento.

The liturgical movement itself has been the object of much serious study, both historical and theological. In "Die geistesgeschichtliche Situation der liturgischen Erneuerung in der Gegenwart," [66] A. L. Mayer is not satisfied with merely treating the various purposes and manifestations of the liturgical movement of today; rather, he digs deep into the cultural, philosophical, theological, and spiritual frame of mind at the turn of the century out of which the liturgical renewal arose. He shows that, far from being a fad, the movement was a cultural necessity.

E. B. Koenker has tried, as a Protestant, to analyze the Roman liturgical movement.[67] He is guided by deep sympathies for the movement and often sees operative in it many of the principles that inspired the early Reformers. Sometimes, naturally, he is inclined to see many of these principles as specifically Protestant

---

[63] New York, Herder and Herder, 1962.
[64] Notre Dame, University of Notre Dame Press, 1960.
[65] All published by Longmans, London.
[66] *Archiv für Liturgiewissenschaft* 4, 1955, 1-51.
[67] *The Liturgical Renaissance in the Roman Catholic Church*, Chicago, University of Chicago Press, 1954.

rather than springing from the common heritage of all Christian churches.

The only book written on the liturgical movement in English by a Catholic is that of L. C. Sheppard, *The Liturgical Movement*.[68] It not only reviews the history of the movement, but also discusses the principles behind it. While Sheppard offers quite a bit of information, he does not go so deeply into questions as does O. Rousseau, O.S.B.,[69] or W. Trapp.[70]

The Protestant liturgical movement has also of late come in for some analysis. In "Offizielle und inoffizielle liturgische Bestrebungen in der evangelischen Kirche Deutschlands," [71] W. Blankenburg reports on the efforts within the Lutheran Church of Germany. M. H. Shepherd tries to do the same for American Protestantism in "The Liturgical Movement in American Protestantism." [72]

However, the first significant attempt at a descriptive synthesis of the liturgical renewal now taking place among American Protestants has been made by M. J. Taylor, S.J.[73] It is welcomed by both Protestants and Catholics alike because of its eminent objectivity and fairness. Unfortunately, Taylor has omitted consideration of the Episcopalians, since they have been traditionally liturgical. Though reasonable, this omission leaves out a very important dimension for a proper understanding of the Protestant renewal, for there have been constant liturgical interactions between the Episcopal and other Protestant traditions in America.

Since the appearance of Jungmann's two-volume work on the Mass, one of the most valuable contributions to the history of the liturgy in the West, especially of what is now called the Roman rite, has been made by S. J. P. Van Dijk, O.F.M., and J. Hazeldon Walker in *The Origins of the Modern Roman Liturgy*.[74] Their scholarly approach to problems and the abundant use of manuscript material are the best indication of their scientific spirit. The

[68] New York, Hawthorn, 1964.

[69] *The Progress of the Liturgy*, Westminster, Newman, 1951.

[70] *Vorgeschichte und Ursprung der liturgischen Bewegung*, Regensburg, 1940.

[71] *Liturgisches Jahrbuch* 13, 1963, 70-83.

[72] *Yearbook of Liturgical Studies* 3, 1962, 35-61.

[73] *The Protestant Liturgical Renewal. A Catholic Viewpoint*, Westminster, Newman, 1963.

[74] Westminster, Newman, 1960.

Franciscan influence on the evolution of the Roman rite has always been a difficult problem. The question about which this book is concerned centers on who composed the breviary and missal used by Haymo in his revision of 1242-1244. The authors are inclined to believe that the Friars themselves did so, adapting source material from the Papal Curia to their own needs.

LANGUAGE

We are all well aware of the quantity of writing done on the subject of the vernacular in the liturgy; at one time or another, we very likely have all waxed eloquent and heated on one or other side of the debate. Of the many studies published few deserve to be singled out.

A. De Marco, O.F.M., offers a readable and interesting account of the liturgical use of various languages throughout the history of the Roman rite in *Rome and the Vernacular*.[75] However, the author's interpretative power proves to be weak when he addresses himself to Trent's decisions on the vernacular. He likewise falls into the facile but futile distinction between the fore-Mass and the sacrificial banquet. Furthermore, he leaves altogether too much unsaid. The best historical and doctrinal-pastoral treatment remains H. Schmidt's *Liturgie et langue vulgaire*.[76]

From this decade, more to the point are *La Maison-Dieu* 53, 1958: *Le problème des langues en liturgie*; and the well-balanced symposium edited by C. R. A. Cunliffe.[77] Although dedicated to an explanation of the discipline of the Eastern rites, C. Korolevsky's work[78] also brings out some little known facts about the use of the vernacular in the Western rites. P. Winninger[79] offers a strong and courageous plea for the vernacular; the great pastoral needs of the present absolutely exclude a rigorously Latin liturgy.

[75] Westminster, Newman, 1961.
[76] Rome, Università Gregoriana, 1950.
[77] *English in the Liturgy*, Springfield, Templegate, 1956.
[78] *Living Languages in Catholic Worship*, Westminster, Newman, 1957.
[79] *Langues vivantes et liturgie*, Paris, Cerf, 1961.

LITURGICAL YEAR

Though the liturgical year receives ample attention in the works we have thus far mentioned, it has also been the object of special studies. I myself have endeavored to draw up a theological analysis of the liturgical year and evaluate the Caselian theory in this regard.[80] An entire issue of *La Maison-Dieu* (65, 1961: *Le Christ hier, aujourd'hui, toujours. La liturgie et le temps*) is devoted to the relationship of the Church's worship and time, and investigates the meaning of *Hodie* in her festal formulas.

In a profoundly analytic study[81] R. Berger provides an important insight into the two major axes of the liturgical year, Easter and Christmas. They celebrate the same thing: the glorification of the Lord. There is this difference: Easter concentrates on the process, his *being* glorified, while Christmas dwells on the result, his glorified *state*. Easter focuses attention on the triumph over the powers of hell, Christmas on the reunion of God and man. The Church year is thus nothing else but an ever recurring celebration of the coming of the glorified Lord to his community.[82]

An excellent introduction to the problems and spirit governing the evolution of the Church year may be found in N. M. Denis-Boulet, *The Christian Calendar*.[83] Perhaps the most stimulating chapter of this book is the one that discusses the reforms needed to make our calendar serve its purpose more effectively.

Naturally, with the restoration of Holy Week by Pius XII, it was to be expected that much attention be paid to analyzing and evaluating the reform, its historical precedents, the significance of its rites, and the pastoral effectiveness of the restoration. Of the immense material published, there are particular interest and value in the studies provided by entire issues of *La Maison-Dieu*: 41, 1955:

[80] See "Theology of the Liturgical Year," *American Ecclesiastical Review* 138, 1958, 221-230.

[81] "Ostern und Weihnachten, zum Grundgefüge des Kirchenjahres," *Archiv für Liturgiewissenschaft* 8, 1963, 1-20.

[82] In the same vein, H. Jenny examines the Easter theme throughout the liturgical year: *The Paschal Mystery in the Christian Year* (Notre Dame, Fides, 1961). And J. A. Jungmann, S.J., offers the fruit of much reflection in "The History of Holy Week as the Heart of the Liturgical Year," *The Furrow* 10, 1959, 287-310.

[83] New York, Hawthorn, 1960.

La Semaine sainte; 45, 1956: *Restauration de la Semaine sainte;* 49, 1957: *La catéchèse de la Semaine sainte;* 67 and 68, 1961: *La liturgie du mystère pascal.* In a monumental two-volume work,[84] H. Schmidt, S.J., has amassed all the historical sources, commentaries, and texts pertinent to a study of Holy Week.

Much discussion has also centered on the origin and meaning of Advent. Louis Bouyer, in his *Liturgical Piety,*[85] claims that the more ancient and more obvious sense of the Advent texts expresses an expectation of the Parousia. An historical investigation of the evolution of the Advent texts, however, leads W. Croce, S.J., to the conclusion that such a theme with all its penitential apparatus was not native to the Roman rite, but was introduced under the influence of Gallican hands.[86] *La Maison-Dieu* gives an excellent summary of the history and meaning of this part of the Church year in number 59 (1959): *Avent. Noël. Epiphanie.* And we must not omit mention of the reprint of B. Botte's excellent monograph, *Les origines de la Noël et de l'Epiphanie.*[87]

THE MASS

Of fundamental importance for the historical development and theology of the Mass is the small symposium edited by J. Delorme.[88] For the benefit of the liturgical scholar as well as the teacher who does not have the competence of a biblical specialist, this work presents not only fresh insights into the biblical background, content and practice of the Eucharist, but also a good introduction to the literature on the subject.[89]

While no one has yet attempted to approach the superb history of the Mass written by J. A. Jungmann, S.J., *The Mass of the Ro-*

---

[84] *Hebdomada Sancta,* Rome, Herder, 1956-1957.
[85] Pp. 200-214.
[86] See especially his "Die Adventsmessen des römischen Missale in ihrer geschichtlichen Entwicklung," and "Die Adventsliturgie im Licht ihrer geschichtlichen Entwicklung," *Zeitschrift für katholische Theologie* 74, 1952, 277-317; 76, 1954, 257-296.
[87] Louvain, Mont-César, 1961.
[88] *The Eucharist in the New Testament,* Baltimore, Helicon, 1964.
[89] L. Bouyer's book, *Liturgical Piety,* to which reference has already been made, also offers a good account of the scriptural framework of the Mass.

man Rite,[90] or his small but inspiring brochure on the Canon of the Mass,[91] F. Amiot does provide an excellent encyclopedic view of the historical evolution of the Mass rites,[92] and attention should also be called to the second volume of B. Capelle's collected works.[93]

The function of the extra prayer between the Collect and the Secret in the Gelasian and Leonine sacramentaries has for a long time been a problem for historians of the liturgy. A. Chavasse[94] shows that this prayer is a remnant of the ancient diaconal litany that followed the Gospel; it was the priest's oration that concluded the litany.

De Jong has devoted a rather lengthy essay to the origin and meaning of the rite of commingling in the Mass.[95] According to him, Syria (specifically the East Syrian Nestorians) is the place of origin of the fraction-commingling rite. He sees a connection between the epiclesis and commingling. The anaphora has two phases: 1) The words of institution over separate species present the Lord's death in symbolic fashion; 2) the epiclesis-commingling present the Resurrection of the Lord. The epiclesis speaks of the coming of the Spirit of God; the commingling symbolically shows his coming, that is, the Spirit producing the Resurrection, making the Lord *pneuma*. Thus the commingling is the connecting link between consecration and communion. In the consecration Christ dies, in the commingling he rises, becomes Spirit, able in communion to give us his Spirit, make us divine.

In keeping with the emphasis on the ecclesial-sacramental nature of the liturgy, much attention has been given to the distribution of roles in the liturgical celebration. A very good summary of such doctrine is *La Maison-Dieu* 60, 1959: *Les acteurs de la célébration liturgique*. Of particular interest to American readers will be the

[90] Two volumes, New York, Benziger, 1951, 1955; one-volume edition, *ibid.*, 1959.

[91] *The Eucharistic Prayer*, Notre Dame, Fides, 1956.

[92] *History of the Mass*, New York, Hawthorn, 1959.

[93] *Travaux liturgiques* 2, *Histoire. La messe*, Louvain, Mont-César, 1962.

[94] "L'oraison *super sindonem* dans la liturgie romaine," *Revue bénédictine* 70, 1960, 313-323.

[95] J. P. de Jong, "Le rite de la commixtion dans la messe romaine dans ses rapports avec les liturgies syriennes," *Archiv für Liturgiewissenschaft* 4, 1956, 245-278; 5, 1957, 33-79.

timely doctoral dissertation of J. McGowan, R.S.C.J.[96] After a very thought-provoking Foreword by Frederick R. McManus, pleading the cause of the Eucharist as the sacrament of unity and the cause of liberty for those priests who wish to concelebrate or participate in a community celebration of Mass rather than celebrate individually, Mother McGowan offers a very thorough exposé of the history of the practice of concelebration and a finely balanced summary of the positions on it taken by dogmatic theologians and documents of the magisterium. It is the most complete work on the subject to date.

Finally, H. A. Reinhold's *Bringing the Mass to the People*[97] is an excellent pastoral application of all the work done on the theology and history of the Mass. Scholars will not always agree with his proposals for reform, but his book is a necessary starting point for anyone who would understand the reforms now being undertaken by the Church in an official way. Again, the introduction by F. R. McManus is an important contribution to the over-all question of reform.

Office

Of the many articles and books written about the Divine Office, four ought to be singled out for special attention. The first is A. Baumstark, *Nocturna Laus. Typen frühchristlicher Vigilienfeier und ihr Fortleben vor allem im römischen und monastischen Ritus.*[98] Though completed by 1938, this work remained unpublished because of World War II. The editor, O. Heiming, O.S.B., brought the work up to date before publishing it in the series, "Liturgiewissenschaftliche Quellen und Forschungen," but he took care to keep his corrections and additions to footnotes identified by his own initials. Baumstark's basic thesis is that the Benedictine *cursus* suffered little direct influence from the Roman. Any likeness, besides the Old Testament canticles, must be ascribed to a supposed

[96] *Concelebration. Sign of the Unity of the Church*, New York, Herder, and Herder, 1964.
[97] Baltimore, Helicon, 1960.
[98] Münster, Aschendorff, 1957.

intermediary community in the vicinity of Monte Cassino or to a direct and independent borrowing from the East. The author also shows that Matins is a monastic development of a purely private vigil observed by many fervent Christians at home. To the psalmody and prayer, the element proper to the ascetic's vigil, were joined readings and responsories, the portion proper to the occasional public vigils in the ancient Church. He also points to Syria as the place of origin of the three nocturns.

J. A. Jungmann's contributions to the history of the Divine Office have been reprinted in his volume *Pastoral Liturgy*.[99] He has also edited the *Brevierstudien* containing the papers given by J. Pascher, Jungmann, H. Rahner, B. Fischer, Th. Schnitzler, and P. Salmon during a special study day on the Divine Office held in conjunction with the Assisi Pastoral Liturgical Congress, September 14-17, 1956.[100]

Perhaps the most significant work on the Office during this decade is that of P. Salmon, O.S.B., *The Breviary Through the Centuries*.[101] It contains some of his previously published articles, and some entirely new material. While it is hard to pick and choose from among so many good things, his chapters on "The History of the Obligation of Reciting the Office," and "The Office as Said among Urban Churches from the Fifth to the Eighth Century," are unquestionably of greatest interest for our present-day situation.

For centuries, the Divine Office was not the prayer of the universal Church; it was the prayer of a concrete, particular church. At the same time, clerics were ordained for the service of these particular churches. The concern of the early centuries was with a living prayer: Each cleric was celebrating in his own church the office of his own church as an extension of that of the cathedral.

Furthermore, there was no question of the daily celebration of all the hours of the Office in each church. This might have been done in the cathedrals where there was a sufficiently large *presbyterium*, or where the clergy of different churches took part in a single celebration, but in accordance with a distribution of hours

[99] Pp. 105-214.
[100] Trier, Paulinus, 1958.
[101] Collegeville, Liturgical Press, 1962.

and personnel throughout different sanctuaries of the city or diocese. In other words, neither each church nor the clergy in general
had the obligation of all the hours of the Office as we know them.
It seems to have been a general custom for the clergy to take turns
so that Lauds and Vespers could be celebrated each day in each
church as truly parochial services. Matins or vigils were celebrated
only on Sundays or feast days or perhaps daily in the principal
churches (again the clergy of neighboring sanctuaries taking turns).
The first instance of the entire Office being celebrated each day in
the one church by a fixed group of clerics was in the monastic
houses or basilicas. The practice of secular churches in time modeled itself on that of the monastic. Synods and bishops also came in
time to impose on the individual cleric what started out as a monastic discipline, namely, a cleric who missed the choral Office had
to make it up in private. Soon private recitation came to be defended as a general practice; in time, it was the only obligation
spoken of by moralists.

It is clear that the basis of personal obligation for reciting the
Office was not ordination or an ecclesiastical benefice. It was
simply attachment to the service of a specific church. There was no
such thing as a private Office, no such thing as an obligation to
recite one. Private recitation merely supplied for choral recitation.

In short, our modern problem consists precisely in imposing on
all—even to the extent of private recitation—an Office which was
never intended in its entirety for all.

ORIENTAL LITURGIES

It would be impossible to report all the work that has been done
during this decade in the area of Oriental studies. The most important single work for the general and scholarly reading public is the
two-volume revised work of Donald Attwater, *The Christian
Churches of the East*.[102] I. H. Dalmais, O.P., in addition to his
encyclopedia volume,[103] has written a series of highly informative
articles on different aspects of the Eastern rites: "Le *Triduum Sacrum* dans la liturgie byzantine" (*La Maison-Dieu* 41, 1955, 118-

[102] Milwaukee, Bruce, 1961².
[103] *Eastern Liturgies*, New York, Hawthorn, 1960.

127); "Le dimanche dans la liturgie byzantine" (*ibid.*, 46, 1956, 60-67); "Les commémorations des saints dans l'office quotidien et hebdomadaire des liturgies orientales" (*ibid.*, 52, 1957, 98-108); "La liturgie du mariage dans les Eglises orientales" (*ibid.*, 50, 1957, 58-69.; "Le sacrement du pénitence chez les Orientaux" (*ibid.*, 56, 1958, 22-29); "Le temps de préparation à Noël dans les liturgies syrienne et byzantine" (*ibid.*, 59, 1959, 25-36). Finally, there is a valuable study on the marriage rites of the East by A. Raes, S.J.[104]

PREACHING

With the renewal of the liturgy there has gone an increased emphasis on the importance and nature of preaching, especially of the homily as a liturgical act. In this area, one of the most significant pieces of writing was done by a Protestant, R. H. Fuller, *What is Liturgical Preaching?*[105] It is a superb treatment of the liturgical homily, showing how important it is *in* the liturgical action, and providing some interesting examples of the procedure one should follow in constructing a homily.[106] An altogether outstanding work for source material for homilies is the series published under the direction of the Abbey of St. André in Bruges: *Assemblée du Seigneur;* begun in 1962, some eighty-nine volumes are projected.

REFORM

In the extended discussion of reform of the liturgy, though good résumés could be cited, we will limit ourselves to two. We have already mentioned H. A. Reinhold's book, *Bringing the Mass to*

---

[104] *Le mariage dans les Eglises d'Orient*, Chevetogne, Editions de Chevetogne, 1959.

[105] London, SCM, 1957.

[106] Several other valuable studies should be mentioned here: *La Maison-Dieu* 39, 1954: *Aux sources de la prédication;* the very important article of W. J. O'Shea, S.S., "The Sermon is Part of the Mass," *Homiletic and Pastoral Review* 60, 1960, 517-526; W. Kahles, "Glaubensverkündigung aus dem Geiste der liturgischen Erneuerung," *Archiv für Liturgiewissenschaft* 6, 1960, 417-454; J. D. Crichton, "Liturgical Preaching," *The Clergy Review* 45, 1960, 725-733; A. M. Roguet, O.P., "La prédication du temps liturgique," *Questions liturgiques et paroissiales* 38, 1957, 110-118; A. Kirchgässner, "Die Predigt in der Messe," *Liturgisches Jahrbuch* 14, 1964, 146-151.

the People. While this work deals expressly with the Mass, its author (and the author of the Introduction) lays down principles of reform that apply to the whole of the liturgy. He is no friend of antiquarianism; rather, he establishes two rules that should guide all reform: 1) a workable and profound knowledge of true historical tradition to insure continuity and to prevent arbitrariness; 2) an honest appraisal of pastoral need and an intelligent response to it.

Of greater proportions and much wider perspective is the work of A. Nocent, O.S.B., *The Future of the Liturgy.*[107] It is an attempt to analyze some of the historical factors that have led to the liturgy's being out of touch with life. Nocent points out the errors in such approaches to the liturgy as "validism," "rubricism," and the desire for absolute uniformity. He calls for a healthy combination of historical appreciation of the liturgy's past and a critical awareness of the pastoral needs of the time in any attempt to reform the liturgy. The balance with which he treats liturgical problems, the sense of urgency he imparts, and the truly pastoral understanding of the liturgy that he displays make this work a very important landmark in the current effort to revitalize the Church's life.

SACRAMENTAL

In this last category, we will touch on those studies which have dealt with sacramental ceremonial, whether of the sacraments or the sacramentals.

What J. A. Jungmann, S.J., achieved for the history of the Mass in his monumental two-volume work, *The Mass of the Roman Rite,* Thierry Maertens, O.S.B., has done for Baptism in his remarkable book, *Histoire et pastorale du rituel du catéchuménat et du baptême.*[108] Anyone familiar with Maertens' many learned studies in the history and pastoral nature of the liturgy will not be surprised to hear that this present work is the most complete and up-to-date contribution on the question that has been written. It is outstanding, not only for the thoroughness with which he treats

[107] New York, Herder and Herder, 1963.
[108] Bruges, Biblica, 1962.

the historical development of the ritual, but also for the uncanny instinct he displays for revealing the pastoral anomalies contained in our present baptismal procedure, and for pointing out the steps necessary for its realistic and satisfactory reform. After two introductory chapters dealing with the Old Testament antecedents of and the New Testament witness to Baptism, he painstakingly investigates the step-by-step evolution of the sacramental ceremonial: first the patristic testimony of the first to the third century, then that of the *Apostolic Tradition* of Hippolytus, the full blossoming of the ritual for the catechumenate and Baptism in the fourth to sixth century, the use of adult ceremonial for infants in the sixth and seventh centuries, and finally the ritualism and clericalization due to the Gallican churches. The final chapter, a magnificent synthesis, treats the doctrinal and pastoral attitudes discernible in the various stages of the ritual's development, and offers clear-cut suggestions for reform.

Though often slovenly written and less thorough than Maertens' work, *Die Taufe*, by A. Stenzel, S.J., gives a valuable overview of the genetic evolution of baptismal rites in the West.[109] And Jungmann, in a paper given at a liturgical study day held at the Abbey of Montserrat in September, 1958, while trying to distinguish primary from secondary elements in the baptismal ritual of the Roman rite, delineated the master plan of the sacramental ceremonial.[110]

Of great interest also are several essays on the blessing of baptismal waters. While Olivar summarizes the research done to date on the Roman consecration of baptismal water,[111] de Jong traces the genetic development of the consecration ritual up to the time it assumed the form it had in the ancient sacramentaries.[112] See also J. Lécuyer, C.S.Sp., "La prière consecratoire des eaux."[113]

Max Thurian of Taizé has made a genuine contribution to an

[109] Innsbruck, Rauch, 1958.
[110] "Aufbauelemente im römischen Taufritus," *Liturgisches Jahrbuch* 9, 1959, 1-15.
[111] A. Olivar, "Vom Ursprung der römischen Taufwasserweihe," *Archiv für Liturgiewissenschaft* 6, 1959, 62-78.
[112] J. P. de Jong, "Benedictio Fontis," *Archiv für Liturgiewissenschaft* 8, 1963, 21-46.
[113] *La Maison-Dieu* 49, 1957, 71-95.

ecumenical understanding of Baptism and Confirmation in his recent work *Consecration of the Layman*.[114] He begins with a detailed examination of the sources, both biblical and patristic, and produces a theology that is in the most ancient and finest tradition of the Church; it is primarily and profoundly the fruit of the life of worship and prayer within the context of community. His broad conclusions are also in harmony with those of many Roman theologians: 1) Christian initiation traditionally embraced a) a Baptism in water, b) Baptism in the Spirit, and c) a catechesis leading to and d) reception of the Eucharist; 2) Baptism in the Spirit is distinct from yet inseparably linked to Baptism in water; 3) to separate Confirmation either in time (until after the reception of the Eucharist) or in thought from Baptism and to limit it to some such notion as a (delayed) "completion of Baptism" or as the conferral of grace *ad robur* is to misunderstand its position in the total process of Christian initiation.[115]

For the sacrament of Penance there are three studies worthy of mention: *La Maison-Dieu* 55 and 56 (1958): *La pénitence*; P. Anciaux, *The Sacrament of Penance*,[116] and B. Poschmann, *Penance and the Anointing of the Sick*.[117] All of them give excellent overviews of the development of sacramental practice.

The recent doctoral dissertation of B. Kleinheyer[118] offers a most comprehensive historical treatment of Roman ordination ceremonial reaching from the utter simplicity of the early Roman ritual to the complex confusion caused by the fusion of Roman and Gallican traditions in the late Middle Ages.

Truly monumental is the work of K. Ritzer, O.S.B., *Formen, Riten und religiöses Brauchtum der Eheschliessung in den christlichen Kirchen des ersten Jahrtausends*.[119] In Part 1-1, Ritzer describes the matrimonial ritual among the peoples of antiquity and the Christians of the first three centuries; in Part 1-2, the Eastern Christian rites of the fourth to the eleventh century. The whole of Part 2 is dedicated to the nuptial rites in the West. It is an incredi-

---

[114] Baltimore, Helicon, 1963.
[115] See also the entire issue 54 of *La Maison Dieu* (1958): *La confirmation*.
[116] New York, Sheed & Ward, 1962.
[117] New York, Herder and Herder, 1964.
[118] *Die Priesterweihe im römischen Ritus*, Trier, Paulinus, 1962.
[119] Münster, Aschendorff, 1962.

bly rich and valuable work as it reports all the pertinent material up to the tenth century. While unable to solve all difficulties (for example, why the nuptial blessing was and is imparted only for first marriages), Ritzer draws some interesting conclusions from his research.

In the first three centuries, we find no specifically ecclesiastical marriage ceremony; Ignatius of Antioch's admonition to contract marriage with the approval of the bishop seems to have been left generally unheeded. More or less private participation in wedding feasts by priests were not unheard of, however; but no church confirmation is to be found in these centuries. At the end of the fourth century, the Church in Greece began to adopt marriage rites from secular practice. In Cappadocia, we find a priest or bishop crowning the bride, a privilege belonging to the bride's father.

The non-Greek Christian Churches exercised a significant influence on the development of the Greek-Byzantine liturgy of Matrimony. The Syrians were the first to make the betrothal formality a part of the liturgy, and the role of the priest was also an essential part of the ceremony. Furthermore, they made the church ceremony the essential way of contracting marriage, but neither Basilius I nor Leo the Wise distinguished between the betrothal and the wedding as the actual marriage. Alexius Comnenus I finally created a pre-betrothal formality for *impuberes* and, with far-reaching effects, reserved the betrothal for marriageable persons.

As regards the West, we find an official marriage ritual in use at Rome and in Italy already from the second half of the fourth century. The chief ceremony of this was the *velatio* or the veiling of the bridal pair by the priest as part of the Mass. And we find a special nuptial Mass formulary in the three oldest Roman sacramentaries.

In Gaul, the sixth century apparently knew only of a priestly blessing on the marriage the evening of the wedding day and in the bridal chamber. The Bobbio Missal, an Irish book, contains a *benedictio in thalamo* that seems to have originated in Spain. But Caesarius of Arles, following the Roman liturgy, had the ceremony take place in church. The Roman liturgy eventually displaced the *in thalamo* rite, but the latter traveled over the continent in the ninth to the eleventh century benedictionals, pontificals, and rituals. A new feature in these books was the blessing of the ring.

Particularly rich and festive matrimonial rites are found in the Spanish liturgy. Besides the *Benedictio in thalamo*, we find a betrothal ceremonial; there is a proper Office for the wedding day, a nuptial Mass with proper orations, lessons and chants, and a special wedding ceremony that takes place towards the end of Mass and in which the *velatio* occurs.

While in the East the church ceremony became the universally binding marriage rite, in the West no particular nuptial ceremony was considered the essential "form." Simple consent made the marriage. A pseudo-Isidore reform party, in one of its jobs of falsification, sharply emphasized a public and legal procedure for Matrimony and gave rise to the ideal of a church-conducted wedding. The fact that the West took longer than the East to make an ecclesiastical matrimonial rite necessary for the validity of marriage was due to insistence of Roman law that consent alone made the marriage. Blossoming canonical and Scholastic science led to a sharper formulation of the Roman concept, but it was not until the Council of Trent that a definite "form" of exchange of consent was prescribed. True, the Fourth Lateran Council's proscription of clandestine marriages was a milestone on the way to Trent's decision. Marriage *in facie ecclesiae* acquired its liturgical form in the Norman church-door wedding ceremony. It is to this rite that the Roman Ritual's emphasis on the exchange of consent can be traced.[120]

It is fitting that we close with a brief notice of studies concerning the burial of the dead. By far the most interesting is that of H. R. Philippeau, "Textes et rubriques des *Agenda mortuorum*," [121] which discusses the break in liturgical tradition that occurred in 1614 upon the promulgation of the new rites for the dead in the *Rituale Romanum*. The older prayers were concerned first and

[120] Other studies on Matrimony to be singled out are: G. Huard, "La liturgie nuptiale dans l'Eglise romaine: les grandes étapes de sa formation," *Questions liturgiques et paroissiales* 38, 1957, 197-205; and *La Maison-Dieu* 50, 1957: *Le mariage*. In the most complete work that has appeared to date on the consecration of virgins, *La consécration des vierges dans l'Eglise romaine*, by R. Metz (Strasbourg, Presses Universitaires, 1954), there is an Appendix on the ritual of marriage (3671410).

[121] *Archiv für Liturgiewissenschaft* 4, 1955, 52-72.

foremost with the salvation of the deceased; the new turned attention to the bereaved, their consolation as well as their amendment. The older prayers sought to quicken one's faith and hope in the power of Christ's redemption; they did not seek to instill fear of damnation or cause tears.[122]

Bibliography

DOCTRINE

BEAUDUIN, L. *Mélanges Liturgiques*, Louvain, Mont-César, 1954.

BERNARD, B. "Peut-on passer de la liturgie?" *Vie spirituelle* 102, 1960, 5-32.

BOUYER, L. *Liturgical Piety*, Notre Dame, University of Notre Dame Press, 1955.

————. "Liturgie et contemplation," *Vie spirituelle* 102, 1960, 406-409.

————. *Rite and Man. Natural Sacredness and Christian Liturgy*, Notre Dame, University of Notre Dame Press, 1963.

BRASO, G. *Liturgy and Spirituality*, Collegeville, Liturgical Press, 1960.

CAPELLE, B. *Travaux liturgiques* 1. *Doctrine*, Louvain, Mont-César, 1955.

CASEL, O. *The Mystery of Christian Worship*, Westminster, Newman, 1962.

CONGAR, Y. *Lay People in the Church*, Westminster, Newman, 1957.

DALMAIS, I. H. *Introduction to the Liturgy*, Baltimore, Helicon, 1961.

————. "Liturgie et mystère du salut," in A. G. Martimort, *L'Eglise en prière*, Tournai, Desclée et Cie., 1961.

DAVIS, C. *Liturgy and Doctrine*, New York, Sheed & Ward, 1960.

DELORME, J., BENOIT, P., DUPONT, P., BOISMARD, M. E., MOLLAT, D. *The Eucharist in the New Testament*, Baltimore, Helicon, 1964.

DIEKMANN, G. *Come, Let Us Worship*, Baltimore, Helicon, 1961.

[122] Also to be consulted: H. Frank, O.S.B., "Römische Herkunft der karolingischen Beerdigungsantiphonen, *Mélanges en l'honneur de Mgr. M. Andrieu*, Strasbourg, Palais Universitaire, 1956, 161-171; "Die älteste erhaltene römische *Ordo Defunctorum*," *Archiv für Liturgiewissenschaft* 7, 1962, 360-415; and the entire number 44 of *La Maison-Dieu* (1955): *Les funerailles chrétiennes*.

DURRWELL, F. X. *The Resurrection*, New York, Sheed & Ward, 1960.

FILTHAUT, The *Die Kontroverse über die Mysterienlehre*, Warendorf, Schnell, 1947; FT *La théologie des mystères. Exposé de la controverse*, Tournai, Desclée et Cie., 1954.

FISCHER, B. "Liturgy and the Risen Christ," *Theology Digest* 8, 1960, 123-126. Original: "Der verherrlichte Mensch Christus und die Liturgie," *Liturgisches Jahrbuch* 8, 1958, 205-217.

GAILLARD, J. "La théologie des mystères," *Revue thomiste* 57, 1957, 510-551.

——. "Noël, memoria ou mystère," *La Maison-Dieu* 59, 1959, 37-70.

HOUTRYVE, I. VAN. "Liturgie et contemplation," *Questions liturgiques et paroissiales* 41, 1960, 105-110.

JUNGMANN, J. A. "Pia Exercitia and Liturgy," *Worship* 33, 1959, 616-622.

LABOURDETTE, M. M. "Principes pour la prière liturgique," *Vie spirituelle* 102, 1960, 493-505.

LÉCUYER, J. *What is a Priest?* New York, Hawthorn, 1959.

——. "Théologie de l'initiation chrétienne chez les Pères," *La Maison-Dieu* 58, 1959, 5-26.

LEFÈBVRE, G. "Oraison et liturgie," *Vie spirituelle* 102, 1960, 428-439.

MARITAIN, J. AND R. "Liturgy and Contemplation," *The Spiritual Life* 5, 1959, 94-131. (= *Liturgy and Contemplation*, New York, Kenedy, 1960.)

MARTIMORT, A. G. "L'assemblée liturgique, mystère du Christ," *La Maison-Dieu* 40, 1954, 5-29.

—— (editor). *The Liturgy and the Word of God*, Collegeville, Liturgical Press, 1959.

——. *The Signs of the New Covenant*, Collegeville, Liturgical Press, 1963.

MATTHIJS, M. "Mysteriengegenwart secundum sanctum Thomam," *Angelicum* 34, 1957, 393-399.

McNAMARA, K. "Aspects of the Layman's Role in the Mystical Body," *Irish Theological Quarterly* 25, 1958, 124-143.

MILLER, J. H. "The Nature and Definition of the Liturgy," *Theological Studies*, 18, 1957, 325-356.

——. "The Theology of the Liturgical Year," *American Ecclesiastical Review* 138, 1958, 221-230.

——. "Until He Comes—The Eucharist and the Resurrection,"

Proceedings of 23rd North American Liturgical Week, 1962, Washington, Liturgical Conference, 1963.

――――. *Signs of Transformation in Christ*, Englewood Cliffs, Prentice-Hall, 1963.

MUSSNER, F. "Kirche als Kultgemeinde," *Liturgisches Jahrbuch* 6, 1956, 50-67.

NEUNHEUSER, B. "Ende des Gesprächs um die Mysteriengegenwart? *Archiv für Liturgiewissenschaft* 4, 1956, 316-324.

――――. "Neue Aeusserungen zur Frage der Mysteriengegenwart," *Archiv für Liturgiewissenschaft* 5, 1958, 333-353.

――――. *Opfer Christi und Opfer der Kirche*, Düsseldorf, Patmos, 1960.

O'NEILL, C. "The Instrumentality of the Sacramental Character," *Irish Theological Quarterly* 25, 1958, 262-268.

――――. "The Role of the Recipient and Sacramental Signification," *The Thomist* 21, 1958, 257-301, 508-540.

PASCHER, J. *L'evolution des rites sacramentels*, Paris, Cerf, 1952.

――――. "Thesen über das Gebet im Namen der Kirche. Ergänzungen zu dem gleichnamigen Aufsatz von Karl Rahner," *Liturgisches Jahrbuch* 12, 1962, 58-62.

RAHNER, K. "Thesen über das Gebet im Namen der Kirche," *Zeitschrift für Katholische Theologie* 83, 1961, 307-324.

RÉGAMEY, P. "L'orientation contemplative de la prière liturgique," *Vie spirituelle* 102, 1960, 469-492.

REINHOLD, H. A. "Liturgy and Contemplation," *Spiritual Life* 6, 1960, 207-217.

ROGUET, A. M. "Liturgie et prière personelle," *La Maison-Dieu* 72, 1962, 99-119.

SALM, C. LUKE (editor). *Studies in Salvation History*, Englewood Cliffs, Prentice-Hall, 1964.

SCHILLEBEECKX, E. H. *Christ the Sacrament of the Encounter with God*, New York, Sheed & Ward, 1963.

SCHLECK, C. A. "The Lay Priesthood and the Mass," *Sciences ecclésiastiques* 12, 1960, 83-103.

SCHMAUS, M. "Die Liturgie als Lebensausdruck der Kirche," *Liturgisches Jahrbuch* 5, 1955, 80-95.

SCHÜRMANN, H. "Die Eucharistie als Repräsentation und Applikation des Heilsgeschehens nach Joh. 6.53-58," *Trierer theologische Zeitschrift* 68, 1959, 30-45, 108-118.

SEMMELROTH, O. "Towards a Unified Concept of the Church," *Yearbook of Liturgical Studies* 2, 1961, 85-102.

STEVENS, G. "Liturgy and Contemplation," *American Ecclesiastical Review* 142, 1960, 108-115.

SULLIVAN, C. STEPHEN (editor). *Readings in Sacramental Theology*, Englewood Cliffs, Prentice-Hall, 1964.

VAGAGGINI, C. *Il senso teologico della liturgia*, Rome, Paoline, 1957.

——. *Theological Dimensions of the Liturgy*, Collegeville, Liturgical Press, 1959.

——. "Contemplazione durante l'atto liturgico e contemplazione extraliturgica," *Rivista di ascetica e mistica* 7, 1962, 8-34.

VANDENBROUCKE, F. "Prière individuelle et prière communautaire," *La Maison-Dieu* 64, 1960, 143-158.

WARNACH, V. "Taufe und Christusgeschehen nach Römer 6," *Archiv für Liturgiewissenschaft* 3, 1954, 284-366.

——. "Die Tauflehre des Römerbriefes in der neueren theologischen Diskussion," *Archiv für Liturgiewissenschaft* 5, 1958, 274-332.

WEGENAER, P. *Heilsgegenwart*, Münster, Aschendorff, 1958.

Worship 34, October, 1960: *Liturgy and the Spiritual Life.*

GENERAL

Assisi Papers, Collegeville, Liturgical Press, 1957.

BRASO, G. *Liturgy and Spirituality*, Collegeville, Liturgical Press, 1960.

DALMAIS, J. H. *Introduction to the Liturgy*, Baltimore, Helicon, 1961.

EISENHOFER, L. AND LECHNER, J. *The Liturgy of the Roman Rite*, New York: Herder and Herder, 1961.

JUNGMANN, J. A. *Public Worship. A Survey*, Collegeville. Liturgical Press, 1957.

KING, J. W. *The Liturgy and the Laity*, Westminster, Newman, 1963.

LEONARD, W. J. (editor). *Liturgy for the People*, Milwaukee, Bruce, 1963.

MAGSAM, CH. M. *The Inner Life of the Liturgy*, St. Meinrad, Grail, 1958.

MARTIMORT, A. G. (editor). *L'Eglise en prière*, Tournai, Desclée et Cie., 1961.

MCMANUS, F. R. (editor). *The Revival of the Liturgy*, New York, Herder and Herder, 1963.

MILLER, J. H. *Fundamentals of the Liturgy*, Notre Dame, Fides, 1960.

O'SHEA, W. J. *The Worship of the Church*, Westminster, Newman, 1957.

PEIL, R. A *Handbook of the Liturgy*, New York, Herder and Herder, 1960.

QUINN, J. R. "The Necessity of an Ecclesial Formation of Seminarians," *Yearbook of Liturgical Studies* 3, 1962, 63-89.

SCHMIDT, H. A. P. *Introductio in liturgiam occidentalem*, Rome, Herder, 1960.

SHEPPARD, L. C. (editor). *True Worship*, Baltimore, Helicon, 1963.

HISTORY

ANDRIEU, M. *Les Ordines Romani du haut moyen-âge* 4-5, Louvain, Spicilegium Sacrum Lovaniense, 1956, 1961.

ASHWORTH, H. "Gregorian Elements in some Early Gelasian Sacramentaries," *Traditio* 13, 1957, 431-442.

————. "Did St. Augustine bring the *Gregorianum* to England?" *Ephemerides Liturgicae* 72, 1958, 39-43.

————. "In Quest of the Primitive *Gregorianum*, " *Ephemerides Liturgicae* 72, 1958, 319-322.

————. "St. Gregory the Great and the Gregorian Sacramentary," *Liturgy* 31, 1962, 12-15.

BLANKENBURG, W. "Offizielle und inoffizielle liturgische Bestrebungen in der evangelischen Kirche Deutschlands," *Liturgisches Jahrbuch* 13, 1963, 70-83.

BOTTE, B. *La Tradition Apostolique de saint Hippolyte. Essai de reconstitution*, Münster, Aschendorff, 1963.

CHAVASSE, A. *Le sacramentaire Gélasien*, Tournai, Desclée et Cie., 1958.

————. "La discipline romaine des sept scrutins pré-baptismaux," *Recherches de science religieuse* 48, 1960, 227-240.

COEBERGH, C. "Le sacramentaire Gélasien ancien," *Archiv für Liturgiewissenschaft* 7, 1961, 45-88.

DANIÉLOU, J. *The Bible and the Liturgy*, Notre Dame, University of Notre Dame Press, 1956.

————. *From Shadows to Reality*, Westminster, Newman, 1960.

————. *Primitive Christian Symbols*, Baltimore, Helicon, 1963.

GAMBER, K. "Hat Gregor der Grosse ein Sakramentar verfasst?" *Ephemerides Liturgicae* 73, 1959, 139-140.

HAMMAN, A. *Early Christian Prayers*, Chicago, Regenery, 1961.

HANSSENS, J. M. *La liturgie d'Hippolyte*, Rome, Istituto Orientale, 1959.

JUNGMANN, J. A. *The Early Liturgy*, Notre Dame, University of Notre Dame Press, 1960.

————. *Pastoral Liturgy*, New York, Herder and Herder, 1962.

KING, A. A. *Liturgies of the Religious Orders*, London, Longmans, 1956.

———. *Liturgies of the Primatial Sees*, London, Longmans, 1957.

———. *Liturgies of the Past*, London, Longmans, 1959.

KOENKER, E. B. *The Liturgical Renaissance in the Roman Catholic Church*, Chicago, University of Chicago Press, 1954.

LANG, A. P. *Leo der Grosse und die Texte des Altgelasianums*, Steyl, Steyler Verlagsbuchhandlung, 1957.

MAYER, A. L. "Die geistesgeschichtliche Situation der liturgischen Erneuerung in der Gegenwart," *Archiv für Liturgiewissenschaft* 4, 1955, 1-51.

MOHLBERG, K. AND SIFFRIN, P. (editors). *Sacramentarium Veronense*, Rome, Herder, 1956.

———. *Missale Francorum*, Rome, Herder , 1957.

———. *Missale Gallicanum Vetus*, Rome, Herder, 1958.

———. *Missale Gothicum*, Rome, Herder, 1961.

SALMON, P. *Etude sur les insignes du pontife dans le rite romain*, Rome, Officium libri catholici, 1955.

SHEPPARD, L. C. *The Mass in the West*, New York, Hawthorn, 1961.

———. *The Liturgical Books*, New York, Hawthorn, 1962.

———. *The Liturgical Movement*, New York, Hawthorn, 1964.

SHEPHERD, M. H. "The Liturgical Movement in American Protestantism," *Yearbook of Liturgical Studies* 3, 1962, 35-61.

TAYLOR, M. J. *The Protestant Liturgical Renewal. A Catholic Viewpoint*, Westminster, Newman, 1963.

VAN DIJK, S. J. P., AND WALKER, J. H. *The Origins of the Modern Roman Liturgy*, Westminster, Newman, 1960.

VOGEL, C. "Précisions sur la date et l'ordonnance primitive du pontifical romano-germanique," *Ephemerides Liturgicae* 74, 1960, 145-162.

LANGUAGE

CUNLIFFE, C. R. A. *English in the Liturgy. A Symposium*, Springfield, Templegate, 1956.

DE MARCO, A. *Rome and the Vernacular*, Westminster, Newman, 1961.

KOROLEVSKY, C. *Living Languages in Catholic Worship*, Westminster, Newman, 1957.

La Maison-Dieu 53, 1958: *Le problème des langues en liturgie*.

SCHMIDT, H. A. *Liturgie et langue vulgaire*, Rome, Università Gregoriana, 1950.

WINNINGER, P. *Langues vivantes et liturgie*, Paris, Cerf, 1961.

LITURGICAL YEAR

BERGER, R. "Ostern und Weihnachten, zum Grundgefüge des Kirchenjahres," *Archiv für Liturgiewissenschaft* 8, 1963, 1-20.

DENIS-BOULET, N. M. *The Christian Calendar*, New York, Hawthorn, 1960.

HILD, J. "L'Avent," *La Maison-Dieu* 59, 1959, 10-25.

JENNY, H. *The Paschal Mystery in the Christian Year*, Notre Dame, Fides, 1961.

La Maison-Dieu 41, 1955: *La semaine sainte.*

La Maison-Dieu 45, 1956: *Restauration de la Semaine sainte.*

La Maison-Dieu 46, 1956: *Les dimanches verts.*

La Maison-Dieu 49, 1957: *La catéchèse de la Semaine sainte.*

La Maison-Dieu 52, 1957: *Le sanctoral.*

La Maison-Dieu 59, 1959: *Avent. Noël. Epiphanie.*

La Maison-Dieu 65, 1961: *Le Christ hier, aujourd'hui, toujours. La liturgie et le temps.*

La Maison-Dieu 67 and 68, 1961: *La liturgie du mystère pascal.*

MILLER, J. H. "Theology of the Liturgical Year," *American Ecclesiastical Review* 138, 1958, 221-230.

SCHMIDT, H. A. *Hebdomada Sancta*, 2 volumes, Rome, Herder, 1956-1957.

SOOS, M. B. DE. *Le mystère liturgique d'après saint Léon le Grand*, Münster, Aschendorff, 1958.

MASS

AMIOT, F. *History of the Mass*, New York, Hawthorn, 1959.

CAPELLE, B. *Travaux liturgiques 2. Histoire. La Messe*, Louvain, Mont-César, 1962.

CHAVASSE, A. "L'oraison *super sindonem* dans la liturgie romaine," *Revue bénédictine* 70, 1960, 313-323.

DELORME, J. *The Eucharist in the New Testament*, Baltimore, Helicon, 1964.

JONG, J. P. DE. "Le rite de la commixtion dans la messe romaine dans ses rapports avec les liturgies syriennes," *Archiv für Liturgiewissenschaft* 4, 1956, 245-278; 5, 1957, 33-79.

JUNGMANN, J. A. *The Mass of the Roman Rite*, 2 volumes, New York, Benziger, 1951, 1955. 1 volume edition, *ibid.*, 1959.

————. *The Eucharistic Prayer. A Study of Canon Missae,* Notre Dame, Fides, 1956.

La Maison-Dieu 60, 1959: *Les acteurs de la célébration liturgique.*

McGowan, J. *Concelebration. Sign of the Unity of the Church,* New York, Herder and Herder, 1964.

OFFICE

Baumstark, A. *Nocturna Laus. Typen frühchristlicher Vigilienfeier und ihr Fortleben vor allem im römishen und monastichen Ritus,* Münster, Aschendorff, 1957.

Jungmann, J. A. *Pastoral Liturgy,* New York, Herder and Herder, 1962.

————— (editor). *Brevierstudien,* Trier, Paulinus, 1958.

Salmon, P. *The Breviary Through the Centuries,* Collegeville, Liturgical Press, 1962.

ORIENTAL

Attwater, D. *The Christian Churches of the East,* 2 volumes, Milwaukee, Bruce, 1961².

Dalmais, I. H. "Le *Triduum Sacrum* dans la liturgie byzantine," *La Maison-Dieu* 41, 1955, 118-127.

————. "Le dimanche dans la liturgie byzantine," *La Maison-Dieu* 46, 1956, 60-67.

————. "La liturgie du mariage dans les Eglises orientales," *La Maison-Dieu* 50, 1957, 58-69.

————. "Les commémorations des saints dans l'office quotidien et hebdomadaire des liturgies orientales," *La Maison-Dieu* 52, 1957, 98-108.

————. "Le sacrement du pénitence chez les Orientaux," *La Maison-Dieu* 56, 1958, 22-29.

————. "Le temps de préparation à Noël dans les liturgies syrienne et byzantine," *La Maison-Dieu* 59, 1959, 25-36.

————. *Eastern Liturgies,* New York, Hawthorn, 1960.

Raes, A. *Le mariage dans les Eglises d'Orient,* Chevetogne, Editions de Chevetogne, 1959.

PREACHING

Assemblée du Seigneur, Bruges, Biblica, 1962-. Eighty-nine volumes projected.

Crichton, J. D. "Liturgical Preaching," *The Clergy Review* 45, 1960, 725-733.

FULLER, R. H. *What is Liturgical Preaching?* London, SCM, 1957.

KAHLES, W. "Glaubensverkündigung aus dem Geiste der liturgischen Erneuerung," *Archiv für Liturgiewissenschaft* 6, 1960, 417-454.

KIRCHGÄSSNER, A. "Die Predigt in der Messe," *Liturgisches Jahrbuch* 14, 1964, 146-151.

La Maison-Dieu 39, 1954: *Aux sources de la prédication*.

MALLON, V. P. "Scripture and Liturgy in the Homiletic Training of Seminarians," *Proceedings of the 22nd North American Liturgical Week, 1960,* Washington, Liturgical Conference, 1961.

O'SHEA, W. J. "The Sermon is Part of the Mass," *Homiletic and Pastoral Review* 60, 1960, 517-526.

ROGUET, A. M. "La prédication du temps liturgique," *Questions liturgiques et paroissiales* 38, 1957, 110-118.

REFORM

HOFINGER, J. (editor). *Liturgy and the Missions,* New York, Kenedy, 1960.

NOCENT, A. *The Future of the Liturgy,* New York, Herder and Herder, 1963.

REINHOLD, H. A. *Bringing the Mass to the People,* Baltimore, Helicon, 1960.

SACRAMENTAL

ANCIAUX, P. *The Sacrament of Penance,* New York, Sheed & Ward, 1962.

FRANK, H. "Römische Herkunft der karolingischen Beerdigungsantiphonen," *Mélanges en l'honneur de Mgr. M. Andrieu,* Strasbourg, Palais Universitaire, 1956.

———. "Die älteste erhaltene römische *Ordo Defunctorum,*" *Archiv für Liturgiewissenschaft* 7, 1962, 360-415.

HUARD, G. "La liturgie nuptiale dans l'Eglise romaine: les grandes étapes de sa formation," *Questions liturgiques et paroissiales* 38, 1957, 197-205.

JONG, J. P. DE. "Benedictio Fontis," *Archiv für Liturgiewissenshaft* 8, 1963, 21-46.

JOUNEL, P. "La liturgie romaine du mariage," *La Maison-Dieu* 50, 1957, 30-57.

JUNGMANN, J. A. "Aufbauelemente im römischen Taufritus," *Liturgisches Jahrbuch* 9, 1959, 1-15.

KLEINHEYER, B. *Die Priesterweihe im römischen Ritus,* Trier, Paulinus, 1962.

LÉCUYER, J. "La prière consécratoire des eaux," *La Maison-Dieu* 49, 1957, 71-95.

MAERTENS, TH. *Histoire et pastorale du rituel du catéchuménat et du baptême*, Bruges, Biblica, 1962.

La Maison-Dieu 44, 1955: *Les funerailles chrétiennes*.

La Maison-Dieu 50, 1957: *Le mariage*.

La Maison-Dieu 54, 1958: *La confirmation*.

La Maison-Dieu 55 and 56, 1958: *La pénitence*.

METZ, R. *La consécration des vierges dans l'Eglise romaine*, Strasbourg, Presses Universitaires, 1954; Appendix, "Le rituel du mariage."

OLIVAR, A. "Vom Ursprung der römischen Taufwasserweihe," *Archiv für Liturgiewissenschaft* 6, 1959, 62-78.

PHILIPPEAU, H. R. "Textes et rubriques des *Agenda mortuorum*," *Archiv für Liturgiewissenschaft* 4, 1955, 52-72.

POSCHMANN, B. *Penance and the Anointing of the Sick*, New York, Herder and Herder, 1964.

RITZER, K. *Formen, Riten und religiöses Brauchtum der Eheschliessung in den christlichen Kirchen des ersten Jahrtausends*, Münster, Aschendorff, 1962.

ROGUES, J. "La préface consécratoire du Chrême," *La Maison-Dieu* 49, 1957, 35-49.

STENZEL, A. *Die Taufe*, Innsbruck, Rauch, 1958.

THURIAN, M. *Consecration of the Layman*, Baltimore, Helicon, 1963.

Theology in Transition

ELMER O'BRIEN, S.J.

No one however little aware of either its abiding nature or its more recent history should be surprised that theology is in a state of transition at the moment. Growth and development—transition therefore—is characteristic of any science worthy of the name and theology, we are not infrequently reminded, is the very queen of the sciences. And, indeed, there has been growth and development latterly; consciously or unconsciously, we have all been its beneficiaries as the preceding papers have served indirectly to attest.

But I would suggest that there is rather more than mere growth and development taking place just now. One hesitates to use so total a term to describe it, yet some such word as "transformation" is simply forced upon one by the facts. A transition, therefore, which is in some sense a transformation.

In the sense of a "new theology" being the likely outcome? One can only hope not. Unless it is true that the only thing we learn from history is that we learn nothing from history, it should be obvious to just about everybody by now that all "new" theologies are always essays in the unreal. The kerygmatic theology of the early thirties, so admirable in its concern for the proclamation of the word of God and so alert to the inadequacies of textbook theology for the achieving of that highly Christian purpose, was clearly one instance of this.[1] The theology stemming chiefly from France in the late forties and dubbed by its noisier

[1] I would wish it clear that I speak here only of those early and abortive essays at a different and distant theology that were made by the Innsbruck theologians, especially Jungmann, Lakner, Dander, and Hugo Rahner. Who could bring himself to speak ill of the latter-day emphasis upon the kerygmatic aspect of theology which has been so fruitful in its consequences, in

critics as precisely *la nouvelle théologie* was another. In both instances, a deliberate effort was made to meet contemporary needs by forming a theology in terms of those needs. For new needs, a new theology. What, on the face of it, could have been more reasonable? It would have been more reasonable, one can now say with the wisdom born of hindsight, to have reëxamined—in the very cause of practicality—the existing theology. For directly one attempts to meet practically a concrete situation by framing—in the very cause of practicality—a new science to meet it, the impractical results. What, for instance, theology can bring to a concrete situation is in large part lost because filtered through this or that notion of this or that particular need. By far the majority of "theologies" of the lay state have served latterly to document this truth anew: the attempt to meet the needs of Catholic Action or, more recently, of the laity generally with those needs—real or imagined —as the determinants has resulted inevitably in the superficial and the banal however apocalyptically presented. Needs which a science can meet are genuinely met—indeed, are genuinely recognized—only if the science is most fully and properly itself. Theology is no exception.

Theology these days is undergoing a transformation. It is becoming, it would seem, more like its old self. If to say that sounds as though theology has long been ailing and is now recuperating, so be it. The fabulous invalid passed on to us of the twentieth century by the theologians of the eighteenth century, who with more zeal than judgment twisted it out of shape in order to meet the needs of their rationalist era, is beginning to regain its proper stance. It no longer has to lean its weight upon philosophic crutches but stands, its weight pretty well distributed throughout itself, on its own two feet. It is in an almost upright position once more, almost able to face up to revelation fully. And, in that confrontation, daily more direct, with revelation as mediated through the life of the Church by Scripture and tradition and liturgical practice, theology

particular for catechetics? Readers familiar with J. A. Jungmann's *Die Frohbotschaft und unsere Glaubensverkündigung* (Regensburg, Pustet, 1936; ET *The Good News Yesterday and Today*, New York, Sadlier, 1962), which was in effect the reasoned manifesto of the early kerygmaticists, will find the revised edition, *Glaubensverkündigung im Lichte der Frohbotschaft* (Innsbruck, Tyrolia, 1963), of exceptional interest in this connection.

is becoming more able to speak meaningfully to contemporary needs.

But of course theology exists, upright or bent, sick or healthy, nowhere except in the minds of theologians. The theologian's present pressing duty is to contribute to its continuing convalescence, the which he will find easier to fulfill (easier without being particularly easy) because of the advances, reported in these pages, that have been made in the areas of knowledge so intimately related to the theological enterprise as scriptural studies, patristic studies, liturgical studies.

Of even more help, of course, is what has recently been done in strictly theological studies. To that area, accordingly, we now address ourselves anew.

REFERENCE WORKS

Clearly, first place must be given to the latest edition of that hardy perennial, the *Enchiridion Symbolorum* edited by Heinrich Denzinger over a century ago and referred to pretty much ever since, whether in malediction or in blessing, as simply "Denzinger." [2] The present editor has fortunately not been content to do as did his predecessors, who for the most part merely added on further bits and pieces from Papal and Commissional pronouncements which might have appeared since a previous edition. He has included for the first time many documents of the past that are directly relevant to the theologian's task and has excised others, so faithfully republished through decades, which never were. In brief introductory paragraphs he has attempted with a large measure of success to insert all documents within their historical contexts. With not infrequent footnotes he has corrected, in the light of recent scholarship, the more usual misinterpretations of the documents. He has, finally, appended a new *Index Systematicus Rerum* that is no longer a simple transcript of the table of contents one would find in just about any seminary manual of the last century or so but is in accord with the emphases and interests of contemporary theology and, perhaps, with the abiding nature of theology itself. And,

[2] Adolf Schönmetzer, *Enchiridion Symbolorum*, Freiburg, Herder, 1963[33].

to put everybody in a good mood, he has prefaced it all with an urbane and witty Introduction.

It is allowable, if not mandatory, to be skeptical of the theologian whose sole book is "Denzinger." But even such a one should prove, with this "Denzinger" the chief subject of his meditations, somewhat more worthy of respect. Indeed, all theologians can become better theologians because of it. The indisputable truth would seem to be that little (except, now and again, heresy) has ever come from theologizing in the ivory-tower privacy of one's head, that one must as theologian come into constant and direct encounter with the realities of the Church's long doctrinal life. Now one can avoid the first and achieve the second rather easily with this edition. More than that, the editor has managed to set in disarray the vicious circle of "Denzinger theology" so much deplored by the previous editor:[3] earlier editors selected texts according to the current theses of seminary courses; theology professors felt that the selection of texts was the norm for what questions were to be treated in theology; theology professors, therefore, for years inelegantly pursued their own tails. The greater amplitude of texts now provided, the historical notes appended, and—especially —the new *Index Systematicus* should (one would hope) put an end to that all too familiar, all too disedifying spectacle.

One difficulty with "Denzinger" even now is the unavoidable brevity of the texts that are given, particularly the Conciliar texts. Hence the great value of *Conciliorum Oecumenicorum Decreta*,[4] a single volume which sits as easily to the hand as it does to one's pocketbook, which contains the decrees of all the Ecumenical Councils in their entirety. Now the theologian is able to do at his ease what formerly was possible only by having recourse to the large, multivolumed, costly editions of the *Acta* of the Councils: read texts in their literary context and avoid thereby whole large areas of misapprehension. Obviously, this relatively small volume can be no substitute for the large *Acta* in the most serious theo-

---

[3] Karl Rahner. See, for instance, his *Schriften zur Theologie* 1 (Einsiedeln, Benziger, 1954), 11, n. 2. ET *Theological Investigations* 1 (Baltimore, Helicon, 196), 3, n. 2.

[4] Edited by Giusèppe Alberigo, *et al.*, Freiburg, Herder, 1962².

logical work. For one thing, it does not provide transcriptions of discussion or of the voting. But it is pleasantly close to being a substitute: variant readings are scrupulously given; historical introductions, with references to the better recent studies, preface each major section; discreet and knowledgeable footnotes adorn at need certain of the stickier passages; the Latin is given throughout, yet Greek originals and Armenian or Arabic versions (as for Florence) are given as well. In fine, a wholly admirable piece of work.

The *Dictionnaire de théologie catholique* has served the theologian long and well. It is serving him even better these days with its *Tables générales*.[5] So lengthy an interval was it between the issuing of its first volume (1903) and of its last (1950), some of the *DTC* was inevitably already out of date when at long last it was complete. The *Tables générales* are being made to fulfill two happy functions, the conventional business of indexing (here done with an almost Germanic thoroughness) and the less usual one of providing corrective supplements to some of the older articles or new articles on subjects it would never have occurred to theologians of the earlier part of this century to treat. Unfortunately, it is not so complete a rehandling as characterizes the addition to the *Dictionnaire de la Bible* which, modestly dubbed *Supplément*, is an almost totally new *Dictionnaire*. Yet, amid the special perplexities of putting out what is in effect not a dictionary but an encyclopedia of theology, the publishers have shown themselves to be most realistic. Recognizing in advance the inescapable *longueurs* of so monumental an enterprise, they published the briefer, more expeditiously achieved, *Dictionnaire des connaissances religieuses* to fill the temporary gap. To it has now succeeded their *Catholicisme*,[6] which, although latterly it has been suffering its own *longueurs*, it is a pleasure to recommend as singularly clear, alive, objective, contemporary.

At least two of these qualities, the aliveness and the contemporaneity, mark the latest edition of *Die Religion in Geschichte und Gegenwart*.[7] Walter Burghardt has already recommended the *RGG* for its patristic articles, but it would be churlish of me not to

5 Paris, Letouzey, 1951-.
6 Paris, Letouzey, 1948-.
7 Six volumes, Tübingen, Mohr, 1957-1962[3].

commend in passing its brief theological articles of an historical cast: Bonaventure, for instance, is presented as reliably and informatively as, say, Barth. But the chief reason for the theologian's being happy to have the *RGG* constantly at hand is its extended doctrinal expositions, which in their sum offer a good transcript of European (mainly Protestant) theology at present and, in the majority of instances, can act as salutary prods to one's own theological reflection.

Much the same can be said of the second edition of the *Lexikon für Theologie und Kirche*,[8] which has been coming out at a regular pace of at least one magnificent volume each year since 1957. But, whereas *RGG*, produced under Protestant auspices, reveals the strong influence of Martin Heidegger and Rudolf Bultmann on its doctrinal articles, the Catholic *LTK* reveals that of Karl Rahner. Indeed, it is Rahner who has taken it to himself to treat just about all the major theological topics (seventy-nine of them up to the early part of the letter "R"); there is even the rumor afloat that in his capacity of co-editor he has tailored the articles of others to fit the pattern of his own thought. Whether the rumor be true or no, this much is certain: the second edition of *LTK* has a personal, one-man quality about it that is lacking in the first edition and is hardly to be expected in any encyclopedia. The volumes so far are, theologically, a sort of lexicon of Karl Rahner's doctrine. To say that, however, is by no means to condemn it; we would all be immeasurably the poorer if Rahner did not exist.

An astonishingly complete and much more compendious presentation of Rahner's doctrine is to be found in the *Kleines theologisches Wörterbuch* of Rahner and his energetic alter ego, Herbert Vorgrimler.[9] Its chief value would seem to be for the beginning student in theology who must, early rather than late, acquire a genuinely theological perspective. This small book, using to the full that admirable system of cross reference rather than repetition for which German editors of doctrinal dictionaries are justly famous, has the inquirer in his search for light on one question read of necessity not one but several articles. In this way, the native coherence of theology, the fashion in which one mystery can cast light

[8] Freiburg, Herder.
[9] Freiburg, Herder, 1961.

on another, the depths to which any proper theological query reaches are inexorably, yet painlessly, brought home to him. He becomes not only theologically informed, but theologically *formed*.

That, in contrast, it is only theological information that is available in the *Theologisch Woordenboek*[10] should not have anyone think lightly of it because the information is about the highly progressive theologizing of those Dutch and Flemish Catholic scholars (chiefly Dominican) whose impact on the theologizing of all of us will, one can only hope, be most marked in the years immediately ahead. In *TW* is most happily to be found the sacramental theology of E. H. Schillebeeckx, O.P., refracted through the numerous articles he has contributed; this presentation can serve in part to keep one informed and to allay impatience as we await the long-delayed completion of his masterly *De sacramentele Heilseconomie*.

The Catholic theologians of the Lowlands are, in the good sense, progressive. Those of the British Isles are, also in the good sense, conservative. The procedure of making do with what one has in preference to breaking new ground is thus rather generally prominent in *A Catholic Dictionary of Theology*,[11] and the result is as healthful as it is, these days, novel. A good illustration is its editorial policy of not having articles simply on, say, "Augustine" or "Bonaventure," but on "Augustine and His Influence," "Bonaventure, Influence of," etc. Clearly, the intent is that history be able to make its indispensable contribution to contemporary theological understanding. At times, the choice of topic is surely questionable theologically (for example, "Agapetae") or the treatment theologically a zero (for example, "Art in the Church"). But only at times. Most often, the *Dictionary* achieves a freshness of both intent and execution that sets it quite apart and above all similar contemporary efforts so that one looks forward to its completion with much impatience.

In a way, the best has here been kept to the last. Of the *Handbuch theologischer Grundbegriffe*[12] one can use, I am happy to state, only unqualified superlatives. More objective than either the

10 Three volumes, Roermond, Romen & Zonen, 1952-1958.
11 Edited by H. Francis Davis *et al.*, New York, Nelson, 1962-.
12 Edited by Heinrich Fries, 2 volumes, Munich, Kösel, 1962, 1963.

RGG or the *LTK,* and more ample in its treatment of the one hundred and fifty-seven topics selected than either *Catholicisme* or *A Catholic Dictionary of Theology,* it provides one of the best expositions of Catholic theology available today in any language.

SURVEYS

At the outset of our period, as if with some premonition that 1954-1964 was to be truly a "decisive decade," global assessments of the Catholic theological scene appeared of which two have lost little of their value in the intervening years for making one more sensitive to the particular cultural context in which theology today—Catholic and non-Catholic—must seek to accomplish its task.[13] Significantly, the operative word in the titles of each is "Problems," for it had not been the custom previously to admit that theology had problems. Answers it had in abundance. But not problems. Yet the hardy realism of these volumes does not end there. They have an openness to contributions from whatever school which we might do well to attempt recapturing these days, threatened as we are by the prospect of theologians solidifying their positions as either "progressives" or "conservatives" to the likely impoverishment of all. Finally, that they should have appeared, balanced and forthright, so soon after *Humani generis* adds to their present value an historical dimension of considerable continuing importance.

However, of even more abiding worth is *Fragen der Theologie heute.*[14] It is a survey as are the others. But it is rather less concerned with reporting and assessing the state of theology than indicating (if it is allowable to engage here in a small play on words) the questionable coinage of theology—those that demand more attentive examination precisely because they have been around so long that they have become largely worn smooth of significance. So well did the various contributors fulfill their task, of such a probity was the unrelenting weighing and questioning they engaged in, many of the determinations they arrived at have already become

[13] *Problemi scelti di teologia contemporanea,* "Analecta Gregoriana" 68, Rome, Università Gregoriana, 1954; *Problemi e orientamenti di teologia dommatica,* 2 volumes, Milan, Marzorati, 1957.
[14] Edited by Johannes Feiner, *et al.,* Einsiedeln, Benziger, 1957, 1960[3].

permanent acquisitions in our theologizing. However, that most happy consummation is no excuse for anyone's not having first-hand acquaintance with the extraordinary *expertise* of *Fragen*.

Experience continues to prove how ridiculously easy it is for one to lose one's sense of direction even in surveys such as these, whose common purpose is to give direction, unless one has some clear notion of which way things were going previously. Once again, therefore, the historical must paradoxically be allowed to enter in if one's theologizing would be contemporary. Much to be recommended in this connection is Eldarov's good-tempered study of a historic incident which was of a sort to stir tempers immoderately, and did: the appearance of the so-called *nouvelle théologie* of the forties.[15] Eldarov's is a deliberately evaluative piece of work, and it is much to his credit that, so close in time to the event itself, he was able to detect what alone was valid in the "new" approach: the emphasis on *ressourcement*, on constant return to the sources and resources of theology. Granted, a "new theology" was in prospect and, as all such ventures must, came to nought. Yet, because of the competence of some of those popularly believed to be involved in it (Daniélou, Congar, de Lubac, *et al.*), a sense of the immediate relevance particularly of the patristic heritage (whether as witness to tradition or carrier of theological insights) for the theological enterprise in our day as in any other was brought home to us to our undoubted (and, one only hopes, continuing) advantage.

The need to know the yesterdays, remote or recent, if we would know today is prominent not only in regard to Catholic theology. The same obtains, for the Catholic theologian, in regard to Protestant theology. My meaning here is not simply that it is needful if one would know Protestant theology; that is too obvious to require mentioning. My meaning rather is this: the influence—in large part happy—of Protestant theology on Catholic theology has been extensive of late. To know, accordingly, the present tasks and pos-

---

[15] G. M. Eldarov, O.F.M. Conv., *Presenza della theologia. Saggio su una recente controversia alla luce dell'enciclica "Humani generis,"* Padua, Il Messaggero di S. Antonio, 1954. The qualities so notably present in this book are as notably absent in *Die Neue Theologie* by Andreas Heinrich Maltha, O.P. (Munich, Manz, 1960).

sibilities of Catholic theology, it is imperative to acquaint oneself
with those influences at their source. There are fortunately multiple aids available to that end. A good beginning can be made with
Mackintosh's small book,[16] initially published in 1937 but now re-
issued because of its continuing value in giving the background
necessary for an understanding of things happening now that have
their origins in cultural and historical areas with which many, the
Catholic especially, would be little familiar. The author dresses out
the entire picture from Schleiermacher to Barth. Then there is
Soper's presentation,[17] more limited and unabashedly *haute vulgar-
isation*. It is especially helpful for an understanding of Tillich, Nels
Ferré, and the Niebuhr brothers because their thought was, at the
time Soper wrote, rather simpler than it was later to become yet of
a piece with it: the child—here as elsewhere—is father of the man
and—here, if not elsewhere—the more easily understood. With
like profit, one might read Bishop J. W. C. Wand's BBC lectures
on Kierkegaard, Barth, Bultmann, Tillich, and Bonhoeffer.[18]

Professor Williams[19] uses a synoptic approach, addressing himself successively not to authors, but to doctrinal areas. The only
pity is that a book so small should have been given a title so vast; it
is not a transcript of what present-day theologians are thinking, but
of what a relatively small handful of them (almost exclusively Protestant) are thinking. However, what it does do it does well. Professor Macquarrie's book does more and does it even better;[20] it is
clear, phenomenally knowledgeable, and as complete as one could
reasonably ask of any single author. Williams discusses five areas;
Macquarrie, twenty-two. Williams reveals little real knowledge of
Catholic contributions; Macquarrie, much. Yet there should really
be no question of choosing between them. Each is recommended.

[16] H. R. Mackintosh, *Types of Modern Theology. Schleiermacher to Barth*,
London, Collins, 1964.
[17] David Wesley Soper, *Major Voices in American Theology. Six Contemporary Leaders*, Philadelphia, Westminster, 1953.
[18] J. W. C. Wand, *The Minds Behind the New Theology*, London, Mowbray, 1963.
[19] Daniel Day Williams, *What Present-Day Theologians Are Thinking*,
New York, Harper, 1959[2].
[20] John Macquarrie, *Twentieth-Century Religious Thought. The Frontiers
of Philosophy and Theology*, 1900-1960, New York, Harper, 1963.

And, be it noted for later reference, each gives attention to the value of methods derived from logical positivism for today's theologian.

In *Subject and Object in Modern Theology*,[21] James Brown considers in turn the doctrines of Kierkegaard, Heidegger, Buber, and Barth. Brown's is a mind of a quite singular analytic ability so that his book performs two worthwhile functions at once. It gives an accurate survey of the not wholly dissimilar views of this theologically most influential quartet. It also indicates a dimension of theological thought that is too often neglected: patterned on insights from Kierkegaard and those coming after him, it makes clear the tension which must be preserved at the very center of theology between man-thinking and God-thought because neither God nor his revelation is simply object—less object, indeed, than subject, less terminal point of theologizing than source. Said as baldly as I am saying it here, it may seem a point so obvious as to be hardly worth making. But, as spelled out by the author, it stands a most necessary and far-reaching lesson for the practicing theologian who can so easily be led astray in his thinking by the surface resemblances of what he is supposed to be doing and what other intellectual disciplines most properly do whose matter is always object, never subject. The least unfortunate *cul de sac* into which he can be led astray is that of a false clarity. Yet that, I dare say, would be—always has been—unfortunate enough.

A double service is also performed by the Archbishop of Canterbury's survey of Anglican theology between 1889 and 1939.[22] It chronicles the period. But Anglican theology, particularly in the British Isles, has had from the early nineteenth century a most respectful and informed concern for the Fathers. So there is here made available much patristic lore in summary fashion under the guise of Anglican theology. Like reasons recommend much of Lewis B. Smedes, *The Incarnation. Trends in Modern Anglican Thought.*[23]

[21] New York, Macmillan, 1955.
[22] Arthur Michael Ramsey, *An Era in Anglican Theology. From Gore to Temple*, New York, Scribner, 1960.
[23] Kampen, Kok, 1953.

Few areas of theology have been given such concerted attention of late as ecclesiology. Indeed, one of the happy distinctions of the "decisive decade" has been the reëxamining, the modifying, the deepening of the theological concept of the Church. Dom Jaki's retrospective review of the work done by Protestant, Catholic, and Orthodox theologians from the middle of the nineteenth century to the middle of the twentieth catalogues the achievements and the failures with a magnificently impartial eye which, however, sees everything mainly in terms of the encyclical *Mystici Corporis*.[24] Yves Congar's view, in his *Sainte Eglise, Etudes et approches ecclé- siologiques*,[25] is rather less constrained. This admirable man to whom we are all so indebted has never kept the promise, made initially some thirty years ago and repeated intermittently ever since, that he would himself write a fundamental theological trea- tise on the Church. He has been carrying about in his head the ingredients of that much desired treatise for decades now, and cer- tain of them have been perceptible in the background of almost everything he has written (most notably in his *Jalons pour une théologie du laïcat*): they have been the tantalizing, unexpressed suppositions of just about every theological statement he has ever made. Well, he appears now to recognize the handwriting on the wall: he will never keep that promise. So, *faute de mieux*, he has published *Sainte Eglise*, an omnibus volume. It contains articles of his from the most various sources, but all concerned with the na- ture and function of the Church. It contains, further, the surveys of work in the theology of the Church which he published in pe- riodicals from 1932 to 1962. Hence we have here the most reliable of entries, many doors wide, into the unwritten Congar ecclesiol- ogy. The articles, of course, are the largest portals of entry. But the surveys, for the circumspect at least, provide genuine access too; thus Congar's approval of the view of, say, Professor X or the rea- sons for his disapproval of the view of Professor Y are of an ex- treme usefulness. The more usual purpose of surveys, that they chiefly catalogue the doctrines of others, they admirably fulfill as

[24] S. Jaki, O.S.B., *Les tendances nouvelles de l'ecclésiologie*, Rome, Herder, 1957.
[25] Paris, Cerf, 1963.

well, and one can there find detailed the context out of which has come the ecclesiology of a Semmelroth[26] or a Küng[27] or a Hamer.[28]

If "Church" has been much to the fore in the decade's theology, "Resurrection" has been only slightly less so. For orientation in a matter whose theological (in contrast with its apologetic) importance becomes daily more obvious, Carlo Martini's survey[29] has much to commend it.

Finally, as a sort of coda or recapitulation, composed with a quite different end in view, of what I have attempted to say earlier about the futility of constructing a theology in terms of contemporary needs, there is the volume by Henry Pitney Van Dusen.[30] The documented apologia (a sort of survey, therefore) which he offers of liberal theology is this: it tries to take its form from present need. Its failure—the Harry Emerson Fosdick sort of thing so on the wane these days—a failure both as theology and as satisfaction of any except the most superficial and spurious needs, is, in Van Dusen's pages, most clear. It is with sadness that one encounters pages such as these because they are an anguished cry in favor of what the author has long and notably identified himself with and now beholds melting away before his eyes. Sadder, the reader should also be the wiser because of it.[31]

PHILOSOPHY AND THEOLOGY

The last ten years have witnessed the reappearance on the theological horizon of a problem that is as old as theology itself: the

[26] Otto Semmelroth, S.J., *Das Geistliche Amt. Theologische Sinndeutung,* Frankfurt, Knecht, 1958.

[27] Hans Küng, *Strukturen der Kirche,* Freiburg, Herder, 1962.

[28] Jérôme Hamer, O.P., *L'Eglise est une communion,* Paris, Cerf, 1962.

[29] *Il problema storico della risurrezione negli studi recenti,* Rome, Università Gregoriana, 1959. Gerhard Koch's *Die Auferstehung Jesu Christi* (Tübingen, Mohr, 1959) is, aside from its own positive theological contribution, a most incisive survey of Protestant theologizing on the Resurrection.

[30] *The Vindication of Liberal Theology. A Tract for the Times,* New York, Scribner, 1963.

[31] Besides volumes of the sort noted in this section which, either in intent or simply in fact, provide surveys of recent theology, the comprehensive coverage provided by the book reviews of *Nouvelle revue théologique* and the doctrinal chronicles of *Revue des sciences philosophiques et théologiques* can best serve to keep the theologian abreast of what is happening.

philosophy-theology relationship. Probably because philosophy has become somewhat more sophisticated of late, the problem itself seems now to possess a more dignified and responsible character and to merit new consideration. In any case, it has been getting it.

1.

A thing that would have been wholly impossible as little as two decades ago has quietly, this last while, taken place: logical positivism is accepted now as one of the poles of the relationship. That the acceptance has been by American and British theologians as distinct from continental theologians should, I think, be a cause of rejoicing rather than of alarm. We theologians, especially the Catholics among us, have been all too prone all too long to live off doctrinal imports from Europe which, by the very nature of things, are largely alien to the mentality here and to the cultural context in which we should be speaking.

The chief reason logical positivism has been accepted is simply that it has become more acceptable. It now no longer limits itself to the experientially verifiable, thrusting out of doors as beneath consideration whatever does not fit wholly within the narrow ambit of human experience. Its operation, rather, has been enlarged to embrace statements of whatever sort, those of theology included, to which it applies analytical techniques of singular reliability on the justified supposition that all statements have *cognitive* import by virtue of their logical relation to those human experiences that are relevant to the judgment of the *truth* of the statements.[32] The theologian speaks in season and out of season of the first person of the Trinity as "Father." How often does he ask himself, "What do I really mean when I use this word?" And, if he does ask, how often has he good prospects of finding out? It is to the accomplishment of this needful task that logical analysis provides what would seem indispensable techniques.

That here the relation of theology to philosophy is not one of method to method or of content to content, but of content to *a* method, does not in any way diminish its importance for one who

[32] See on this Fred Berthold, Jr., "Logical Empiricism and Philosophical Theology," *Journal of Religion* 35, 1955, 207-217.

would use theological language responsibly. All theologians are liable to the occupational hazard of the verbal solution: one familiar word conjures up almost automatically another familiar word which is taken, in whole or in part, as the answer. For theological words, as all words and just about all things else, become worn smooth by usage and tend to caress the mind when they should prod it. A dogmatic slumber that would surprise even a Kant not infrequently results.

It takes a small degree of humility and a large degree of realism for the theologian to put the question to himself, "What do I mean when I say this?" It takes even larger degrees of both for him to have recourse to the techniques of another discipline in order to find out. To such a one the following studies are strongly recommended.

New Essays in Philosophical Theology[33] has proved to be continuingly efficacious in disposing the theologian to take a hard, relatively sophisticated look at his use of language and in initiating him into some of the more elementary methods of doing so. Ian T. Ramsey's *Miracles. An Exercise in Logical Mapwork*[34] demonstrates the method of logical analysis as applied to one sole area, and manages to make pellucidly clear how a single theological statement can contain words which rest on different linguistic levels and should, accordingly, be so understood and so intended. His *Religious Language*[35] illustrates *in extenso* what follows when one grounds theological words and phrases within a religious situation —the which every believing theologian, wittingly or unwittingly, inevitably does.

[33] Edited by Antony Flew and Alasdair MacIntyre, New York, Macmillan, 1956. *Faith and Logic. Oxford Essays in Philosophical Theology* (London, Allen & Unwin, 1957) edited by one of the contributors to *New Essays*, Basil Mitchell, is by comparison somewhat fanciful and farfetched. *Difficulties in Christian Belief* (London, SCM, 1959) by the coeditor of *New Essays*, Alasdair MacIntyre, displays a cautiousness that the author did not have previously and has since abandoned.

[34] Oxford, Clarendon, 1952.

[35] Naperville, Allenson, 1957. His *On Being Sure in Religion* (New York, Oxford University Press, 1963) discusses the theology of F. D. Maurice (1805-1872) in a fashion that is singularly informative about his own theology as well. *Models and Mystery* (London, Oxford University Press, 1964) is concerned to show the affinities as well as the contrasts between various sciences, theology included, according to the tenets of logical analysis.

Ronald Hepburn[36] provides instances of even more marked sophistication. Recognizing that "paradoxical and near-paradoxical language is the *staple* of accounts of God and is not confined to rhetorical extravaganzas," he asks, "When is a contradiction not a *mere* contradiction, but a sublime Paradox, a Mystery? How can we distinguish a viciously muddled confusion of concepts from an excusably stammering attempt to describe what has been glimpsed during some 'raid on the inarticulate,' an object too great for our comprehension, but nonetheless real for that?" And he directs his attention, with these queries in mind, to "encounter" theology, to "Christocentric" theology, to the theological appeal to "history," etc. His suggestion is that religious language has a logic all its own (which is all to the good so long as the one using such language recognizes this distinctiveness and comports himself accordingly).

Hepburn intended to be, and believed he had been, largely destructive in *Christianity and Paradox*. The symposium edited by A. R. Vidler[37] three years later not only intended but succeeded in being destructive (although "exploratory" is the editor's word for it).[38] Less characterized by the methods than by the mood of logical analysis, provoking it surely is. Yet it is provocative as well, particularly in its treatment of contemporary Christologies and the idea of the transcendent. G. F. Woods contributed the latter essay. Such is his quality as there revealed, most readers will be prompted by it to return to his magisterial *Theological Explanation*.[39]

In its passage from Britain to America, this more recent sort of

[36] *Christianity and Paradox. Critical Studies in Twentieth-Century Theology*, New York, Humanities Press, 1959.

[37] *Soundings. Essays Concerning Christian Understanding*, New York, Cambridge University Press, 1962. Even those who disagreed quite violently with *Soundings* persisted in the pretty literary conceit of finding one's titles exclusively in Acts 27. Thus *Up and Down in Adria. Some Considerations of the Volume Entitled* Soundings (London, Faith, 1963) by E. L. Mascall and *Four Anchors From the Stern* (London, SCM, 1963) edited by Alan Richardson.

[38] The more recent, slighter volume edited by Professor Vidler, *Objections to Christian Belief* (London, Constable, 1963), has achieved comparable *succès de scandale* and *succès de librairie* but is not, therefore, without worth for the professional theologian.

[39] Welwyn, Nisbet, 1958.

logical positivism has undergone a sea-change which makes it, if anything, the more meaningful for us. The chief importers have been John Hick and Frederick Ferré.

Professor Hick has shown himself a middleman of exceptional reliability. What he brings to the American theological scene, particularly with his essay towards an epistemology of faith,[40] is a logical analysis whose lineaments are right—and unrigid. It is the traditional *fides quaerens intellectum* that one finds in his pages, but faith seeking precisely to understand itself with the unobtrusive aid of this untraditional discipline.

Professor Ferré, with a like reliability, has made available even more extensive wares. Were I limited to recommending one lone book as being indispensable to the theologian who would make his own these latter-day techniques for tidying up theological language, it would be Ferré's *Language, Logic and God*,[41] where "words-about-God"—whether of the man in the street or of the scholar in his study—are subjected to sustained philosophic scrutiny. Making his own a "functional" analysis (in place of the limited positivistic verificational analysis of the earlier, Cambridge school), Ferré assesses in highly instructive fashion the logic of analogy (the Thomist sort of thing), of obedience (the Barthian), and of encounter (the Buber) before proceeding to his own programmatic of how theological language might best be made behave.[42]

Of course, not everyone shares to the same degree the present writer's enthusiasm for the contribution logical analysis can make to the theological enterprise. The reader would be wise, therefore,

[40] *Faith and Knowledge. A Modern Introduction to the Problem of Religious Knowledge*, Ithaca, Cornell University Press, 1957.

[41] New York, Harper, 1961. See also *Exploring the Logic of Faith* (New York, Association, 1962) in which he and Kent Bendall engage in what they have called *A Dialogue on the Relation of Modern Philosophy to Christian Faith*.

[42] In his *Reason in Religion* (New York, Nelson, 1963), Nels F. S. Ferré has put himself under the tutelage of his son, Frederick. Those of us who have for years been fans of the elder Ferré can feel only dismay at the result. Never has he been so earnest, so careful, and so unconvincing. Could it be that the theology of Ferré *père* was always thus lacking in content and we were merely bewitched by his rhapsodic use (misuse?) of theological language?

to acquaint himself with the reactions of a Clarke[43] or a Cleobury[44] or a Zuurdeeg[45] as well.

2.

Besides the philosophy-theology relationship of a method to content, that—more familiar—of a method to a method has been the object of renewed examination of late.

Among both Protestants and Catholics, it has, although in different ways, commonly taken on a character that would have been quite impossible even a generation ago. The reason, again, is probably the one I suggested in another connection earlier: philosophy itself has become rather more sophisticated of late. In anycase, the result has been a continued reassessing of philosophic method as operative *within* theology, and not (the earlier way) as something preparatory to theology or, at most, complementary to theology.

Among Catholics, the philosophic method that is analyzed as one pole of the relation is no one thing; a curious and not altogether happy variety of philosophies and non-philosophies are, as often as not, invoked—but that need not detain us here. What is of especial interest is the new attention that is being given to Hegelianism and Aristotelianism, each freshly rebaptized.

The French, particularly in the post-war years, have shown themselves the especial champions of Hegelianism. Yet it is the work of German and Austrian scholars, notably instanced in the Innsbruck University symposium,[46] which promises best for theology. In their hands, that seemingly least tractable of philosophic systems reveals itself as methodologically most applicable to the varied tasks imposed by the theologian's operating on the boundaries of knowledge—not simply those of nature-supernature, but

[43] W. Norris Clarke, S.J., "Linguistic Analysis and Natural Theology," *Proceedings of the American Catholic Philosophical Association* 34, 1960, 110-126.
[44] F. H. Cleobury, *Christian Rationalism and Philosophical Analysis*, London, Clarke, 1959.
[45] Willem F. Zuurdeeg, *An Analytical Philosophy of Religion. A Treatment of Religion on the Basis of Methods of Empirical and Existential Philosophy*, London, Allen & Unwin, 1959.
[46] E. Coreth, *et al.*, *Aufgaben der Philosophie*, Innsbruck, Rauch, 1958.

there where all secular disciplines meet—and by the need he has to fashion concepts *there* which will contribute to the better understanding of concepts and problems that are strictly theological.

Aristotelianism in one form or another has been common baggage in the mind of the Christian West for centuries now. The Thomist form (that is, that of the thirteenth-century Thomas Aquinas) has, during the last decade but chiefly because of the historical work done in the two previous decades, in the hands of some been shown to be methodologically most instructive for the felicitous accomplishing of today's theological tasks. To realize just how instructive, one need merely browse in the monographs of Josef Pieper and see him philosophizing there *within* a total theological context.[47] The rationale of all this has been articulated, magisterially and at length, by Bernard J. F. Lonergan, S.J., in his *Insight. A Study of Human Understanding.*[48] One of the truly great books of the decade, *Insight* makes exorbitant demands on the ordinary reader's capacity for speculation, but in due time (an entire decade would not be overmuch) provides proportionate rewards. Already its influence on many of the more influential religious thinkers of the day is detectable. Philosophers have been the first to profit from it. Of late, however, theologians have swelled the ranks to a degree which the future undoubtedly will see greatly increase so long as theologians have sufficient patience with the philosophy that fills by far the greater part of *Insight* so that they may come, knowledgeably alert, to the theological referents towards its end.[49] With those referents as basis, Lonergan has since been engaged on what promises to be a monumental work on theological method.

Among Protestants, the philosophic method that is analyzed as one pole of the philosophy-theology relationship is Heideggerian. The initiative in this was, of course, Rudolf Bultmann's. And, with an ironic twist, it continues to be. His former pupils at Mar-

[47] Especially to be commended in this respect is his *Ueber die Gerechtigkeit* (Munich, Kösel, 1953, 1954²; ET *Justice*, New York, Pantheon, 1955). A similar instance is provided by M. D. Chenu, O.P., *Pour une théologie du travail*, Paris, Seuil, 1955; ET *The Theology of Work. An Exploration*, Dublin, Gill, 1963.

[48] New York, Philosophical Library, 1957.

[49] Pp. 733-734, 739-747.

burg, now occupying just about all the important Scripture profes-
sorships in the German universities, have manifested a touching
pietas towards their former mentor by assembling each year in his
honor to discuss matters biblical and theological. But many of
them are not only his former pupils. In keeping with that noble
Germanic custom whereby—true "wandering scholars"—doctoral
students move about from university to university in the orderly
achieving of their degree, many of them are also former pupils of
Martin Heidegger at Freiburg. From 1953 on, the informal assem-
blies of the "Old Marburgers" became respectfully critical of what
the participants had learned from Bultmann on the basis of what
they had learned from Heidegger. By 1959 ,the matter came to a
head. The relation of Heidegger to theology was the topic of that
year's meeting, which concluded with a day-long seminar on
"Christian Faith and Thinking" conducted by Heidegger himself.
Out of that meeting and succeeding ones several things have been
made clear. First, the Heideggerian doctrine which has held so
large a place in the thinking of Bultmann since his abandonment
of Barth was probably never taught by Heidegger. Second, the later
Heidegger provides a doctrine more relevant to theology than
either his own or Bultmann's expression of his earlier thought. Finally, "hermeneutic"—as the reflective process, deliberately engaged in, of interpretation on whatever level—should be accorded
its role once more in theology.[50]

The best thinking on this entire matter has been divested of its
parochial German character and presented in the first two volumes[51] of what promises to be a most valuable series, "New Frontiers in Theology," edited by James M. Robinson and John B.
Cobb, Jr., whose purpose is to provide the means for theological
interaction between German and American scholars. It is not too
easy to isolate the best among so many good things contained in
these books. Most readers will be especially grateful for the introductory surveys by Professor Robinson, "The German Discussion
of the Later Heidegger" and "Hermeneutic Since Barth." Others

---

[50] A good general introduction to this most fruitful approach is provided
in the papers of both Protestant and Catholic theologians edited by Henrico
Castelli, *Ermeneutica e tradizione* (Rome, Istituto di studi filosofici, 1963).

[51] *The Later Heidegger and Theology*, New York, Harper, 1963; *The New
Hermeneutic*, New York, Harper, 1964.

will be grateful for the translation of such important papers as that
of Heinrich Ott on the nature of systematic theology (it, he con-
tends, is hermeneutical), or that of Gerhard Ebeling on the word
of God and hermeneutic, or that of Ernst Fuchs on the New Testament and the hermeneutical problem. All should find the re-
sponses to the American discussion by Ott and by Fuchs healthily
stimulating and additional inducements to read the entire volumes
pencil in hand. Curiously enough, readers familiar with American-
British logical analysis will be most at home in this highly Germanic sort of theological examination. The function of hereme-
neutic, interpretation which is always "translation" and therefore
"transfer," differs from the technique of logical analysis chiefly in
that the latter is applied to theology from without, while hermeneutic is a philosophic operation within theology itself. Like logical
analysis, it manages in a fashion particularly congenial to the contemporary mentality to face up to the difficulty of the ill-founded
and fuzzy forever masquerading itself as theology.[52]

3.

The most treacherous relationship of philosophy to theology is that
of content to content. The documentation of this statement grows,
unfortunately, with every passing day. The procedure of, you might
say, filling the wine jars of theology with the water of philosophy
and peddling it as wine is so prevalent that many believe it impossible for philosophy to contribute its characteristic content to the
theological enterprise without the tasteless being inevitably the result. Romano Guardini has long proved that it can be done and
that, if anything, a singularly enriched theology is the consequence.
Hence, here, a bibliographical wave of the hand to Professor Guardini, emeritus now in every noble sense of the term.[53]

[52] On a level considerably less adult, the same problematic was faced by John
A. T. Robinson in his *Honest to God* (London, SCM, 1963), on which see
O. Fielding Clarke, *For Christ's Sake. A Reply to 'Honest to God'* (Wallington, Religious Education Press, 1963), or—better!—*The Honest to God Debate*, edited by David L. Edwards (London, SCM, 1963), especially the tem-
perate assessment by Herbert McCabe (pp. 165-180).

[53] A remarkable *fil de conducteur* runs through the following works: *Drei
Schriftauslegungen*, Würzburg, Werkbund-Verlag, 1949, ET *The Word of
God. On Faith, Hope and Charity*, Chicago, Regnery, 1963; *Die Bekehrung*

SYMBOLISM

Of late in theology, the word "symbol" has become a catch-all word. The frequency of its use, daily on the increase, is equaled only by the variety of meanings ascribed to it. The resultant confusion is of a sort that would seem to promise little of value to theology. Yet, if one excludes the work of those theologians who themselves have no definite notion of what they mean by the word, the opposite is the case. As further work is done by theologians who do have a definite notion of what they mean by the word even though they do not all mean the same thing, more exact words will be substituted for the sole word "symbol" and much will accrue of value to theology. Something of value already has. Under the common tag "symbol," theologians have been exploring in depth the personalist dimensions of the religious response, setting theology and aesthetics in fruitful correlation, introducing into the theological enterprise philosophic insights of exceptional worth, and establishing the perduring question of sacramental causality within fresh and highly promising perspectives. That in doing these four different things theologians have in mind four different notions of what "symbol" means, should not induce undue dismay. It would have

des Aurelius Augustinus, der innere Vorgang in seinen Bekenntnissen, Munich, Kösel, 1950[2], ET *The Conversion of Augustine*, Westminster, Newman, 1960; *Das Ende der Neuzeit. Ein Versuch zur Orientierung*, Basel, Hess, 1950, ET *The End of the Modern World. A Search for Orientation*, New York, Sheed & Ward, 1956; *Lebendiger Geist*, Zürich, Verlag der Arche, 1950; *Vom Sinn der Gemeinschaft*, Zürich, Verlag der Arche, 1950; *Das Wesen des Christentums*, revised edition, Würzburg, Werkbund-Verlag, 1953; *Vom Wesen katholischer Weltanschauung*, Basel, Hess, 1953; *Freiheit, Gnade, Schicksal*, Munich, Kösel, 1956[4], ET *Freedom, Grace, and Destiny. Three Chapters in the Interpretation of Existence*, New York, Pantheon, 1961; *Der Dienst am Nächsten in Gefahr*, Würzburg, Werkbund-Verlag, 1956; *Ehe und Jungfraulichkeit*, Mainz, Matthias-Grünewald, 1956; *Die Macht. Versuch einer Wegweisung*, Würtburg, Werkbund-Verlag, 1957[5], ET *Power and Responsibility. A Course of Action for the New Age*, Chicago, Regnery, 1961; *Die Sinne und die religiöse Erkenntnis. Zwei Versuche über die christliche Vergewisserung*, second revised and enlarged edition, Würzburg, Werkbund-Verlag, 1958; *Landschaft der Ewigkeit*, Munich, Kösel, 1958; *Die menschliche Wirklichkeit des Herrn. Beiträge zu einer Psychologie Jesu*, Würzburg, Werkbund-Verlag, 1958; *Wunder und Zeichen*, Würzburg, Werkbund-Verlag, 1959; *In Spiegel und Gleichnis. Bilder und Gedanken*, Mainz, Matthias-Grünewald, 1960[6]. Accordingly the time lag before their appearance in English is less to be deplored than, in most other theologians, would be the case.

been calamitous to have had to await such achievements until after the terminological tangle had been sorted out.

The worthy pioneer of the personalist has been, and continues to be, Jean Mouroux. One can follow him best along the subtle path he takes by beginning with his first work in this area, *Le sens chrétien de l'homme*,[54] going on to his latest, *Le mystère du temps*,[55] and then, after addressing oneself to his *Expérience chrétienne*,[56] coming finally to the minute but masterful *Je crois en Toi*.[57] Using the word "symbol" rather less than most others do herein, Mouroux yet actually plots out what might be called (if that were not to subordinate great things to small) the theological justification of Emerson's "We are symbols and inhabit symbols."

More than one pioneer seems to have been at work latterly in the field of aesthetics-theology; at least, it would be invidious to assert at this early stage any priorities among them. Their explorations are only beginning, but already their achievements are notable. Several theologians, fortunately, might here be mentioned.[58] However, it appears best that two among them be simply noted here, William F. Lynch[59] and Nathan Alexander Scott.[60] Both are thinkers of singular sensibility, theologically as well as aesthetically. That their interest in the aesthetical has so far been limited largely to the literary is all to the good because they have been the beneficiaries, as American intellectuals, of American literary criticism which is the most sophisticated and completely developed there is.

[54] Paris, Aubier, 1945; ET *The Meaning of Man*, New York, Sheed & Ward, 1948.

[55] Paris, Aubier, 1962.

[56] Paris, Aubier, 1952; ET *The Christian Experience. An Introduction to A Theology*, New York, Sheed & Ward, 1954.

[57] Paris, Cerf, 1948; ET *I Believe. The Personal Structure of Faith*, New York, Sheed & Ward, 1959.

[58] For instance, Luis Alonso Schökel for his *El hombre de hoy ante la Biblia* (Barcelona, Flors, 1959; ET *Understanding Biblical Research*, New York, Herder and Herder, 1963) and, especially, for his *Estudios de poética hebrea* (Barcelona, Flors, 1963), in which literary theory is brought to bear upon the operations of biblical theology in a way that should be productive of long needed consequences.

[59] *Christ and Apollo. The Dimensions of the Literary Imagination*, New York, Sheed & Ward, 1960.

[60] *The Tragic Vision and the Christian Faith*, New York, Association, 1957.

Lynch's doctrine of the evocative symbol commends itself in particular to the attention of theologians.

F. W. Dillistone is the best of initial guides into the theology-philosophy area in which most theologians who write much of symbolism disport themselves these days.[61] The philosophy is that of Susanne Langer for the most part along with certain of the happier philosophic categories of Carl Jung.[62] Hence there is a conscious openness, at least, to data available from such professional practitioners of the symbolic as practicing artists. Eric Mascall is the one who, to our common profit, has taken most advantage of the data thus available. In his earlier work,[63] as he strove to extricate himself from the difficulties proposed by logical empiricism to valid theological discourse, he utilized the analogy of art symbols to validate the communicative possibility of the theologian's talking about God. But more recently, he has embraced such philosophic and artistic contributions even more fully.[64] The occasion of his doing so was the appearance of a book by A. C. Bridge,[65] formerly an artist but by then an Anglican curate, in which even the dicta of Chalcedon were most stimulatingly accorded a symbolic dimension. The result in Mascall is an articulated exposition of the central correlation of the imaged and the said in the symbol. If one were so foolhardy as to attempt prophecy, one would say that the word "symbol" will end up meaning, for theologians, just that.

The use of the word "symbol" by the theologians referred to so far has been, whatever the individual differences, to indicate cognitive forms whose signification derives not from the nature of things but from convention; at most, some of these authors (with rather unconvincing recourse to primitive religions) hold for the inevitability of determinate signification.[66] There are, however, theolo-

---

[61] *Christianity and Symbolism*, Philadelphia, Westminster, 1955.

[62] They are not many. The theologian's must in general be the reaction of Martin Buber: "We must really flee all this sparkling ambiguity!" (*Gottesfinsternis*, p. 160).

[63] E. L. Mascall, *Words and Images. A Study in Theological Discourse*, New York, Ronald Press, 1957.

[64] *Theology and Images*, London, Mowbray, 1963.

[65] *Images of God. An Essay on the Life and Death of Symbols*, London, Hodder & Stoughton, 1960.

[66] Karl Rahner provides further documentation in his "Zur Theologie des

gians who go much further. They see an ontological relationship between "symbol" and "symbolized." Although one experiences a mild malaise at their use of "symbol" to designate the undoubted reality with which they are concerned, one can only be grateful for the new vistas they have thus opened up in sacramental theology. As in the Trinity the Son is the symbol of the Father, and as in the human composite the body is the symbol of the soul, so in the sacramental system the rite is the symbol of the grace because, analogously, it exists by it and is expressive of it. This manner of speaking and thinking has made it possible for, most notably, Schillebeeckx and Rahner to suggest new orientations in the problem of sacramental causality by reference to Christ (Schillebeeckx) or to the Church (Rahner) as the primordial sacrament. But more of this, *ex professo*, in the next section.

THE SACRAMENTS

The most important event for sacramental theology in the years 1954-1964 took place in the year 1952. It was then that Schillebeeckx published the first part of a projected two-volume elaboration of the sacramental doctrine of St. Thomas Aquinas.[67] Since then, theologians in ever increasing numbers have been awaiting with poorly concealed impatience the appearance of the second volume to which, in the first volume, Schillebeeckx continually refers his readers for the justification of many of his more basic points. Clearly, in that initial volume, he managed to flush out many more doctrinal rabbits than he felt himself ready to capture and skin and systematically dress. So the second and concluding volume has not yet appeared. But the first one has served us well. With its exploratory sallies, it has restored to sacramental theology entire areas whose existence one would scarcely suspect from a reading of the treatises of the last three centuries so limited to the

---

Symbols," in A. Bea, H. Rahner, H. Rondet, and F. Schwendimann, *Cor Jesu* 1 (Rome, Herder, 1959) 461-505.

[67] E. H. Schillebeeckx, O.P., *De sacramentele Heilseconomie. Theologische bezinning op S. Thomas' sacramentenleer in het licht van de traditie en van de hedendaagse sacramentsproblematiek*, Anvers, 't Groeit, 1952.

clerical, all but exclusively concerned with the conditions for valid administration-reception and with, at best, on occasion an added philosophic fillip about causality.

In 1953, Otto Semmelroth, quite independently of Schillebeeckx, worked out again the basic ecclesial dimension of the sacraments.[68]

In 1954, M. Müller performed a like chore on the personalist dimension.[69]

These three works (largely because they did so much to establish it) illustrate best the pattern of sacramental theology throughout the "decisive decade": Schillebeeckx's, with its emphasis on the large sweep of the *Heilsgeschichte*; Semmelroth's, with its insistence on the Church as the primordial sacrament; Müller's, with its doctrine of encounter.

"Encounter" has since become, not altogether happily, little short of a rallying cry. Both Schillebeeckx[70] and Semmelroth[71] in the event have made it their own. But what precisely one is to understand by "encounter" in the sacramental context has never been made clear. What normally one understands by it in everyday discourse is so general as to be meaningless when it is transferred to theological discourse.[72] What, under the tutelage chiefly of Martin Buber, one is meant to understand by it is theologically inapplicable to the sacraments, for in the sacraments, quite as, more generically, in every faith response, it is question of "knowledge *about*" and not exclusively of "knowledge *of*." But its meaning must be clear at least to Schillebeeckx if one is to judge by the good the-

---

[68] Otto Semmelroth, S.J., *Die Kirche als Ursakrament*, Frankfurt, Knecht, 1953, ET *The Church as Primordial Sacrament*, New York, Herder and Herder, 1965.

[69] M. Müller, O.F.M., *Die Begegnung im Ewigen. Zur Theologie der christlichen Gemeinschaft*, Freiburg, Herder, 1954.

[70] *De Christusontmoeting als sacrament van de Godsontmoeting. Theologische begrijpelijkheid van het heilsfeit der Sacramenten*, Anvers, 't Groeit, 1957.

[71] "Personalismus und Sakramentalismus," in J. Auer and H. Volk, *Theologie in Geschichte und Gegenwart*, Munich, Zink, 1957.

[72] The critical comments of Ronald Hepburn, *Christianity and Paradox*, 24-59, and of Frederick Ferré, *Language, Logic and God*, 94-104, are not irrelevant here.

ology he has of late been producing in terms of "encounter." [73] With Semmelroth the situation seems quite other: Using "encounter" as his key-word, he has been able to provide a sacramental theology at times unjustifiably inclusive and, at other times, just as unjustifiably exclusive, tight, and narrow.[74] The moral herein for lesser theological practitioners than Semmelroth is obvious.

The use to which recent theology has put Semmelroth's great personal insight, the Church as the "primordial sacrament," has been less frenzied and more fruitful. Karl Rahner, on various levels, has worked out its virtualities best,[75] but he is fortunately not alone in his labors as, to take one especially significant instance among many, the Schmaus symposium attests.[76]

One common characteristic of this sacramental theology, whether its primary emphasis is on *Heilsgeschichte* or on "encounter" or on "Church-as-Sacrament," is a happy openness to data from non-Christian religions. One can scarcely measure the light which an acquaintance with, say, the comparative history of religions is able to cast on the Christian doctrinal heritage especially in sacramental matters. However, the converse is the case when the theologian begins with the data (so very limited actually) from non-Christian religions and then compresses the Christian doctrinal heritage within so limited a framework. Louis Bouyer's otherwise admirable volume[77] is, I fear, an instance of this unhappy, because misplaced, openness.

---

[73] Thus his "Sakramente als Organe der Gottbegegnung," in Johannes Feiner, *et al.*, *Fragen der Theologie heute*, 379-401, and, most especially, the third and revised edition of his *De Christusontmoeting* referred to above: *Christus, Sacrament van de Godsontmoeting*, Bilthoven, Nelissen, 1960; ET *Christ the Sacrament of the Encounter with God*, New York, Sheed & Ward, 1963.

[74] *Vom Sinn der Sakramente*, Frankfurt, Knecht, 1960.

[75] The basic work is *Kirche und Sakramente* (Freiburg, Herder, 1961; ET *The Church and the Sacraments*, New York, Herder and Herder, 1963).

[76] Michael Schmaus (editor), *Aktuelle Fragen zur Eucharistie*, Munich, Hueber, 1960. On the other hand, the title given, by the editor apparently, to a wholly admirable collection of essays by the late Pierre Charles seems a gratuitously deceiving one for our day. Charles was theologically much in advance of his time in seeing the Church always in a sacramental perspective. But *L'Eglise, sacrement du monde* (Bruges, Desclée de Brouwer, 1960) is simply not *Ursakrament* theology.

[77] Louis Bouyer, *Le rite et l'homme. Sacralité naturelle et liturgie*, Paris,

THE THEOLOGY OF MORALS

When one views the moral theology of the past several years, three facts command attention: in no other area of theology has so much been written; in no other area (if one except, perhaps, Mariology) has so little been written that is of value; at no other area have such searing criticisms been leveled. This last, the question of criticism, might most profitably engage our attention briefly here.

The beginning of the decade saw the appearance of the Louvain symposium.[78] That such criticism, which has only increased in the meantime, is in large part justified, it is difficult to deny for this at least is clear: in the theology of morals, we have consistently continued to be bedeviled by the past instead of benefiting from it. Granted that the end of the Middle Ages witnessed the development of a systematic moral teaching suitable to those changing times because framed in terms of fundamental natural precepts of morality which lay beyond the reach of the religious dissensions of the period, and granted, too, that it was equally suitable, after an interval of four centuries, to the age of rationalism, yet such desiccated and sin-centered moralizing is ill-suited to our day, and, as in every day, fits poorly—if at all—into theology. Doubting Thomases need merely consult the *Dictionary of Moral Theology*.[79] Put together, the Preface tells us, as a compilation "in which modern, educated Catholics might find an up-to-date, practical, and effective moral guide," it seems rather, in effect, to be a sizable encyclopedia of the theory and practice of sin. Admittedly, one is brought up short upon arriving at page 663 and finding there an

Cerf, 1962; ET *Rite and Man*, Notre Dame, University of Notre Dame Press, 1963. Compare, for instance, the procedure in Joseph Lécuyer's penetrating *Le sacrifice de la nouvelle alliance* (Le Puy, Mappus, 1962). Paul Palmer, S.J., for his part has made the documents of tradition commodiously available in *Sources of Christian Theology* 1. *Sacraments and Worship. Liturgy and Doctrinal Development of Baptism, Confirmation and the Eucharist*; 2. *Sacraments and Forgiveness. History and Doctrinal Development of Penance, Extreme Unction and Indulgences* (Westminster, 1955, 1959).

[78] *Morale chrétienne et requêtes contemporaines*, Tournai, Casterman, 1954. And see E. Hirschbrich, *Die Entwicklung der Moraltheologie im deutschen Sprachgebiet seit der Jahrhundertwende*, Klosterneuburg, Bernina, 1959.

[79] Compiled under the direction of Francesco Cardinal Roberti and edited under the direction of Pietro Palazzini, Westminster, Newman, 1962; ET of *Dizionario de Teologia Morale*, Rome, Studium, 1954, 1957².

article on "Joy": all, one thinks, is perhaps not sin that engages the talents of the volume's contributors. But one is forthwith disabused as one reads there that "joy cannot be sinful except by participation."

In the first volume of their *Contemporary Moral Theology*, John C. Ford, S.J., and Gerald Kelly, S.J.,[80] give a brief survey of recent complaints about moral theology and of pleas for a change to something more appropriately Christian and theological. With all their monumental sanity, they manage to be basically unsympathetic to any such plaints and programs, a fact which makes one somewhat hesitant to persist in the global condemnation of "traditional" moral theology. But likely they are there so unsympathetic because they are unaware of the volume by Bernard Häring which appeared a full four years before their own.[81] For no one is better founded in his criticisms or more knowledgeable and balanced in his proposals than Häring. And in the succeeding editions of *Das Gesetz Christi* he has implemented his proposals in ever greater detail so that we now have, in at least one instance, a theology of morals which is a theology.[82] Aside from inevitably disputable points of detail, criticisms of his work seem chiefly to stem from a lack of comprehension of what it really is: a *part* of theology. Assertions which seem little probative will be seen to be extremely so

---

[80] Westminster, Newman, 1958.

[81] *Das Gesetz Christi. Moraltheologie dargestellt für Priester und Laien*, Freiburg, Wewel, 1954.

[82] *The Law of Christ. Moral Theology for Priests and Laity* (Westminster, Newman, 1963) is the ET, volume 1, of the fifth edition (1959), and volume 2 of the sixth edition (1960) of *Das Gesetz Christi*. His procedure has received independent confirmation by such studies (of unusual value in their own right) as G. Söhngen's *Gesetz und Evangelium: Ihre analoge Einheit* (Munich, Alber, 1957), where, in the light of the faith-being analogy, the "analogy" of law rooted in *agape* is made explicit; P. Daubercies' *La condition charnelle. Recherches positives pour la théologie d'une réalité terrestre* (Tournai, Desclée et Cie., 1959), in which the area of the *réalité terrestre*—Canon Thils's expression of a decade or so ago—is considered in historical perspective; and Werner Schöllgen's *Aktuelle Moralprobleme* (Düsseldorf, Patmos, 1955; adapted in English, *Moral Problems Today*, New York, Herder and Herder, 1963), where contemporary questions are accorded an ethical treatment which reveals a constant awareness of the findings of contemporary psychology, sociology, political theory, etc.; and, particularly, the multiple studies by Philippe Delhaye, of which those indicated in the Bibliography are especially valuable.

when beheld, as they are meant to be, within the total context of theology.

Achievements even greater than that of Häring are, one trusts, in prospect. When they come, it will be to him one's thanks will be mainly due. Until they come, to him one's thanks are due—unreservedly.

VARIA

There are several signally important works from the period under discussion to which attention should be called but which did not admit, without distortion, being placed in any of the previous categories. Where put, for instance, the rich exploratory studies of Henri Rondet,[83] or that, so immediate to present concern, of J. Dijkman,[84] or the basic statement, now at long last published, of one of the handful of truly great theologians of this century, Emile Mersch?[85] Hence this grab-bag section.

A new and, it would seem, healthy insistence on the theological priority of a doctrine of creation fully situated within the *Heilsgeschichte* has come into existence of late. Essays in this direction, all the way from new interpretations of John 1:1-18 to new interpretations of the *Summa Theologica* of St. Thomas, appear with increasing frequency in the journals. But the man who was the innovator here continues to be the most eloquent champion of this priority, the Swedish theologian Gustaf Wingren. His *Skapelsen och lagen*[86] is, of all his works bearing on this matter, especially deserving of recommendation.

Of the science-theology relationship, much may be learned from T. R. Miles and E. L. Mascall [87] and even more from the highly

[83] Henri Rondet, S.J., *Notes sur la théologie du péché*, Paris, Lethielleux, 1957; *Introduction à l'étude de la théologie du mariage*, Paris, Lethielleux, 1960.

[84] J. Dijkman, S.C.J., *Christus, Offenbarung des Dreieinigen Gottes*, Fribourg, Universitäts-Verlag, 1957.

[85] Emile Mersch, S.J., *Le Christ, l'homme et l'univers*, Bruges, Desclée de Brouwer, 1962.

[86] Lund, Gleerup, 1958; ET *Creation and Law*, Edinburgh, Oliver & Boyd, 1961. But see, as well, M. Flick, S.J. and Z. Alszeghy, S.J., *Il Creatore, L'inizio della salvezza*, Florence, Fiorentina, 1959.

[87] T. R. Miles, *Religion and the Scientific Outlook*, London, Allen & Unwin, 1959; E. L. Mascall, *Christian Theology and Natural Science. Some Questions on Their Relations*, London, Longmans, 1956.

specialized and professional H. Dolch.[88] At the very least, a too prevalent naïveté of theologians in our technological age might be in part dispersed by an immediate acquaintance with such works as these. Whether the naïveté is ours or Canon Dewar's, acquaintance with his study[89] (scientifically based?, pseudo-scientifically based?) of the role of the Holy Spirit in the Christian assembly has at least a freshness of approach to recommend it; taking William James's hint of a half century ago that the area of supernatural influences might well be the subliminal, Dewar suggests that it is through the unconscious that the grace of the Spirit is operative. L. Monden, transferring the entire discussion from the pseudo-scientific, is the pioneer of miracles considered within a properly theological context.[90]

The problem of speaking in these pages of the work of Bonhoeffer or of Teilhard is not that they would fail to fit into any of the previous categories, but that they fit all too well into all of them. For each of these thinkers, whose influence on theology has become general only in the last decade, has proved himself the sort that undercuts (if he does not actually destroy) all such departmentalization.

Dietrich Bonhoeffer (1906-1945) felt himself a latter-day Antaeus who could draw strength only from contact with the earth; the need for "ground under one's feet" theologically—concreteness, earthiness, sanity, the historical—was his constant preoccupation. From the place where he was convinced he stood, Christianity looked very different. If nothing more, the theologian can achieve a different and provocative perspective on Christianity from a close reading of this extraordinary man's works.[91]

Pierre Teilhard de Chardin (1881-1955) was, in a not wholly

[88] H. Dolch, *Kausalität im Verständnis der Theologen und der Begründer neuzeitlicher Physik*, Freiburg, Herder, 1954.

[89] Lindsay Dewar, *The Holy Spirit and Modern Thought. An Inquiry into the Historical, Theological, and Psychological Aspects of the Christian Doctrine of the Holy Spirit*, New York, Harper, 1960.

[90] L. Monden, *Het wonder. Theologie en apologetiek van het christelijk mirakel*, Antwerp, Standaard-Boekhandel, 1958; FT *Le miracle. Signe de salut*, Bruges, Desclée de Brouwer, 1960.

[91] *Gesammelte Schriften*, 4 volumes, edited by Eberhard Bethge, Munich, Kaiser, 1958-1961. The number of English translations of individual works is steadily on the increase.

dissimilar way, of the earth earthy. But his was an earth in transit, since its origin, to the high consummating point of the divine purpose. The effect so far of the writings of Teilhard [92] has been to make the scales fall from the eyes of many theologians. It is rather too early to expect any of them to see clearly, but the prospects for the future seem good.[93]

THE CONVERGENCE OF TRADITIONS

Many elements have gone to make the years 1954-1964 the "decisive decade," and not a few of them have been remarked in the preceding pages. But, if one were to single out the most distinctive, one would be forced to mention something which has gone unmentioned thus far: the appearance, among Catholic theologians, of "personal" theologies. Just as it was possible, even necessary, to speak of the theology of Barth or the theology of Tillich (quite as, formerly, one spoke of, say, the theology of Schleiermacher) as of cohesive systems distinctively marked by the personalities of their authors, now one was under similar compulsion to speak of the theology of de Lubac or of Rahner or of von Balthasar or of Murray or of Daniélou.

The theologizing of Henri de Lubac has moved on such a variety of levels that its essential and distinctive unity is less immediately perceptible, perhaps, than that of the others. Comparative religion (*Israel et la Foi chrétienne*, 1942; *Aspects du Bouddhisme*, 1951), religious sociology (*Le drame de l'humanisme athée*, 1943; *Proudhon et la Christianisme*, 1945), the history of biblical exegesis (*Histoire et Esprit*, 1950, and especially the magisterial *Exégèse médiévale*[94]), the history of Christian doctrine (*Corpus Mysticum*, 1944; *Surnaturel*, 1946) have all engaged its attention. But, whatever the accuracy of the report thus given of the views of others, the distinctive view of de Lubac himself is everywhere perceptible. And it is the constant in all his directly theological works, from

[92] *Oeuvres*, Paris, Seuil, 1955-. The ET is in process of publication by Harper and Row, New York and Evanston.
[93] A chief reason for optimism here is the fact that the Teilhard insight is pretty much that of Paul (Romans 8).
[94] Paris, Aubier, 1959-.

Catholicisme (1937) to *Sur les chemins de Dieu*[95] (1956): the rich awareness of the social dimension of the Christian commitment.

There is no such problem with Karl Rahner. His early studies under Martin Heidegger made of him a philosophic personalist who throughout his theological career has, not without complications, been consistently attempting to make this one important point: the primacy of the personal. He does so, whether in analyzing the status of the individual in the Church,[96] or in erecting the hypothesis of a "supernatural existential," [97] or in proposing biblical inspiration as mediated through the primitive Church,[98] or in highlighting the charismatic element in the Church of whatever day,[99] or in ranging through questions as diverse as the role of Our Lady in the apostolate and the televising of Masses,[100] or, finally, in probing the meaning of Christian death.[101] The pleasant consequence is that, no matter what one may think of some of his answers, Karl Rahner poses his questions in a fashion that has proved wondrously stimulating to theologians of whatever school or confession.

The concern of Hans Urs von Balthasar has always been, in one way or another, with "the word." This is little surprising in one who is the official translator of the poems of Paul Claudel, the biographer of Georges Bernanos, and himself an accomplished literary artist whether he is writing in German or in French. Theologizing, he has always begun with Christ as the Word of the Father.

[95] Paris, Aubier; ET *The Discovery of God*, New York, Kenedy, 1960.

[96] *Gefahren im heutigen Katholizismus*, Einsiedeln, Johannes, 1950, 1955³; ET the second part of *Nature and Grace*, New York, Sheed & Ward, 1964.

[97] "Würde und Freiheit des Menschen," in *Schriften zur Theologie* 2, Einsiedeln, Benziger, 1955, 247-277, especially 252; ET "The Dignity and Freedom of Man," in *Theological Investigations* 2. *Man in the Church*, Baltimore, Helicon, 1963, 234-263, especially 240. See also his "Natur und Gnade," in Johannes Feiner, *et al.*, *Fragen der Theologie heute*, Einsiedeln, Benziger, 1957, 1960³, 209-230; ET the first part of *Nature and Grace*, New York, Sheed & Ward, 1964.

[98] *Ueber die Schriftinspiration*, Freiburg, Herder, 1957; ET *Inspiration in the Bible*, New York, Herder and Herder, 1961.

[99] *Das Dynamische in der Kirche*, Freiburg, Herder, 1958; ET *The Dynamic Element in the Church*, New York, Herder and Herder, 1964.

[100] *Sendung und Gnade. Beiträge zur Pastoraltheologie*, Innsbruck, Tyrolia, 1959, 1961³; ET of the first third: *The Christian Commitment. Essays in Pastoral Theology*, New York, Sheed & Ward, 1963.

[101] *Zur Theologie des Todes*, Freiburg, Herder, 1958; ET *On the Theology of Death*, New York, Herder and Herder, 1961.

Upon the Word is structured his interpretation of history,[102] his analysis of the nature and function of contemplation,[103] and his pioneering[104] theology of aesthetics.[105] Appropriately, the two volumes of his collected essays are titled *"Verbum Caro"* and *"Sponsa Verbi."* [106] To limit comment to one advantage of so proceeding, I would point out the ease with which von Balthasar[107] solves both the real problem of the faith of Christ and the pseudo-problem of Martin Buber's two types of faith.[108]

When Jean Daniélou disengages himself from his primary occupation of relating the history of primitive Christian doctrine[109] and theologizes, the result is a theology that is subtly Trinitarian to a degree perhaps without parallel since the days of the Greek Fathers. But, where the Fathers were aided (and hampered) by a cumbersome symbolism,[110] he is aided by the sophisticated insights

---

[102] *Theologie der Geschichte. Ein Grundriss*, revised and enlarged edition, Einsiedeln, Johannes, 1959²; ET *A Theology of History*, New York, Sheed & Ward, 1963.

[103] *Das betrachtende Gebet*, Einsiedeln, Johannes, 1955; ET *Prayer*, New York, Sheed & Ward, 1961.

[104] "Pioneering," that is, if one except (as one should) Romano Guardini's pragmatic essay: *Ueber das Wesen des Kunstwerks* (Stuttgart, Wunderlich, 1948).

[105] *Herrlichkeit. Eine theologische Aesthetik 1. Schau der Gestalt*, Einsiedeln, Johannes, 1961.

[106] *Skizzen zur Theologie 1-2*, Einsiedeln, Johannes, 1961.

[107] In *Skizzen zur Theologie 2*, 49-79.

[108] Von Balthasar, of course, initially took up the question briefly in his brilliant *Einsame Zwiesprache. Martin Buber und das Christentum* (Cologne, Hegner, 1958; ET *Martin Buber and Christianity. A Dialogue Between Israel and the Church*, New York, Macmillan, 1962). See, for more such brilliance, *Die Gottesfrage des heutigen Menschen* (Vienna-Munich, Herold, 1956; ET *Science, Religion and Christianity*, Westminster, Newman, 1958).

[109] A most justified exception in a report such as this of *contemporary* theology, attention must here be called to that notable achievement, the first volume of his *The Development of Christian Doctrine Before the Council of Nicaea. The Theology of Jewish Christianity* (New York, McGraw-Hill, 1964). As translated and edited by John A. Baker, it is a marked advance even on the French original, *Théologie du Judéo-Christianisme* (Tournai, Desclée et Cie., 1958), which for the first time made handily available to today's theologian the rich doctrine of a Christian culture that, two generations ago, was not known to have so much as existed.

[110] Of which Daniélou himself has been, as historian, the outstanding champion: *Sacramentum futuri. Etudes sur les origines de la typologie biblique* (Paris, Beauchesne, 1950; ET *From Shadows to Reality*, Westminster, Newman, 1960).

of philosophers such as Gabriel Marcel. No one of his works to date expresses his theology in its entirety. The *Essai sur le mystère de l'histoire*[111] comes closest to doing so. If to it one add his *Dieu et nous,*[112] *Le chrétien et le monde moderne,*[113] and *Approches du Christ,*[114] one will achieve a rather good notion of what this theology is all about. The language it speaks is, as with all real theology, a universal language. But it speaks it, naturally, with a strong European accent.

With John Courtney Murray, S.J., the language is universal, but the accent is refreshingly North American. The distinctiveness, however, of Murray's theology goes rather more deeply than that. The impression persists that each of the theologians just mentioned (with the likely exception of de Lubac) is a theologian *malgré lui:* a philosopher (Rahner), a *littérateur* (von Balthasar), and a historian (Daniélou) who under the stress of circumstances have theologized most admirably. But Murray is the *habitus theologicus* incardinate and, one expects, always was. That a theologian should give due attention, as he has done, to the properly theological dimensions of the problem of God [115] is no occasion for wonderment. But that a theologian should take up the varied issues contained in *We Hold These Truths*[116] and in every instance make manifest their theological pattern is something else again. Only one who is by nature and not by necessity a theologian could have done so. In this nonsubjective sense, then, the Murray theology is the most personal of any being produced these days by a Catholic scholar.

This recent phenomenon of "personal" theologies in the Catholic Church will be found on examination to point to another that is more basic still: the five theologians commented on in this con-

---

[111] Paris, Seuil, 1953; ET *The Lord of History. Reflections on the Inner Meaning of History,* Chicago, Regnery, 1958.

[112] Paris, Grasset, 1956; ET *God and the Ways of Knowing,* New York, Meridian, 1957.

[113] Tournai, Desclée et Cie., 1959.

[114] Paris, Grasset, 1960; ET *Christ and Us,* New York, Sheed & Ward, 1961.

[115] *The Problem of God. Yesterday and Today,* New Haven, Yale University Press, 1964.

[116] Subtitled *Catholic Reflections on the American Proposition,* New York, Sheed & Ward, 1960.

nection have all been in close contact with Protestant theology throughout their productive careers. Each of them has profited by this contact in a number of ways but chiefly in the bringing into existence of their own theologies because such contact gave them a deeper awareness of their Catholic theological tradition. Even if one say that Protestant theology has been for them no more than a catalytic agent, there seems no denying the fortunate results. It is actually possible to document the matter further by referring to the achievements of other theologians who, although they have not as yet produced "personal" theologies, have produced much of the most alert work of the past several years: each of them has long been engaged in ecumenical work. Their dean, of course, is Karl Adam, whose *Der Christus des Glaubens. Vorlesungen über die kirchliche Christologie*[117] could never have been realized in a Catholic theological ghetto. And then there is the magnificent Yves Congar who, without abandoning Thomistic categories, has thus managed to speak so meaningfully to our day.[118] Or, again, George H. Tavard who can present a tradition-fraught today,[119] who can make positive theological contributions equally well in a monograph on one theologian[120] or in an extensive historical study[121] because of his long familiarity with other Christian theologies.[122] Or, again, that stormy petrel Hans Küng; his doctoral dissertation[123]

[117] Düsseldorf, Patmos, 1954, 1956²; ET *The Christ of Faith. The Christology of the Church*, New York, Pantheon, 1957.

[118] Yves M. J. Congar, O.P., *Le Christ, Marie et l'Eglise*, Bruges, Desclée de Brouwer, 1952, ET *Christ, Our Lady and the Church*, Westminster, Newman, 1957; *Jalons pour une théologie du laïcat*, Paris, Cerf, 1953, ET *Lay People in the Church*, Westminster, Newman, 1957; *Esquisses du mystère de l'Eglise* and *La Pentecôte: Chartres*, Paris, Cerf, 1956, ET *The Mystery of the Church*, Baltimore, Helicon, 1960; *Le Mystère du Temple*, Paris, Cerf, 1958, ET *The Mystery of the Temple*, Westminster, Newman, 1962; *Sacerdoce et Laïcat devant leurs tâches d'évangélisation et de civilisation*, Paris, Cerf, 1962.

[119] George H. Tavard, *The Church, the Layman and the Modern World*, New York, Macmillan, 1959.

[120] *Paul Tillich and the Christian Message*, New York, Scribner, 1962.

[121] As in *Holy Writ or Holy Church. The Crisis of the Protestant Reformation*, New York, Harper, 1960, and *The Quest for Catholicity. A Study in Anglicanism*, New York, Herder and Herder, 1964.

[122] See, for instance, his *A la rencontre du protestantisme*, Paris, Centurion, 1954; ET *The Catholic Approach to Protestantism*, New York, Harper, 1955.

[123] *Rechtfertigung. Die Lehre Karl Barths und eine katholische Besinnung*, Einsiedeln, Johannes, 1957.

on the doctrine of justification in Trent and in Karl Barth introduced him early and most effectively to this kind of contact; his
subsequent, rather hasty works[124] are yet big with the promise of an
eventual outstanding theologian.[125]

The way, of course, was prepared for Küng's *Rechtfertigung* by
Louis Bouyer's brilliant exploration of the Protestant and Catholic
theological traditions, *Du protestantisme à l'Eglise.*[126]

It is in this convergence of theological traditions, which have
been so long maintained in unhappy separation, that one must
seek the most significant and durable contribution of the "decisive
decade."

Explicitly contributory to this end, Walter Horton's pioneering
work (whose value increases with each successive edition), *Christian Theology. An Ecumenical Approach,*[127] is much to be recommended. Under some seven headings, it gives, first, the consensus
among Christians and, second, the doctrinal divergences to be
found in the different confessions. A like service is provided by the
fat volume published in celebration of Otto Karrer's seventieth
birthday. Edited by a Protestant, Oscar Cullmann, and a Catholic,
Maximilian Roesle, *Begegnung der Christen*[128] contains seventeen

[124] *Konzil und Wiedervereinigung. Erneuerung als Ruf in die Einheit,* Freiburg, Herder, 1960, ET *The Council, Reform and Reunion,* New York, Sheed
& Ward, 1962; *Strukturen der Kirche,* Freiburg, Herder, 1962.

[125] It takes no prophet to detect similar promise in Gregory Baum if one
judge from his achievement thus far: *That They May Be One. A Study of
Papal Doctrine, Leo XIII-Pius XII* (Westminster, Newman, 1958); *The Jews
and the Gospel. A Re-examination of the New Testament* (Westminster, Newman, 1961); *Progress and Perspectives. The Catholic Quest for Christian
Unity* (New York, Sheed & Ward, 1962).

[126] Paris, Cerf. 1954, 1955²; ET *The Spirit and Forms of Protestantism,*
Westminster, Newman, 1956. See also his *Parole, Eglise et sacrements dans le
protestantisme et le catholicisme* (Bruges, Desclée de Brouwer, 1960; ET *The
Word, Church and Sacraments in Protestantism and Catholicism,* New York,
Desclée, 1961). Pleasantly obvious is the added perceptiveness that such continued contact has accorded such other of his studies as *Le Trône de la Sagesse. Essai sur la signification du culte marial* (Paris, Cerf, 1957; ET *Seat of
Wisdom,* New York, Pantheon, 1962) and *La Bible et l'évangile, Le sens de
l'Ecriture. Du Dieu qui parle au Dieu fait homme* (revised edition, Paris, Cerf,
1958²; ET *The Meaning of Sacred Scripture,* Notre Dame, University of
Notre Dame Press, 1958).

[127] Revised and enlarged edition, New York, Harper, 1958.

[128] Frankfurt, Knecht, 1960². An especial interest attaches to the papers of
Wilhelm Andersen and Heinrich Fries on "Theologische Studien. Stand und

theological or historical-theological topics, most treated in turn by a Protestant and a Catholic scholar.

Yet even more convincing of the indispensable theological values to be achieved by the convergence of traditions are such things as the Moeller-Philips volume[129] on the doctrine of grace, and certain parts of the Harvard symposium,[130] for in them are had transcripts of the actual *viva voce* theologizing in concert by theologians of diverse traditions.

To judge from the past, it is in that sort of thing that our best theological future lies.

Bibliography

Because of their unusual impact on the years 1954-1964, works are included here whose publication was actually prior to 1954.

REFERENCE WORKS

ALBERIGO, GIUSÈPPE, *et al.* (editors). *Conciliorum Oecumenicorum Decreta*, Freiburg, Herder, 1962².

A *Catholic Dictionary of Theology*, New York, Nelson, 1962-.

Catholicisme, Paris, Letouzey, 1948-.

Dictionnaire de théologie catholique. Tables générales, Paris, Letouzey, 1951-.

FRIES, HEINRICH (editor). *Handbuch theologischer Grundbegriffe*, 2 volumes, Munich, Kösel, 1962, 1963.

Lexikon für Theologie und Kirche, Freiburg, Herder, 1957²-.

RAHNER, KARL, and VORGRIMLER, HERBERT (editors). *Kleines theologisches Wörterbuch*, Freiburg, Herder, 1961.

Hoffnungen" (501-545); see also, in this connection, *Theology and the University, An Ecumenical Investigation*, edited by John Coulson (Baltimore, Helicon, 1964), and Clyde A. Holbrook, *Religion, a Humanistic Field* (Englewood Cliffs, Prentice-Hall, 1963).

[129] C. Moeller and G. Philips, *Grâce et oecuménisme*, Chevetogne, Editions de Chevetogne, 1957; ET *The Theology of Grace and the Oecumenical Movement*, London, Mowbray, 1962.

[130] *Ecumenical Dialogue at Harvard. The Roman Catholic-Protestant Colloquium*, edited by Samuel H. Miller and G. Ernest Wright, Cambridge (Mass.), Harvard University Press, 1964.

Die Religion in Geschichte und Gegenwart, 6 volumes, Tübingen, Mohr, 1957-1962. Index volume in preparation.

SCHÖNMETZER, ADOLF (editor). *Enchiridion Symbolorum,* Freiburg, Herder, 1963[33].

Theologisch Woordenboek, 3 volumes, Roermond, Romen & Zonen, 1952-1958.

SURVEYS

BROWN, JAMES. *Subject and Object in Modern Theology,* New York, Macmillan, 1955.

CONGAR, YVES M. J. *Sainte Eglise. Etudes et approches ecclésiologiques,* Paris, Cerf, 1963.

ELDAROV, G. M. *Presenza della teologia. Saggio su una recente controversia alla luce dell'enciclica "Humani generis,"* Padua, Il Messaggero di S. Antonio, 1954.

FEINER, JOHANNES, *et al.* (editors). *Fragen der Theologie heute,* Einsiedeln, Benziger, 1957, 1960[3].

JAKI, S. *Les tendances nouvelles de l'ecclésiologie,* Rome, Herder, 1957.

KOCH, GERHARD. *Die Auferstehung Jesu Christi,* Tübingen, Mohr, 1959.

MACKINTOSH, H. R. *Types of Modern Theology. Schleiermacher to Barth,* New York, Scribner, 1937. London, Collins, 1964.

MACQUARRIE, JOHN. *Twentieth-Century Religious Thought. The Frontiers of Philosophy and Theology, 1900-1960,* New York, Harper, 1963.

MALTHA, ANDREAS HEINRICH. *Die Neue Theologie,* Munich, Manz, 1960.

MARTINI, CARLO M. *Il problema storico della risurrezione negli studi recenti,* Rome, Università Gregoriana, 1959.

Problemi e orientamenti di teologia dommatica, 2 volumes, Milan, Marzorati, 1957.

Problemi scelti di teologia contemporanea, "Analecta Gregoriana" 68, Rome, Università Gregoriana, 1954.

RAMSEY, ARTHUR MICHAEL. *An Era in Anglican Theology. From Gore to Temple,* New York, Scribner, 1960.

SMEDES, LEWIS B. *The Incarnation. Trends in Modern Anglican Thought,* Kampen, Kok, 1953.

SOPER, DAVID WESLEY. *Major Voices in American Theology. Six Contemporary Leaders,* Philadelphia, Westminster, 1953.

VAN DUSEN, HENRY PITNEY. *The Vindication of Liberal Theology. A Tract for the Times*, New York, Scribner, 1963.

WAND, J. W. C. *The Minds Behind the New Theology. Kierkegaard, Barth, Bultmann, Tillich, and Bonhoeffer*, London, Mowbray, 1963.

WILLIAMS, DANIEL DAY. *What Present-Day Theologians Are Thinking*, New York, Harper, 1959[2].

PHILOSOPHY AND THEOLOGY

1.

BENDALL, KENT, and FERRÉ, FREDERICK. *Exploring the Logic of Faith. A Dialogue on the Relation of Modern Philosophy to Christian Faith*, New York, Association, 1962.

BERTHOLD, FRED, JR. "Logical Empiricism and Philosophical Theology," *Journal of Religion* 35, 1955, 207-217.

CLARKE, W. NORRIS. "Linguistic Analysis and Natural Theology," *Proceedings of the American Catholic Philosophical Association* 34, 1960, 110-126.

CLEOBURY, F. H. *Christian Rationalism and Philosophical Analysis*, London, Clarke, 1959.

FERRÉ, FREDERICK. *Language, Logic and God*, New York, Harper, 1961.

FERRÉ, NELS F. S. *Reason in Religion*, New York, Nelson, 1963.

FLEW, ANTONY, and MACINTYRE, ALASDAIR (editors). *New Essays in Philosophical Theology*, New York, Macmillan, 1956.

HEPBURN, RONALD W. *Christianity and Paradox. Critical Studies in Twentieth-Century Theology*, New York, Humanities Press, 1959.

HICK, JOHN. *Faith and Knowledge. A Modern Introduction to the Problem of Religious Knowledge*, Ithaca, Cornell University Press, 1957.

MACINTYRE, ALASDAIR. *Difficulties in Christian Belief*, London, SCM, 1959.

MASCALL, E. L. *Up and Down in Adria. Some Considerations of the Volume Entitled* Soundings, London, Faith Press, 1963.

MITCHELL, BASIL (editor). *Faith and Logic. Oxford Essays in Philosophical Theology*, London, Allen & Unwin, 1957.

RAMSEY, IAN T. *Mircles. An Exercise in Logical Mapwork*, Oxford, Clarendon, 1952.

———. *Religious Language. An Empirical Placing of Theological Phrases*, Naperville, Allenson, 1957.

———. *On Being Sure in Religion*, New York, Oxford University Press, 1963.

———. *Models and Mystery*, London, Oxford University Press, 1964.

RICHARDSON, ALAN (editor). *Four Anchors From the Stern*, London, SCM, 1963.

VIDLER, A. R. (editor). *Soundings. Essays Concerning Christian Understanding*, New York, Cambridge University Press, 1962.

——— (editor). *Objections to Christian Belief*, London, Constable, 1963.

WOODS, G. F. *Theological Explanation*, Welwyn, Nisbet, 1958.

ZUURDEEG, WILLEM F. *An Analytical Philosophy of Religion. A Treatment of Religion on the Basis of Methods of Empirical and Existential Philosophy*, London, Allen & Unwin, 1959.

2.

CASTELLI, HENRICO (editor). *Ermeneutica e tradizione*, Rome, Istituto di studi filosofici, 1963.

CHENU, M. D. *Pour une théologie du travail*, Paris, Seuil, 1955. ET *The Theology of Work. An Exploration*, Dublin, Gill, 1963.

CLARKE, O. FIELDING. *For Christ's Sake. A Reply to 'Honest to God'*, Wallington, Religious Education Press, 1963.

CORETH, E., *et al. Aufgaben der Philosophie*, Innsbruck, Rauch, 1958.

EDWARDS, DAVID L. (editor), and ROBINSON, JOHN A. T. *The Honest to God Debate*, London, SCM, 1963.

LONERGAN, BERNARD J. F. *Insight. A Study of Human Understanding*, New York, Philosophical Library, 1957.

PIEPER, JOSEF. *Ueber die Gerechtigkeit*, Munich, Kösel, 1953, 1954². ET *Justice*, New York, Pantheon, 1955.

ROBINSON, JAMES, and COBB, JR., JOHN (editors). *The Later Heidegger and Theology*, New York, Harper, 1963.

——— (editors). *The New Hermeneutic*, New York, Harper, 1964.

ROBINSON, JOHN A. T. *Honest to God*, London, SCM, 1963.

3.

GUARDINI, ROMANO. *Drei Schriftauslegungen*, Würzburg, Werkbund-Verlag, 1949. ET *The Word of God. On Faith, Hope and Charity*, Chicago, Regnery, 1963.

———. *Die Bekehrung des Aurelius Augustinus, der innere Vorgang in seinen Bekenntnissen*, Munich, Kösel, 1950²; ET *The Conversion of Augustine*, Westminster, Newman, 1960.

———. *Das Ende der Neuzeit. Ein Versuch zur Orientierung*, Basel,

Hess, 1950. ET *The End of the Modern World. A Search for Orientation*, New York, Sheed & Ward, 1956.

———. *Freiheit, Gnade, Schicksal*, Munich, Kösel, 1956[4]; ET *Freedom, Grace, and Destiny. Three Chapters in the Interpretation of Existence*, New York, Pantheon, 1961.

———. *Der Dienst am Nächsten in Gefahr*, Würzburg, Werkbund-Verlag, 1956.

———. *Ehe und Jungfraulichkeit*, Mainz, Matthias-Grünewald, 1956.

———. *Die Macht. Versuch einer Wegweisung*, Würzburg, Werkbund-Verlag, 1957[5]. ET *Power and Responsibility. A Course of Action for the New Age*, Chicago, Regnery, 1961.

———. *Die Sinne und die religiöse Erkenntnis. Zwei Versuche über die christliche Vergewisserung*, second revised and enlarged edition, Würzburg, Werkbund-Verlag, 1958.

———. *Landschaft der Ewigkeit*, Munich, Kösel, 1958.

———. *Die menschliche Wirklichkeit des Herrn. Beiträge zu einer Psychologie Jesu*, Würzburg, Werkbund-Verlag, 1958.

———. *Wunder und Zeichen*, Würzburg, Werkbund-Verlag, 1959.

———. *In Spiegel und Gleichnis. Bilder und Gedanken*, Mainz, Matthias-Grünewald, 1960[6].

SYMBOLISM

ALONSO SCHÖKEL, LUIS. *El hombre de hoy ante la Biblia*, Barcelona, Flors, 1959. ET *Understanding Biblical Research*, New York, Herder and Herder, 1963.

———. *Estudios de poética hebrea*, Barcelona, Flors, 1963.

BRIDGE, A. C. *Images of God. An Essay on the Life and Death of Symbols*, London, Hodder & Stoughton, 1960.

DILLISTONE, F. W. *Christianity and Symbolism*, Philadelphia, Westminster, 1955.

LYNCH, WILLIAM F. *Christ and Apollo. The Dimensions of the Literary Imagination*, New York, Sheed & Ward, 1960.

MASCALL, E. L. *Words and Images. A Study in Theological Discourse*, New York, Ronald Press, 1957.

———. *Theology and Images*, London, Mowbray, 1963.

MOUROUX, JEAN. *Le sens chrétien de l'homme*, Paris, Aubier, 1945. ET *The Meaning of Man*, New York, Sheed & Ward, 1948.

———. *Je crois en Toi. Structure personnelle de la foi*, Paris, Cerf, 1948. ET *I Believe. The Personal Structure of Faith*, New York, Sheed & Ward, 1959.

———. *Expérience chrétienne. Introduction à une théologie*, Paris,

Aubier, 1952. ET *The Christian Experience. An Introduction to A Theology*, New York, Sheed & Ward, 1954.

———. *Le mystère du temps. Approche théologique*, Paris, Aubier, 1962.

RAHNER, KARL. "Zur Theologie des Symbols," in A. Bea, H. Rahner, H. Rondet, and F. Schwendimann, *Cor Jesu* 1, Rome, Herder, 1959.

SCOTT, NATHAN ALEXANDER (editor). *The Tragic Vision and the Christian Faith*, New York, Association, 1957.

SACRAMENTS AND CHURCH

BOUYER, LOUIS. *Le rite et l'homme. Sacralité naturelle et liturgie*, Paris, Cerf, 1962. ET *Rite and Man*, Notre Dame, University of Notre Dame Press, 1963.

CHARLES, PIERRE. *L'Eglise, sacrement du monde*, Bruges, Desclée de Brouwer, 1960.

CONGAR, YVES M. J. *Sainte Eglise. Etudes et approches ecclésiologiques*, Paris, Cerf, 1963.

HAMER, JÉROME. *L'Eglise est une communion*, Paris, Cerf, 1962.

KÜNG, HANS. *Strukturen der Kirche*, Freiburg, Herder, 1962.

LÉCUYER, JOSEPH. *Le sacrifice de la nouvelle alliance*, Le Puy, Mappus, 1962.

MÜLLER, M. *Die Begegnung im Ewigen. Zur Theologie der christlichen Gemeinschaft*, Freiburg, Herder, 1954.

PALMER, PAUL F. *Sources of Christian Theology* 1. *Sacraments and Worship. Liturgy and Doctrinal Development of Baptism, Confirmation and the Eucharist*; 2. *Sacraments and Forgiveness. History and Doctrinal Development of Penance, Extreme Unction and Indulgences*, Westminster, Newman, 1955, 1959.

RAHNER, KARL. *Kirche und Sakramente*, Freiburg, Herder, 1961; ET *The Church and the Sacraments*, New York, Herder and Herder, 1963.

SCHILLEBEECKX, E. H. *De sacramentele Heilseconomie. Theologische bezinning op S. Thomas' sacramentenleer in het licht van de traditie en van de hedendaagse sacramentsproblematiek*, Anvers, 't Groeit, 1952.

———. *De Christusontmoeting als sacrament van de Godsontmoeting: Theologische begrijpelijkheid van het heilsfeit der Sacramenten*, Anvers, 't Groeit, 1957, pp. 169; third revised and enlarged edition: *Christus, Sacrament van de Godsontmoeting*,

Bilthoven, Nelissen, 1960; ET *Christ the Sacrament of the Encounter with God*, New York, Sheed & Ward, 1963.

———. "Sakramente als Organe der Gottbegegnung," in Johannes Feiner, *et al.*, *Fragen der Theologie heute*, Einsiedeln, Benziger, 1957, 1960³.

SCHMAUS, MICHAEL (editor). *Aktuelle Fragen zur Eucharistie*, Munich, Hueber, 1960.

SEMMELROTH, OTTO. *Die Kirche als Ursakrament*, Frankfurt, Knecht, 1953.

———. "Personalismus und Sakramentalismus," in J. Auer and H. Volk, *Theologie in Geschichte und Gegenwart*, Munich, Zink, 1957.

———. *Das Geistliche Amt. Theologische Sinndeutung*, Frankfurt, Knecht, 1958.

———. *Vom Sinn der Sakramente*, Frankfurt, Knecht, 1960.

THE THEOLOGY OF MORALS

DAUBERCIES, P. *La condition charnelle. Recherches positives pour la théologie d'une réalité terrestre*, Tournai, Desclée et Cie., 1959.

DELHAYE, PHILIPPE. "Le recours à l'Ancien Testament dans l'étude de la théologie morale," *Ephemerides Theologicae Lovanienses* 31, 1955, 637-657.

———. "Le recours à l'Ecriture sainte dans l'enseignement de la théologie morale," *Bulletin des Facultés catholiques de Lyon* 77, 1955, 5-19; 78, 1956, 5-26.

———. *Rencontre de Dieu et de l'homme. Vertus théologales en général*, Tournai, Desclée et Cie., 1957.

———. "Les bases bibliques du traité de la conscience," *Studia Montis Regis* 4, 1961, 229-251.

———. "L'obligation morale dans les Evangiles," *Ami du Clergé* 71, 1961, 321-329, 369-373.

———. *Permanence du Droit Naturel*, Louvain, Nauwelaerts, 1961.

———. "L'orientation religieuse des actes moraux d'après la Sainte Ecriture et la Théologie," *Mémorial Gelin*, Le Puy, Mappus, 1961.

———. *Le Décalogue et sa place dans la morale chrétienne*, Brussels, La Pensée Catholique, 1963.

Dizionario de Teologia Morale, Rome, Studium, 1954, 1957²; ET *Dictionary of Moral Theology*, Westminster, Newman, 1962.

FORD, JOHN C., and KELLY, GERALD. *Contemporary Moral Theology*, 2 volumes, Westminster, Newman, 1958, 1963.

HÄRING, BERNARD. *Das Gesetz Christi. Moraltheologie dargestellt für Priester und Laien*, Freiburg, Wewel, 1954; ET (of the fifth edition, 1959) volume 1 and (of the sixth edition, 1960) volume 2, *The Law of Christ. Moral Theology for Priests and Laity*, Westminster, Newman, 1961, 1963.

HIRSCHBRICH, E. *Die Entwicklung der Moraltheologie im deutschen Sprachgebiet seit der Jahrhundertwende*, Klosterneuburg, Bernina, 1959.

Morale chrétienne et requêtes contemporaines, Tournai, Casterman, 1954.

SCHÖLLGEN, WERNER. *Aktuelle Moralprobleme*, Düsseldorf, Patmos, 1955. Adapted in English, *Moral Problems Today*, New York, Herder and Herder, 1963.

SÖHNGEN, G. *Gesetz und Evangelium. Ihre analoge Einheit*, Munich, Alber, 1957.

VARIA

BONHOEFFER, DIETRICH. *Gesammelte Schriften*, 4 volumes, edited by Eberhard Bethge, Munich, Kaiser, 1958-1961.

DEWAR, LINDSAY. *The Holy Spirit and Modern Thought. An Inquiry into the Historical, Theological, and Psychological Aspects of the Christian Doctrine of the Holy Spirit*, New York, Harper, 1960.

DIJKMAN, J. *Christus, Offenbarung des Dreieinigen Gottes*, Fribourg, Universitäts-Verlag, 1957.

DOLCH, H. *Kausalität im Verständnis der Theologen und der Begründer neuzeitlicher Physik*, Freiburg, Herder, 1954.

FLICK, M., and ALSZEGHY, Z. *Il Creatore, L'inizio della salvezza*, Florence, Fiorentina, 1959.

MASCALL, E. L. *Christian Theology and Natural Science, Some Questions on Their Relations*, London, Longmans, 1956.

MERSCH, EMILE. *Le Christ, l'homme et l'univers*, Bruges, Desclée de Brouwer, 1962.

MILES, T. R. *Religion and the Scientific Outlook*, London, Allen & Unwin, 1959.

MONDEN, L. *Het Wonder. Theologie en apologetiek van het christelijk mirakel*, Antwerp, Standaard-Boekhandel, 1958; FT *Le Miracle. Signe de salut*, Bruges, Desclée de Brouwer, 1960.

RONDET, HENRI. *Notes sur la théologie du péché*, Paris, Lethielleux, 1957.

————. *Introduction à l'étude de la théologie du mariage*, Paris, Lethielleux, 1960.

Teilhard de Chardin, Pierre. *Oeuvres*, Paris, Seuil, 1955-.

Wingren, Gustaf. *Skapelsen och lagen*, Lund, Gleerup, 1958; ET *Creation and Law*, Edinburgh, Oliver & Boyd, 1961.

The Convergence of Traditions

Adam, Karl. *Der Christus des Glaubens. Vorlesungen über die kirchliche Christologie*, Düsseldorf, Patmos, 1954, 1956²; ET *The Christ of Faith. The Christology of the Church*, New York, Pantheon, 1957.

Andersen, Wilhelm. "Die Reform des theologischen Studiums als theologisches Problem," in Maximilian Roesle and Oscar Cullmann, *Begegnung der Christen*, Frankfurt, Knecht, 1960².

Balthasar, Hans Urs von. *Theologie der Geschichte. Ein Grundruss*, revised and enlarged edition, Einsiedeln, Johannes, 1959²; ET *A Theology of History*, New York, Sheed & Ward, 1963.

―――. *Das betrachtende Gebet*, Einsiedeln, Johannes, 1955; ET *Prayer*, New York, Sheed & Ward, 1961.

―――. *Die Gottesfrage des heutigen Menschen*, Vienna-Munich, Herold, 1956; ET *Science, Religion and Christianity*, Westminster, Newman, 1958.

―――. *Einsame Zwiesprache. Martin Buber und das Christentum*, Cologne, Hegner, 1958; ET *Martin Buber and Christianity. A Dialogue Between Israel and the Church*, New York, Macmillan, 1962.

―――. *Herrlichkeit. Eine theologische Aesthetik 1. Schau der Gestalt*, Einsiedeln, Johannes, 1961.

―――. *Skizzen zur Theologie 1. Verbum Caro; 2. Sponsa Verbi*, Einsiedeln, Johannes, 1961; ET of *Verbum Caro* (in 2 volumes): *Word and Revelation. Essays in Theology 1*, and *Word and Redemption. Essays in Theology 2*, New York, Herder and Herder, 1964, 1965. *Sponsa Verbi* is scheduled for ET publication in 1966.

Baum, Gregory. *That They May Be One. A Study of Papal Doctrine, Leo XIII-Pius XII*, Westminster, Newman, 1958.

―――. *The Jews and the Gospel. A Re-examination of the New Testament*, Westminster, Newman, 1961.

―――. *Progress and Perspectives. The Catholic Quest for Christian Unity*, New York, Sheed & Ward, 1962.

Bouyer, Louis. *Du protestantisme à l'Eglise*, Paris, Cerf, 1954, 1955²; ET *The Spirit and Forms of Protestantism*, Westminster, Newman, 1956.

————. *La Bible et l'évangile, Le sens de l'Ecriture. Du Dieu qui parle au Dieu fait homme*, revised edition, Paris, Cerf, 1958²; ET *The Meaning of Sacred Scripture*, Notre Dame, University of Notre Dame Press, 1958.

————. *Le Trône de la Sagesse. Essai sur la signification du culte marial*, Paris, Cerf, 1957; ET *Seat of Wisdom*, New York, Pantheon, 1962.

————. *Parole, Eglise et sacrements dans le protestantisme et le catholicisme*, Bruges, Desclée de Brouwer, 1960; ET *The Word, Church and Sacraments in Protestantism and Catholicism*, New York, Desclée, 1961.

CONGAR, YVES M. J. *Le Christ, Marie et l'Eglise*, Bruges, Desclée de Brouwer, 1952; ET *Christ, Our Lady and the Church*, Westminster, Newman, 1957.

————. *Jalons pour une théologie du laïcat*, Paris, Cerf, 1953; ET *Lay People in the Church*, Westminster, Newman, 1957.

————. *Esquisses du mystère de l'Eglise* and *La Pentecôte. Chartres*, Paris, Cerf, 1956; ET *The Mystery of the Church*, Baltimore, Helicon, 1960.

————. *Le Mystère du Temple*, Paris, Cerf, 1958; ET *The Mystery of the Temple*, Westminster, Newman, 1962.

————. *Sacerdoce et Laïcat devant leurs tâches d'évangélisation et de civilisation*, Paris, Cerf, 1962.

COULSON, JOHN (editor). *Theology and the University. An Ecumenical Investigation*, Baltimore, Helicon, 1964.

DANIÉLOU, JEAN. *Sacramentum futuri. Etudes sur les origines de la typologie biblique*, Paris, Beauchesne, 1950; ET *From Shadows to Reality*, Westminster, Newman, 1960.

————. *Essai sur le mystère de l'histoire*, Paris, Seuil, 1953; ET *The Lord of History. Reflections on the Inner Meaning of History*, Chicago, Regnery, 1958.

————. *Dieu et nous*, Paris, Grasset, 1956; ET *God and the Ways of Knowing*, New York, Meridian, 1957.

————. *Théologie du Judéo-Christianisme*, Tournai, Desclée et Cie., 1958; ET *The Development of Christian Doctrine Before the Council of Nicaea 1. The Theology of Jewish Christianity*, translated and edited by John A. Baker, New York, McGraw-Hill, 1964.

————. *Le chrétien et le monde moderne*, Tournai, Desclée et Cie., 1959.

————. *Approches du Christ*, Paris, Grasset, 1960; ET *Christ and Us*, New York, Sheed & Ward, 1961.

FRIES, HEINRICH. "Die theologischen Studien, Stand und Hoffnung," in Maximilian Roesle and Oscar Cullmann, *Begegnung der Christen*, Frankfurt, Knecht, 1960².

HOLBROOK, CLYDE A. *Religion, a Humanistic Field*, Englewood Cliffs, Prentice-Hall, 1963.

HORTON, WALTER MARSHALL. *Christian Theology. An Ecumenical Approach*, New York, Harper, 1958².

KÜNG, HANS. *Rechtfertigung. Die Lehre Karl Barths und eine katholische Besinnung* (mit einem Geleitbrief von Karl Barth), Einsiedeln, Johannes, 1957.

————. *Konzil und Wiedervereinigung. Erneuerung als Ruf in die Einheit*, Freiburg, Herder, 1960; ET *The Council, Reform and Reunion*, New York, Sheed & Ward, 1962.

————. *Strukturen der Kirche*, Freiburg, Herder, 1962.

LUBAC, HENRI DE. *Sur les chemins de Dieu*, Paris, Aubier, 1956; ET *The Discovery of God*, New York, Kenedy, 1960.

————. *Exégèse médiévale. Les quatre sens de l'Ecriture*, Paris, Aubier, 1959-.

MILLER, SAMUEL, and WRIGHT, G. ERNEST (editors). *Ecumenical Dialogue at Harvard. The Roman Catholic-Protestant Colloquium*, Cambridge (Mass.), Harvard University Press, 1964.

MOELLER, C., and PHILIPS, G. *Grâce et oecuménisme*, Chevetogne, Editions de Chevetogne, 1957; ET *The Theology of Grace and the Oecumenical Movement*, London, Mowbray, 1962.

MURRAY, JOHN COURTNEY. *We Hold These Truths. Catholic Reflections on the American Proposition*, New York, Sheed & Ward, 1960.

————. *The Problem of God. Yesterday and Today*, New Haven, Yale University Press, 1964.

RAHNER, KARL. *Gefahren im heutigen Katholizismus*, Einsiedeln, Johannes, 1950, 1955³; ET the second part of *Nature and Grace*, New York, Sheed & Ward, 1964.

————. "Würde und Freiheit des Menschen," in *Schriften zur Theologie* 2, Einsiedeln, Benziger, 1955; ET "The Dignity and Freedom of Man," in *Theological Investigations* 2. *Man in the Church*, Baltimore, Helicon, 1963.

————. "Natur und Gnade," in Johannes Feiner, *et al.*, *Fragen der Theologie heute*, Einsiedeln, Benziger, 1957, 1960³; ET the first part of *Nature and Grace*, New York, Sheed & Ward, 1964.

——. *Ueber die Schriftinspiration*, Freiburg, Herder, 1957; ET *Inspiration in the Bible*, New York, Herder and Herder, 1961.

——. *Das Dynamische in der Kirche*, Freiburg, Herder, 1958; ET *The Dynamic Element in the Church*, New York, Herder and Herder, 1964.

——. *Zur Theologie des Todes*, Freiburg, Herder, 1958; ET *On the Theology of Death*, New York, Herder and Herder, 1961.

——. *Sendung und Gnade. Beiträge zur Pastoraltheologie*, Innsbruck, Tyrolia, 1959, 1961³; ET of the first third: *The Christian Commitment. Essays in Pastoral Theology*, New York, Sheed & Ward, 1963.

ROESLE, MAXIMILIAN, and CULLMANN, OSCAR (editors). *Begegnung der Christen*, Frankfurt, Knecht, 1960².

TAVARD, GEORGE H. *A la rencontre du protestantisme*, Paris, Centurion, 1954; ET *The Catholic Approach to Protestantism*, New York, Harper, 1955.

——. *The Church, the Layman and the Modern World*, New York, Macmillan, 1959.

——. *Holy Writ or Holy Church. The Crisis of the Protestant Reformation*, New York, Harper, 1960.

——. *Paul Tillich and the Christian Message*, New York, Scribner, 1962.

——. *The Quest for Catholicity. A Study in Anglicanism*, New York, Herder and Herder, 1964.

Notes on Contributors

Walter J. Burghardt, S.J., M.A., Ph.L., S.T.D., Professor of Patrology and Patristic Theology in Woodstock College, Coeditor of *Ancient Christian Writers*, and President of The Patristic Academy of America, is the author of *The Image of God in Man according to Cyril of Alexandria*, *The Testimony of the Patristic Age concerning Mary's Death*, *All Lost in Wonder: Sermons on Theology and Life*, and co-author with William F. Lynch, S.J., of *The Idea of Catholicism*.

John J. Collins, S.J., M.A., S.S.L., D.H.L., is Professor of the New Testament and Biblical Greek, Weston College. Past President of the Catholic Biblical Association of America, he was one of the founders in 1956 and has been since its inception Editor of *New Testament Abstracts*.

Joseph Hugh Crehan, S.J., M.A. (Oxon.), Ph.D., D.D., Editor of the encyclopedic *Catholic Dictionary of Theology* has written, among other works, *Early Christian Baptism and the Creed* and edited and translated *Athenagoras, Embassy and Resurrection from the Dead*.

John H. Miller, C.S.C., Ph.B., S.T.L., S.T.D., Associate Professor of Theology, University of Notre Dame, is on leave of absence to serve as Liturgical Editor of the *New Catholic Encyclopedia*. On the Board of Advisers of the World Center for Liturgical Studies and a Consultor to the Post-Conciliar Liturgical Commission, he is the founder and Editor of the *Yearbook of Liturgical Studies*.

Roland E. Murphy, O.Carm., M.A., S.T.D., S.S.L., Professor of Old Testament in the Catholic University of America and Visiting Professor (1964-1965) in Pittsburgh Theological Seminary, is Editor-in-

Chief of *The Catholic Biblical Quarterly.* A frequent contributor to the learned journals, he is also author of *The Dead Sea Scrolls and the Bible* and *Seven Books of Wisdom.*

Elmer O'Brien, S.J., Ph.L., S.T.L., S.T.D., is Chairman of the Department of Theology, Loyola College, Montreal, and Director of the Contemporary Theology Institute. He is Editor of CONTEMPORARY THEOLOGY and the author of *The Essential Plotinus* and *Varieties of Mystic Experience.*

INDEXES

Subject Index

Name Index

Walker, J. H., 188, 207
Wand, J. W. C., 11, 35, 221, 250
Warnach, V., 178, 205
Waszink, J. H., 135
Weber, K. O., 157n, 173
Wegenaer, P., 22n, 37, 178, 205
Weigel, G., 162n
Weiser, A., 43, 70
Wellhausen, J., 55
Werner, M., 127n
Westermann, C., 51, 52, 72
Weyman, C., 124
Wikenhauser, A., 102, 113, 115, 118
Williams, C. S. C., 113
Williams, D. D., 221, 251

Wilson, E., 65
Wingren, G., 241, 257
Winninger, P., 189, 208
Winter, P., 110
Wolfson, H. A., 130, 131, 166
Woods, G. F., 227, 252
Wright, G. E., 53n, 57, 65, 67, 69, 72, 73, 76, 77, 249n, 259
Wright, W., 124
Würthwein, E., 65n, 76
Wyclif, J., 13

Young, F. W., 102

Zimmerli, W., 44, 51-52, 70
Zuurdeeg, W. F., 229, 252